The Courage to Set
Healthy Boundaries

Also by Robert Jackman

Healing Your Lost Inner Child
Healing Your Lost Inner Child Companion Workbook
Healing Your Wounded Relationship
The Tender Path of Grief and Loss

Praise for *The Courage to Set Healthy Boundaries*

"Through impressive wisdom on every page and real-life examples, *The Courage to Set Healthy Boundaries* reads like a treasure map to your emotional freedom and spotlights how to deal with manipulators in your life. True to form, Robert Jackman pens another love letter to the inner child with this approach to self-love. Finally, we have a boundary-focused book that siphons through all the traumatic reenactments of our past to foster strength and healing in the present day. This book will help you write your own narrative and start protecting yourself with boundaries."

— Scott Gleeson, LCPC, Psychotherapist, and co-author
of Amazon #1 bestseller *Until My Last Breath*

"I'm seriously blown away at how good this book is. So much of what is covered are the exact words I use with my clients, and I learned some new things as well. *The Courage to Set Healthy Boundaries* is a simple yet sophisticated guide to the complex task of establishing and navigating appropriate boundaries for lasting and healthy relationships. Readers are guided through gentle, thought-provoking exercises so they can better understand their unique Boundary Protection System."

— Carol Dafesh, MS, LMFT

"As a practicing clinical psychologist, boundary work is necessary with most of my patients. This inspired book explains the importance of understanding 'the place where I end and the other begins.' Providing examples and exercises, Robert Jackman teaches us that with healthy boundaries, we feel whole. An excellent tool for individuals and clinicians alike—highly recommended! Robert's work is amazing, and I can't wait to use this book with my patients."

— Karen A. Baker, PsyD, Licensed Clinical Psychologist,
co-owner of Goodman Psychologist Associates,
and Founder of Delta Foundation for Spiritual Studies

"*The Courage to Set Healthy Boundaries* is Robert Jackman's fifth book and may be his best yet. His warmth, empathy, and intellect make it feel like he is personally reassuring and guiding readers to understand boundaries. If only our parents had taught us what Jackman does so masterfully. As in his other books, Robert effortlessly explains complex psychological concepts while providing practical techniques for problem-solving.

Readers will undoubtedly feel a strong sense of urgency, enthusiasm, and confidence to apply the book's wisdom to their own lives. If you're looking to develop self-love and respect through better boundaries but have never received guidance on the subject, this is an absolute must read. This book is so essential it should sit on the coffee table in every mental health practitioner's office!"

— Ross Rosenberg, M.Ed., LCPC, CADC, Psychotherapist, and CEO of Self-Love Recovery Institute

The Courage to Set
Healthy Boundaries

Stand Strong in Your Truth,
Feel Whole and Respected

ROBERT JACKMAN

MS, LCPC, NCC

Published by
PRACTICAL WISDOM PRESS
www.theartofpracticalwisdom.com

ISBN (paperback) 978-1-7354445-8-1
ISBN (e-book) 978-1-7354445-9-8

Editing by Jessica Vineyard, Red Letter Editing
Book design by Christy Day, Constellation Book Services

Printed in the United States of America

To my loving grandparents and all those who came before me for your courage to face triumphs and tragedies, many of which are unknown to me, so that I could be here today.

Contents

Author's Note

In Zen gardens, the empty space between the rocks, plants, and raked sand bring forth feelings of serenity and tranquility. In traditional Japanese aesthetics this principle is known as Yohaku no bi, "the beauty of blank space." The raked sand often represents water and movement, fluidity and change, evoking a sense of impermanence in life. The careful placement of rocks represents mountains or islands and are meant to evoke a sense of permanence and stability. The rocks, often arranged in odd numbers, bring forth a sense of balance. All of these design elements are meant to promote stillness, being present in the moment, and contemplation.

The quiet or blank spaces in the garden have as much meaning as the more prominent features as they each play a role in creating this harmony. In this way, I am using the Zen garden image on the cover to represent a person's (rocks) interaction with life (raked sand) that is ever changing and evolving. The positioning of the raked sand and the rocks symbolically represent the boundaries between life elements and how we each learn from our engagement and reflection on life. The boundaries define and allow the space and interaction for quiet stillness, while honoring the interplay within life itself. This is a simple, yet sophisticated synergy and, like us, each Zen garden is a unique and beautiful expression.

The Power of No

Where did I get the selfless notion that saying yes instead of no, to others and myself, somehow made me a better person? Maybe this came from parochial school and a shame-based heritage, where I was instructed that others needed what they wanted more than I needed what I wanted. A willing supplicant, I took this to heart and began to discard my needs, abandoning them in a crumpled pile along with any sense of personal power. I dreamed that others would somehow secretly know of my relinquished wishes; then I could stay righteously selfless in my newly minted myopic reality of pleasing others and neglecting myself. I unconsciously became a smaller, curated version of myself, freely giving away yesses like Monopoly money, bringing smiles to others and a confused resentment inside of me.

Then I began to heal my needless and wantless self. What would happen if I broke my uneasy silence? Cautiously, quietly, I said no instead of yes. In the breathless silence, I waited. Waited for family and friends to erupt in anger or laughter at my spoken needs. I pondered how they would get their needs met if I said no instead of yes. Ultimately, my inner healer chose a middle path, where I learned how to honor myself and not carry someone else's agenda.

Over time and with practice I realized that saying no didn't isolate me, it joined me with others, for they heard my truth for the first time. I was saying yes to myself, that I mattered, and consequently, I began to feel more whole. Some could hold my reality and respect it, and some self-centered people wanted me to go back to the before time, when their needs mattered more than mine. In the end, my ability to say no saved me. I reclaimed my once-abandoned power that I had heaped in the corner of my diminished idea of myself. Surprisingly to me, others began to want to know of my once-unspoken needs. Others saw the authentic me, not the selfless version I had been instructed to be. After decades of being lost in someone else's dream, I came home, openly, heartfully, authentically saying yes to me while embracing the power of no.

Robert Jackman

Acknowledgments

I'd like to first acknowledge the wayshowers I have known throughout my life who, by example, showed me all the ways we can set boundaries, bringing us closer or keeping us separate. These were not grand, teachable moments; they were everyday examples of seeing others clearly speak their truth or declare when something didn't work for them, even if that meant disappointing someone. I thought this was their unique personality, that they were born this way, but I now realize that it was consistent boundary practice on their part that helped them craft intentional lives.

I came to understand that many of them worked hard to heal themselves and their intergenerational emotional pain through therapy, coming out the other side more whole. I see now how small and large boundary gestures made their lives easier. Their examples informed my boundary system and helped me to create a solid and balanced life for myself. I am grateful to all of them for showing me the way.

Thank you also to those who taught me boundary lessons the hard way—the manipulators, the boundary deflectors, and those who disrespected my boundaries in overt and covert ways. Each of you was a mirror, reflecting back to me my own wounding and where I needed to heal so I could learn to set healthy boundaries. You were my teachers, and the lessons were hard-won. Thank you for the gift of showing me my shadow.

Thank you to Drew Caldwell, my partner of more than thirty-six years. You inspire me, encourage me, believe in me, and are my biggest champion. You give me the gentle, honest feedback I need and always support my ideas no matter how "out there" they are. What a lucky guy I am to have you in my life. I love you. And thank you to my loving and supportive family and friends. You consistently give me courage and comfort.

I want to acknowledge all of those who have helped me on my book publishing path and helped to bring *The Courage to Set Healthy Boundaries* and my *Practical Wisdom Healing Series* to market. A heartfelt thank you to Jessica Vineyard, with Red Letter Editing; Christy Day and Maggie McLaughlin, with Constellation Book Services; Martha Bullen, with Bullen Publishing Services; and my foreign rights agent, Deanna Leah, with HBG Productions. All of you help me bring my books to fruition. This work would not be the same without your guidance and deep knowledge of the publishing industry.

Finally, thank you to my 100,000+ readers throughout the world. Your loyalty and feedback encourage me to continue writing my books to impart the wisdom I have to help others heal.

Introduction

Being kind does not mean having no boundaries. There is a big difference between holding the door and being the doormat.
—PAMELA STORCH

You have probably noticed that some people have an ease about them. Things seem to go well for them, and they have very little drama in their life. Their life isn't perfect, but it has a flow and a straightforward simplicity. It's as if they hold some secret of the universe that opens doors to a life of fulfillment and authenticity. What they manifest in their life is possible because they have mastered the art of boundary setting. They have learned that there is a big payoff when, through patience and practice, they consistently set boundaries instead of hoping others will read their minds and do the hard work for them. They have learned to not give away their power, to speak their truth and defend their needs. In the shelter of good boundaries, many good things can grow, and a life of ease will manifest.

As with any skill, practice makes the process look effortless, but what we don't see is the day-to-day effort that creates the manifested expertise. With consistent practice, people who have good boundaries strengthen and shape how they interact with themselves and others by using their boundary system on a daily basis. They define and refine what feels good and keep a strong level of trust, respect, and reciprocation in their relationships. Consistent and clear boundaries create the foundation for rewarding relationships. There are still challenges, but boundaries give us the tools to navigate the inevitable peaks and valleys of life.

Like many people, you may have tried to set boundaries and then, when others didn't respect you, despondently resigned yourself to the idea that you just have to go along with what others want. Maybe you have given away your power to someone else to avoid a potential conflict, or always say yes to try to be liked and loved—but even this doesn't work. These are the relationship dynamics a lot of people find themselves spinning in, and they don't know how to change this pattern.

You may see boundary setting as a lot of work that causes more problems than it's worth, that it's easier to go along to get along, imagining the emotional reactions of others, all of which takes up a lot of rent-free space in your head. Words get stuck in your throat, and you shut down any attempt to speak up for yourself. Understandably, the biggest thing most of us worry about before we state a boundary is that we don't want to make things worse or make someone else mad or sad. This sense of futility often pushes people away from boundary setting, but usually the issue isn't our boundary, it's others not respecting it. Most of us eventually get tired of being walked all over and want to have our voice heard, but we don't know how to go about creating boundaries. This book will give you the boundary tools to protect yourself, your needs, and your truth.

In reality, we practice boundaries of some sort every day without even thinking about it. We say no when we don't want to do something—or ignore our true feelings and say yes when we want to say no. We may not recognize these as boundaries, but we claim and defend what we like, don't like, need, and don't need. Learning how to set healthy boundaries is akin to learning a new language. As you develop your unique boundary language and system to protect yourself, you will recognize when you find the sweet spot where you feel safe both within yourself and with others. This work will help you to be more intentional with your communications and interactions so you can curate the life you want.

My intention is to teach you how to create a set of core-strength boundary tools you can use in all of your relationships so that you can feel masterful and drama-free. This work will help you move from simply surviving in your relationships to feeling alive and thriving. You will learn to be a conscious creator of your life instead of going on autopilot and hoping for the best. You will learn to trust your gut instinct—your gut-level reaction—as this is an instant barometer that tells you whether you like or don't like something. For us to be open and vulnerable in our relationships, we need to feel the emotional safety that healthy boundaries provide. Boundaries help us feel anchored in an emotional storm. They help us to understand our needs and the needs of others.

Throughout these chapters, you will learn how to stand strong in your truth and state your boundaries with confidence. I will be giving you many descriptions of what boundaries look like and lots of examples of how these situations show up in daily life. You will be learning how to separate out your feelings, ideas, and perspectives from someone else's—which sounds simple but takes practice to recognize. You will learn how to be clear with your boundaries and not apologize for them. You will learn that your boundaries are not bad or wrong just because someone doesn't like them. You will learn the difference between an ask, a request, and a boundary. You will learn that for boundaries to have meaning, you need to have consequences in mind if your boundaries are not honored.

You will learn that your boundaries are your internal source of truth that helps you know what feels right and what does not. You will see that setting boundaries becomes easy once you identify a feeling word that reflects your state of being, and like a key in a lock, this truth opens a pathway to your healing. You will learn about the two pillars of respect and reciprocity that support your boundary protection system. Without these present, your ability to set healthy boundaries gets derailed. The material within this book will help you build a foundational understanding of what boundaries are and then give you practical and accessible skills you can begin to use right away.

Healthy boundaries have the power to bring us together, deepen relationships, and encourage growth, while unhealthy boundaries break down relationships, foster division and isolation, and keep us spinning in a dysfunctional drama. Boundary setting is a capable resource that helps us keep our sense of direction in the slipstream of life. When we listen to ourselves and take care of our side of the street, we create genuine and authentic lives. Boundaries are about caring for ourselves and others. They are about helping us form bridges of connection and joining.

As you start out with boundary setting, it's important to know that the people in your life may not be used to you stating your boundaries and may even reject them at first. Know that, in time, you will learn how to use opening boundary statements as a way to become acclimated to stating your boundaries and others hearing them. You will learn how to use this useful communication tool to get your needs met instead of feeling left out.

You will be learning about inherited boundaries from your childhood family and how, as a boy, I had few boundaries and was enmeshed with my parents' dramas. My sense of self was "melted" in a wounded soup with them, not knowing where I ended and they began. For this book, I dug deep and went to a tender place to relate my no-boundaries inner child wounding origin story for you. When we see through the lens of someone else's experiences, we find a part of ourselves in their journey.

You will be learning how we use a mix of defensive boundaries and avoidance strategies or putting up walls when we feel threatened because of past or current traumas. You will learn how trauma wounding influences our ability to set boundaries, shutting down our voice and robbing us of feeling safe. You will learn about internal and external boundaries, boundary violations, and how behaviors such as numbing out or being passive-aggressive can be seen as nonverbal defensive boundaries. You will read about unique boundary situations and stories of how boundary setting plays out in everyday life. (All of the stories except my own come from a blend of situations to help make the boundary points relatable and accessible. Any connection to anyone living or dead is purely coincidental.)

You may notice that the people in some of the stories display heightened wounded emotions, which can be a common occurrence when people are first learning how to bring their boundaries forth. This is especially true if the feelings have been marinating for a long time. It's important to know you don't need to be in an agitated state to express boundaries. In my examples, I wanted to show what happens in real life, not sugar-coated, idealistic versions that would not help you learn what it's really like to set boundaries.

Boundaries and our emotions can be messy, especially when we are learning a new language skill. Some boundary statements I will give you may sound formal and not the language you would use. For your boundaries to work, you will need to personalize them using your own words and phrasing. I am simply giving you examples for foundations that you can build on. I encourage you to read each section even if you think it doesn't apply to you, as you may find some gems that will help your particular situation.

You will learn how to set boundaries and consequences with those who are lost in the throes of addiction so you don't get lost in their pain. You will learn how to set boundaries and consequences with manipulators, narcissists, and other challenging people and situations. And you will learn about the grief and loss that comes with setting boundaries with those who don't understand or respect your boundaries. Throughout the book you will complete exercises and answer questions that are designed to take you deeper into your work. These practical exercises will give you a clearer understanding of how your boundaries show up in all spheres of your life. By bringing all of this knowledge together, you can create an emotionally fulfilling life for yourself because you are creating a strong boundary protection system that you can rely upon.

When you work the exercises and answer the questions, it will be helpful to have a notebook to write deeper reflections as they come to you. Each chapter builds on and reinforces the next, so you will begin to develop a clear sense of your boundary system and those of others. Keep your notes to look back on so you can see your progress.

If boundary setting is a new concept to you, this book will take you on a step-by-step journey to teach you when, where, and how to use boundaries to help you shape your interactions with life. If you are familiar with boundary setting, the stories, question prompts, and cognitive behavioral therapy techniques and exercises will take you deeper into your work and help to refine your boundary style. I humbly hope that you find this material practical and helpful.

Much of what I relate to you I had to learn the hard way. Everything I'm asking you to do, I've done. Through trial and error and from many great teachers, I've learned the perils and triumphs of going from having very few boundaries to learning how to respect and love myself with healthy boundaries. It's my intention to bring forth everything I know about this subject to give you the tools I wish I had early on. I work on my boundary system every day to strengthen that muscle.

Our inner child wounding greatly influences how we relate to others and ourselves. You will learn how to recognize when this wounded aspect of yourself shows up and how to heal this repeating pattern so you can feel safe in all of your interactions. For example, you may have had a fuzzy boundary system as a child that worked for you then, but in adulthood you realize your boundaries need to be much stronger and more robust. Our boundaries are adaptable and dynamic, and as we heal, our boundary awareness expands. The boundary process you are learning here is an extension of the work in my book *Healing Your Lost Inner Child*.

I don't mean to oversell that your life will be perfect once you start to set boundaries more consistently, as you will still have unexpected things happen, joyful experiences and surprises, but that's life. I will tell you from my own experience that my life and relationships became simpler, more direct, and I wasn't flooded with guilt, self-doubt, second-guessing, or mind reading once I started to set healthier boundaries. You will have what I call clean transactions with others—you will be able to clean up loose ends in your relationships so you don't get snagged on them later. Boundaries set us free from the codependent wounded patterns that often feel baked in. You will learn how to say no instead of saying yes and later feeling resentful.

Whenever I talk about boundaries people say, Why isn't this taught in school?! I think this statement highlights the importance and power that boundaries have to make our lives more functional and enjoyable once we learn and consistently practice a few skills. Boundaries lay the groundwork for a mutually respectful and reciprocal connection with everyone we encounter. These are the communication tools most of us would love to have known about when starting our adult life.

Through the process of learning skillful boundary setting, you will become more aware of this expression and new ways of refining your messages with clarity. Your awareness of boundaries, both your own and those of others, will change and grow as you heal. You will learn many new boundary tools to help make your life flow with ease and help you reach a state of contentment.

There is a great sense of emotional freedom that comes with boundary setting. There is a courage deep inside that is awakening within, preparing you to own your truth, speak your truth, and claim your power. As you go through this work, you may experience a magical moment that others have told me and I have seen myself, when, after study, observation, and practice, you will suddenly start to set boundaries reflexively. Just like that, it begins to happen. You carry a feeling of standing strong with a deep knowing that you are protecting yourself, speaking your truth in ways that you may never have before, and connecting with your inner healer. You will be protecting yourself in ways that you always needed to but didn't have the words or boundary knowledge to do so.

A bigger, more expanded version of you is patiently waiting to step into a new, unfolding reality that was always there, hidden in plain sight. Treasure this moment, as you deserve to feel safe, loved, and respected. Find and embrace the courage to set healthy boundaries. Welcome to the adventure.

CHAPTER ONE

A Foundation of Boundaries

Daring to set boundaries is about having the courage to love ourselves even when we risk disappointing others.
—BRENÉ BROWN

Most people drift through life with a vague notion of what boundaries are, yet they do not consciously know that boundaries help us to create a more fulfilling life when we use them consistently. Some people have boundaries that are not defined and are always shifting, a loose collection of wishes they hope others will magically know. Some are armored up, rigidly shutting out others, with a trepidation that their safe cocoon will be penetrated by fears, both real and imagined. The goal with boundary setting is to speak our truth in such a way as to be heard and to create the lives we desire. To be successful in this work, it is helpful to learn what healthy boundaries are and what they are not, then find the courage to state a boundary when necessary.

Like a mama bear with her cubs, healthy boundaries act as powerful guardrails around our interactions with others, defining where we end and they begin. Whether we consciously know it or not, we all have a line in the sand or a deal breaker when it comes to certain behaviors and experiences, but often we do not verbalize them to others or even consciously recognize them within ourselves. We just know that when something happens that offends us or doesn't feel right, a boundary has been crossed. Many of us push aside the boundary violation and hope they won't do it again, or swallow our frustration each time they do. Healthy boundaries help us to create balance in our lives by acknowledging a boundary violation, where we can create the experiences that help our authentic selves step forward and live more fully. Boundaries are about helping us to connect, join, and feel whole.

Boundaries are one of the main ways we define and shape our relationships regarding what we will and won't tolerate. Without clear boundaries, we leave ourselves open for our relationships and situations to be defined by others—but there is a cost to both setting and not setting boundaries. We can either state a boundary up front so others know where we stand, we can go along and not say anything, or we can say yes but feel a no inside—paying the price later with regret, hurt, and resentment. A lot of people feel guilty even thinking about setting a boundary. At the beginning, it's natural to vacillate between giving up and shutting down, and standing in our convictions, feeling healed and grounded, knowing our truth.

You will be learning about many types of healthy boundaries throughout this work, and I will invite you to practice boundary setting when you're ready. To get you started, here are a few examples of situations where you may already be setting healthy boundaries. Ask yourself how well you respond with boundaries in these situations:

- Saying no (or yes) when you have an opinion or need.
- Accepting when others say no.
- Not compromising your values for others.
- Sharing personal information in a respectful way.
- Letting the other person have their own experience and not try to micromanage.
- Reassuring yourself that things are going to be okay. (*I don't know how it's going to work out, but I'm going to do my best.*)
- Honoring what you want or how you want to approach a situation.
- Removing yourself from situations that are uncomfortable or harmful.
- Stating your physical or sexual safety boundaries firmly; not apologizing for your boundaries.
- Expressing what you want or need to yourself and others.

If you are able to set many of these boundaries, congratulations, as you are ahead of the curve. These are examples of healthy boundary tools you can use to keep yourself emotionally, physically, mentally, and sexually safe.

These examples may also highlight some areas of your life where you need to reinforce healthier boundaries to protect yourself. The better care you take of your needs and the boundary needs of others, the better you can connect with your authentic self and create balance. By attending to your needs first, you establish a strong internal base, giving strength and fortitude to your ability to set boundaries with others.

Where We End and Others Begin

*In kindness, stand firm in your boundary statement.
Over time, others will see your consistency as an
indication that you know yourself and your needs.*

Boundaries set us free from the patterns that have kept us stuck. They are the tools that help us find the way through and out of recycled pain and into a place of emotional freedom. They are the limits of what we determine to be acceptable and needed in our lives. Boundaries can be a statement to others (using our voice), an action (behavior), or a silent promise to ourselves. We enter into an agreement with ourselves when we embrace the power of stating healthy boundaries. They are a necessary and normal part of the communication and interaction in our relationships.

Using boundary tools every day reinforces and helps us to recognize our needs in each of our life spheres. With healthy boundaries in place, we can discern if our needs are being honored and respected in all of our relationships—in other words, we learn to see the red flags when someone does not honor our boundaries. Over time, this discernment becomes second nature. Engaging with healthy boundaries creates the foundational blueprint for respect and reciprocation in our relationships. You know where you end and others begin.

Boundaries are about saying no, but as you will learn, they are about much more than that. Healthy boundaries involve developing specific tools that you need to make your relationships successful. With healthy boundaries, you can feel, at a deep level, that you are strong, you know your feelings, and you can show up authentically, feeling safe and vulnerably available.

When we start to think of boundaries as needs, naming and claiming our boundaries is less mysterious and we can see them as a necessary means to an end. In order to meet our needs ourselves and have them met by others, we have to express them. Others may know us well, but they can't read our minds. The only way others know what our needs are and whether they are being met is through this interaction. When we state our needs, we speak our truth and allow our boundaries to protect and look after our needs. Without these declarations, our needs may never be known or met, creating a feeling of disappointment and invalidation. We define and shape our reality through our boundaries.

Stating boundaries is about stating our needs,
which helps us to show up authentically.

Sometimes people don't respect our boundaries no matter what we do or how we say them. Maybe you've tried many times to set boundaries to no avail, and you're just worn out. Maybe you are too hurt by another to even contemplate setting a boundary with them; you just no longer want to have anything to do with them. Know that that's okay and that you are worth protecting and being cared for. Your emotional safety is worth more than trying to reconnect and establish boundaries with someone who is not interested in your feeling of safety. Boundary work is not about convincing someone to respect your boundaries. Either they respect you or they don't, and when you have this clarity and conviction of your boundaries, this truth will be self-evident.

I have met with thousands of people throughout my career as a psychotherapist, and I've seen that the number one issue that gets in the way of our feeling whole and having healthy relationships is the lack of boundary setting. It seems simple enough to just say no and set a boundary, but for many reasons—most importantly, childhood family programming—it is hard for most of us to do (at first). When others don't respect our boundaries, we can get flummoxed and confused, and struggle to maintain this necessary defense. Yelling our boundaries louder or saying them over and over will not help a disrespectful person to suddenly hear or respect our needs.

An important thing to know about boundaries is that we state a boundary first for ourselves to hear, and then for the other person to hear. When we secure our needs first, then we will be better equipped to address the needs of others. It's great if others hear and respect our boundaries, but it's more important that we hear our own voice and how we are protecting ourselves.

Healthy boundaries are demonstrated with respect for ourselves and the other person. They are solid, firm, and strong. Wobbly boundaries happen when we don't know what to say, don't know the boundary we need, or don't know if it's easier to avoid the situation altogether. The following are examples of wobbly boundaries:

- You sometimes wish people could read your mind instead of having to tell them what you need.
- You insert yourself into someone else's life so you feel in control, or others do that to you.
- You avoid conflict by ignoring people and situations simply because you don't know what to say.
- You get frustrated when others talk over you or tell you how you feel instead of asking you.
- You answer for others instead of asking what they want or need.
- It is easier to give in to what others want from you than to express your desires.
- You have trouble making decisions because you don't want to make others mad.
- You keep others at arm's length so they don't get too close.

These are everyday situations that we have all encountered, but when they happen frequently, they are the indicators of an unhealthy or wobbly boundary system. When we don't fully acknowledge our needs and defend them, others will make up what they think our needs or boundaries should be in the resulting vacuum; others will shape our reality and form our narrative. Stating our boundaries is not about disconnecting or ending a conversation, it's about declaring our needs and sharing with others so they know us better. Healthy boundaries are meant to encourage a deeper conversation and connection. When we verbalize a boundary, others know what our needs are, and we can go from there.

A big part of boundary work is learning the language of boundaries. Boundaries begin with stating our needs clearly, which I reference as an opening boundary. For example, an opening boundary might sound like, *I would really like it if we could snuggle on the couch, as I am feeling lonely and I want to feel closer to you.* This opening boundary is akin to an ask or a request we make. It is without demand and is not an ultimatum. If the opening boundary is not heard, validated, or respected, then we craft a boundary statement with a consequence that is similar to our ask, but with a reinforcement: *I'm feeling lonely and unhappy in our relationship. If we can't create some level of physical intimacy, I will need to determine whether our connection is best for me.* The consequence says that you're serious about your boundaries. Without stating a consequence, it's as if you are speaking only to yourself, and the other person may not take you seriously. To carry this idea further, you can extend the consequence. For example, if your boundary statement is still ignored, the consequence extension might be: *I can't be in a relationship without a physical connection. This relationship doesn't work for me.*

You can build boundary statements as needed, as you don't need to start out stating a boundary with a consequence or reinforcement. Boundaries are about connecting, joining, and having an open-hearted conversation, then seeing where it takes you.

That's the function of opening boundaries. You are saying, *Let's have a conversation about something that is bothering me.* Boundaries with consequence say to others that you are serious about protecting your needs, and you want to join with and participate in life with them. You put yourself out there and, hopefully, those in your life can hold and honor your needs, making sure you are heard and seen. You will learn more about stating boundaries with consequence as you do this work. For now, focus on learning about when and where you need to set boundaries in your life.

When we have clarity and begin to develop our boundaries, we have an acute awareness of those who have good boundaries and those who do not. We begin to see healthy boundaries reflected back to us when others are respectful and reciprocal. Those with unhealthy boundaries reveal their lack of knowing, either by ignoring the line we draw in the sand or by questioning *why* we need to stand up for ourselves. Their glaring lack of boundary awareness tells us more about them, highlighting the difference between those we can trust with a confidence and those who care more about their own needs than ours.

The intention for setting healthy boundaries is to help us have a more fulfilling life and to feel more connected in our relationships. Establishing boundaries with another, even someone we know we can trust, can be like stepping into the unknown as we bring forth a truth that is clear to us. The risk is that we don't know how the other person is going to hear our truth, but at the end of the day, it's our truth, our need, our reality to be brought forth. Stating a boundary is an invitation for others to honor our truth, to join us in a deeper connection so they know our needs better and so we have their recognition of our now-acknowledged truth. When our needs have been held in this way, it's important to honor and thank those who hold our boundary truth because so much of our healing comes from being seen.

*Establishing boundaries requires
courage and vulnerability.*

People who have good boundary skills may have learned them at an early age, but in my experience, most of us learn healthy boundaries as we get older, when we have more life experiences and have learned through trial and error. Through our interactions, we learn that we can be close to some people and remain wary of others, who we can trust with confidences and who we can share only limited information with. If we are successful with our practice of boundary setting, we will develop strong relationships while maintaining our sense of self. We begin to quickly register if someone respects our boundaries and whether or not they have a strong boundary system. We can recognize the red flags much sooner so that we don't spin our wheels with someone who is not good for us. With this new language and understanding, we can evaluate situations and people more accurately to determine whether they are safe and healthy and will respect who we are.

Poor boundaries enable a wounded dance that will stealthily show up in all our spheres of life. We pull from the same boundary toolkit at work and at home, so this toolkit, whether healthy or poorly developed, recreates the same relationship dynamics over and over, just in variations. This is why some people want to run away from their life; they don't have a break because they have the same kinds of issues with people wherever they go. Essentially, they don't use the right boundaries for the situation, so the drama persists. In order to heal and create better boundaries, we need new skills.

Boundary Skill Sets

To be successful with boundary setting, you will need two skill sets. The first skill set is the ability to understand context: who you are setting the boundary with, your relationship to them, the situation, and life juggles with respect to your own well-being. This skill set involves reading the situation and bringing in flexibility and adaptation to state your boundary as clearly as you can for others, as well as trusting your gut, determining risk, and seeing opportunity.

Over the arc of time, we may encounter any one of an infinite number of situations, and through each one we learn as we go, paying attention to our gut reactions and discerning if the situation is respectful and reciprocal. Later, I will give you examples of everyday situations that include boundary violations to help you discern when, where, and how to respond to them. You will read over the examples of healthy boundaries and see how they match a similar situation in your life to help you create the responses you feel are appropriate.

The second skill set includes using various types of boundaries to create guardrails, definition, and walls, if needed, to keep you safe and help you live your best life. This skill set is about self-discipline and creating an emotionally fulfilling life for yourself. You will learn about many types of boundary tools and how and when to employ them to defend your needs. As you apply your new skills, you will be learning how to use these tools to create an internal boundary resource to pull from for the rest of your life. You will use them over and over again, and each time you do, your boundary muscle will become stronger, more dynamic, and more refined. You will embody the tools you need to help you create a sense of emotional freedom in your life. This is the long game of developing your boundary skills.

Speaking your truth and advocating for your needs by using healthy boundaries is the goal. To be able to speak with clarity, you must first determine what your boundary needs are, and then you can wrap words around what you are protecting. When used as a whole, these skills will create the foundation for you to recognize your needs, find your boundary statement or message, and speak or act on your truth.

Here is a thought exercise: Think of someone in your life with whom you have a problem. You feel the need to speak your truth, but you've been hesitant to say something to them because of what they might think or say in response. The feelings you are having right now may indicate the need to set a boundary with this person or situation. As you read the examples of how to state a boundary, begin to imagine how you would set a boundary with this person. Focus on your statement, not on their response.

Respect and Reciprocity

When I began to learn about healthy boundary setting, it was if a curtain were being drawn back, slowly revealing those who were respectful and reciprocal toward me and those who tried to run me over with their agenda, taking from me and giving nothing in return. Before this awakening, I stumbled through my interactions, not understanding why I was upset or disappointed after conversations with some people and why I felt good and whole when I was with others. I was using the only boundary tools I had seen growing up for how to relate to others, and I didn't know any different.

Many of my learned responses at that time were from childhood, and I used them over and over to try to connect and develop relationships in adulthood. I would become triggered and, not having a healthy boundary system, would do things like shut down, people-please, avoid, and try to mind read. These codependent behaviors were the broken boundary tools my lost inner child used to feel safe and in control when I was a kid, and I brought them into my adult relationships. But these wounded tools were developed for another time and place, and only made matters worse. I was lost in this codependent wounding and thought it was just who I was. I didn't know I had options. I didn't know about setting healthy boundaries or that I could use my words to defend my needs.

In order to ensure a healthy boundary system, we need to have mutual respect and a connection that feels reciprocal. Ideally, the receiver will respect our boundary at face value and not question, shame, or demean us. This interaction, ideally, is reciprocal and works both ways, not just where one does all the work while being disrespected. A lack of respect or reciprocity sets the stage to enable codependent patterns, and this dysfunction marinates in our relationships.

In my book *Healing Your Lost Inner Child*, I define codependency as having a higher regard, esteem, love, trust, and respect for another than one has for oneself, and over-relying on others for a sense of self or validation of self. For any interaction or connection to *not* be codependent in nature, there needs to be a healthy exchange, where one expresses a need and the other reciprocates by honoring and respecting the need. Consistent boundaries disengage, disarm, eliminate, and heal codependent patterns in ourselves and our relationships. Boundaries are about protecting ourselves by word or action within the situation we find ourselves in.

As I mentioned earlier, the process has two skill sets: understanding context and applying appropriate boundaries with consequences. Context is the circumstance you find yourself in and your relationship to the other person, and determines how you state your boundary. Following are two examples. The first is in the context of a casual or tertiary relationship (think, a stranger in front of you in line at the grocery store). The second is in the context of a close friendship or interpersonal relationship where there might be more consequences, depending on how the boundary setting process plays out. The examples are similar statements but different in tone related to the context.

Consider the context and how you would state a boundary with someone else or the situation. Notice the boundary statement and then the stated consequence if the behavior continues. Boundaries with a stranger or someone with whom you do not expect future interaction are very short and direct. They might sound like this:

- You're in my personal space. Please stand back. If you don't, I will leave this meeting.
- How you are speaking to me is very shaming. Please stop speaking to me that way or I'm ending the conversation.
- Please don't use my things without my permission. I'm putting a lock on my door.

These statements are direct, clear, and to the point with a stranger or new acquaintance. They are unlike how you would state a boundary with someone close to you. When we interact with people in everyday circumstances who are not respectful or who are repeatedly manipulative, the best way to state boundaries is to be concise and without confusion followed by a consequence. Stating boundaries in this context is meant to protect and look after ourselves in the immediate circumstance we find ourselves in.

There is a need for us to be clear in the moment as we consider the context and how we want to get our information across so the other person can hear us. In the moment, if you feel passionate about your boundaries and don't feel seen or heard, you may be tempted to state them in a brutal way and weaponize your truth out of frustration. If you were to do that, the receiver may not be able to hear your truth and may become defensive, paving the way for arguments and shouting matches. You can evaluate the context and discern the tone and language of how you want to get your point across with your boundary tools. With the context and person in mind, you can start shaping your boundary message.

Stating boundaries with consequence within the context of a friend, partner, or close relative with whom you are likely to have many future interactions may sound like this:

- I feel really hurt when you talk to me like that, as it feels condescending. Please don't speak to me that way or I will have to consider my options for our connection.
- I would appreciate it if you would stand back and give me more room. This feels confining and uncomfortable. If this continues, I will have to leave.
- When you say that you don't have time for my screw-ups, it feels very shaming. If I can't be given feedback in a more supportive and productive manner, then this opportunity is not for me.
- Please ask me if you want to use my things instead of just taking them. This feels violating when you use my things without permission. If this doesn't change, I will not be able to continue as your roommate.

Notice these are similar to the boundary messages as before, with a stranger or acquaintance, but with more words and feelings wrapped around them with respect to the context and the relationship. These statements may sound polite, and they are. In order for us to be respected, we need to be respectful. Your truth is an energetic gift you share with others. When you consider context and consequences, you can present your boundaries in a way others can hear them more clearly. You package your message for the receiver, but not in a manipulative way. Usually, the best way those we are close to can hear our truth is in a gentle, direct, and clear way.

Learning how to set your boundaries and use your words to defend your needs takes effort. This new boundary language is akin to learning a foreign language; it takes time to learn, but when you begin to see the advantages of being clear with others, advocating for yourself, and getting the results you want, it's hard to go back to avoiding boundaries. The many examples I give throughout the book will help you learn how to state boundaries within the context of your life. They are meant as a guide to help you craft your own boundary language. The combination of words you use may sound different from my examples.

I hear from people who are frustrated with their relationships. They say, *I just want to run away from my life; everyone around me keeps telling me what to do*, or, *I don't feel I can say what I really need to say because they will get mad*. These are examples of where the person tried to set a boundary at one time but it wasn't honored, or they thought they or their boundaries were the problem. They opened themselves up, got hurt, and then retreated behind a wall so others couldn't hurt them again. Their inner child wounding of not being heard or seen may have gotten triggered, so they retreat into a hurt space in their shadow.

It takes consistent effort to set boundaries that will show our inner wounded parts that we can protect all of ourselves. This effort helps to heal those parts that at one time felt helpless, bullied, or victimized. There are so many times when we need boundaries, large and small, in our lives. As you read the stories I've included, you may start to think of situations in your life where you need clearer boundaries and consequences to define the connection.

You may find that some of the boundary violators in your life have manipulative and narcissistic traits. They use violating and shaming language as a way to gain dominance, to control you with passive-aggressive behaviors, and to push you into a submissive state. Learning how to set boundaries with these difficult personality types takes time. The more knowledge you have, the better equipped you will feel, and you won't give in to their games so easily. These types of interactions call for a strong boundary system, where you know yourself well and have the tools to navigate these challenging relationships. You will learn more about how to set boundaries in these types of relationships in chapter 9.

People who didn't have good boundary role models as children often have broken or mixed boundaries and are unable to recognize boundary violations or red flags because they grew up in an environment that had fuzzy boundaries or none at all. This lack of boundary awareness has deep-reaching consequences on choices and will present itself in repeating patterns until it is healed. A big part of this work is unlearning boundary types that no longer serve you, while learning more effective strategies to express your needs.

Those who respect us will hear our boundaries and pay attention to our needs. They will be willing to change how they talk to or interact with us because they see us, hear us, and hold space for us in their lives. Respect and reciprocity sound like, *What I hear you saying is . . .*, or, *I know this is important to you, so how can we make it happen?* Those who are more concerned about their own needs than ours and don't respect our boundaries don't treat us very well and disregard our boundaries as a nuisance rather than a need. Recognizing the boundaries or lack thereof in our relationships is a decision point: if we aren't felt, heard, or seen, we can either give up because it's too hard to defend our boundaries or move on from them and honor ourselves and our boundaries.

Who People Are (and Are Not)

Another way to look at context within our boundary system is to recognize that we put people into categories of how close we can pull them in or how far we need to keep them out. This includes things we can and can't do with them, what we can and can't say to them, and what we can and can't ask of them. We know instinctively and from experience what we can and cannot ask of people. We know at a gut level the boundaries we need to use with different people.

- We know who we can trust with money and who we can't.
- We know who we can ask for a favor and who we cannot.
- We know who we can share a secret with and who are loose-lipped.
- We know who we can trust to take care of our pets and who we would not.
- We know who we can trust to look after our kids and who we cannot.
- We know who will be reliable and on time if we ask them for help and who will not.

We set boundaries with each of these folks, but we don't think of these delineations as boundaries; we are just being pragmatic. We know what people are good at and what they are not good at. Others have shown us over time the type of boundaries we need to set with them based on their personalities.

For us to have successful interactions with others and manage our expectations, we need to be discerning and have a clear idea of who we should go to for what, depending on what's going on in our lives. Think about the people in your life not just in terms of what they can do for you but for who they are and the place they hold in your life. This is one of the ways you shape an internal boundary sense with that person.

We look out for ourselves and for the relationship with clarity. We acknowledge how this person fits into our life and how close we can bring them in. We are being realistic with ourselves and the other person by not putting expectations on them or the relationship that cannot be fulfilled. We may leave some connections on the table because of the guardrails we need to set, such as learning that we can't share a confidence with someone, or we disagree with a relative but they are really good with helping our mom, or we don't think a friend would do a good job with money but they're patient with our kids. Paying attention to how you feel about someone else informs your boundary system.

Sometimes relationships become too loaded and crush under the weight of expectations. Do you see others for who they are or who you need them to be?

You may have a relationship with another person who is there but doesn't make an effort. This nonengagement is where, for whatever reason, they have set a boundary about how much or how little they want to participate. This is confusing because even if you ask them to participate more, they do not. In these cases, a good boundary inquiry would be to ask them what is going on. If nothing changes, you will know to not work any harder than they are.

I had to do this with a long-term friendship after we agreed that I was doing more of the work and that he wasn't interested in working that hard to maintain the friendship. It took me a while to realize that the resentment I felt was because of the lack of boundaries on my part, so I stopped checking in and making things happen. I stopped projecting who I needed him to be and saw him for who he was and how he was showing up. I missed the connection, but afterward I felt proud of the way I stepped up and honored my feelings. What I realized in that moment was that he wasn't going to change; that was just who he was. I remembered the words of Maya Angelou: "When someone shows you who they are, believe them the first time." I am still connected to my friend, but it's not the same, and it can't be. I can't go back to doing everything to manufacture what I need him to be, what I need the relationship to be. That wouldn't be fair to me.

Starting to express boundaries is like stepping into a new land with new language. It is an unknown landscape where we are learning new ways to express and defend our deepest needs and improve our relationships so we feel connected, closer, and safer. Not everyone in your life will recognize or respect your boundaries—especially if you've never expressed them before—but the results and benefits will far outweigh the unknowns. There is a new world of emotional freedom, within yourself and your relationships, waiting for you to explore.

Bridget's Story

Bridget, a young mom, was always helping her mom friends, and it was hard for her to say no when anyone asked her for help. She liked seeing the other moms smile and thank her. She felt wanted, needed, and liked—all the things she didn't feel growing up in an emotionally neglectful household.

Bridget would agree to pick up other moms' kids from school and take them to practice or games. She'd always say, *No problem, call me anytime, happy to help you out.* The other moms began to rely on her. Bridget created a dependency in these friendships, which satisfied the wounded, hurting part of her that wanted to feel needed. But by filling her own wounded needs, her kids suffered because she wasn't available for them. She didn't know how to set healthy boundaries for herself or others, so she over-extended herself and became sick, frustrated, shutdown, and withdrawn.

The other moms were sad to hear Bridget was sick, but they didn't offer to help her. She had effectively trained them to be dependent or her, essentially inferring that she didn't have any needs, that her job was to be a people pleaser and serve the needs of others. By making herself indispensable to the other moms, she was unconsciously playing out her childhood wounded needs.

The emotionally wounded part of her needed to be needed so much that she sacrificed her own family's well-being in order to receive validation from others. When we don't have the adult tools we need, we go back to what has worked before.

Bridget grew up in a home with emotionally unavailable parents who were unable to give her the attention she needed. She always helped out around the house to get their attention, but it didn't work, as they were in their own world and had few emotional tools. She would try harder, thinking she was the problem. This unhealthy relationship taught Bridget that she needed to be as helpful as possible to others so others would see her value, would rely on and need her, and finally give her the attention she craved her whole life. Unfortunately, it meant she had little or no boundary skills in her relationships to say no when she needed to. She put her worth in the approval of others.

Through therapy, Bridget is learning to set boundaries with herself first, then with others. She now sees how her inner child wounding of not feeling she is enough sends her into a people-pleasing and overcompensating spiral. She is learning how to love and care for herself in ways that she never received from her parents. She is also learning the boundary language to ask for help or to say no to others when she doesn't have the capacity to help out. This is the first step in healing the inner child wounding: giving ourselves what we needed most in childhood. Bridget is learning to hold the truth that she is enough. She is saying no to other moms now and is learning to hold this feeling.

Don't mistake my kindness for a weakness.

A broken boundary system like Bridget's keeps us looping in a toxic soup, where we set ourselves up for being hurt in some way.

What once worked in our childhood family gets in the way of our feeling authentic and fulfilled in our adult relationships. Yes, we can have boundaries and still be nice, but that doesn't mean we're a pushover. Boundaries help us have a sense of agency over our traumatic past so we don't keep repeating the same mistakes over and over.

You are learning new ways to express and solidly defend yourself. As you gather this knowledge, you will start using your newfound boundary language and will one day feel a sense of pride and maybe even surprise. A feeling of emotional freedom is waiting for you.

If you feel the need to repeat, teach, train, or explain your boundary, chances are the other person isn't respecting your boundary. When you go into explaining mode, you are eroding your boundaries and giving your power away.

Learning What Your Boundaries Are

When you say "yes" to others,
make sure you're not saying "no" to yourself.
—PAUL COELHO

Every boundary we set is in context to a person, place, situation, or timing within each of what I call life spheres. For example, you have a set of boundaries with people you work with and different sets of boundaries with your friends and family. You aren't changing yourself with each group; you just let some people in closer than others. Life spheres are the parts of our life that, combined, help us to feel whole. I identify these spheres to include the areas of emotional health; personal space; intellectual thoughts, ideas, and beliefs; sexual identity and expression; work life; time management; play and creativity; and security. The importance and priorities we place on each life sphere and the protections we give to each become the building blocks that blend together to create our life as we know it. When we give more attention to certain areas, we thrive in those spheres. When we neglect some areas, those spheres go dormant, and in time, we will not feel as fulfilled. For example, say you learned at a young age that you were not deserving of having a loving relationship, so your emotional life sphere became neglected and shut down. Or perhaps you do not have the tools needed to create balance in your time management sphere because you feel you are not "enough," so you overcompensate and overwork, with no time for play.

Our unhealed inner child wounding is a direct contributor to the attention or neglect and the boundary protections we give to each sphere. Through this work, you can observe yourself with a soft gaze and see which spheres you encourage and which need more of your boundary attention. Understanding each life sphere provides the framework for how, when, and where we use boundaries. The goal is to have balance within each of the spheres, which are the main components of a strong boundary protection system.

Learning about your life spheres and boundaries will help you see more clearly the game board of the interactions between all areas of your life. You will begin to see what you do that helps or hurts your relationships and how you feel about yourself. You will see when you make yourself smaller to hide and give power away, and when you puff yourself up to be in control and look big and powerful.

In chapter 5, Healthy Boundaries, you will learn about the internal and external boundaries you can use in each life sphere that will help to create a sense of balance and protect your needs within the context of a situation. For now, think of boundaries in each life sphere as simply saying no or yes.

Life Spheres: A Framework for Boundary Balance

The clarity and focus we have with our boundary setting is linked to the energy and importance we give to each of our life spheres. The complexities of life put demands on us that often pull us in different directions. We can easily get distracted by a situation that is very loud and overpowers everything else, making it hard to see where we need boundaries. The better boundary balance we have in each of our life spheres, the more effective boundaries we have across all spheres. This boundary balance translates to a feeling that our lives are more in control, and we contentedly feel good about things. It's a deep feeling of connection that is hard to pinpoint, but when you have this feeling, you know this feeling.

> *We are the guardians for each of our life spheres.*
> *Without good boundaries, creating and protecting*
> *our dreams and desires will be challenging.*

Following is a detailed description of each life sphere and possible boundaries that work within each. After reading the description for each life sphere, you will rate how well you think you manage your boundaries for that sphere. Don't worry if you have trouble assessing your boundaries within these spheres right now. Boundaries take time to understand and integrate. For now, just think of them as where and when you do a good job of saying no or yes in a way that helps you achieve balance within each life sphere.

The emotional life sphere relates to how we feel regarding our overall mood and our relationships. The boundaries we use in the emotional life sphere form the backbone of our relationships to ourselves and others. Clear boundaries in this sphere help others know how we want to be treated. Healthy emotional boundaries put brackets around what we feel comfortable sharing and not sharing of our personal or private information. With a healthy boundary, there is a natural unfolding of personal and private information over the course of a relationship; we don't divulge everything at once. This sphere is more in balance when we acknowledge our feelings internally; share this tender part of ourselves with others; and feel heard, seen, and valued.

How well do you look after your emotional needs? Do you make the emotional needs of others more important than your own? On a scale of one to five, with five being the best, rate how well you meet the needs of your emotional life sphere and the boundaries you use to achieve balance in this sphere.

The personal space life sphere is about our sense of personal space and physical touch (not including intimate touch). This is where we check in with ourselves to see if, for example, we are okay being in a crowded place or prefer to be with a smaller group. Personal space boundaries are violated when others touch or hug us without permission, ignore our limits, or rummage through our things (including phones).

We determine if it's okay for others to shake our hand, stand close to us, or give us a hug, but no one can read our minds or know our physical boundaries until we state them. We set a boundary in our own words, in our own way, around these behaviors. This sphere is more in balance when we consciously honor our physical boundary needs and feel at a deep level that we are protecting ourselves.

Do you stand up for yourself, or do you feel that others violate your space? Rate from one to five how well you meet the needs of your personal space life sphere and the boundaries you use to achieve balance in this sphere.

(As a note, our bodies remember trauma. If you have a history of physical trauma, your body won't always allow you to be open and will often reject physical closeness, or you may have no physical boundaries because of a prior violation and let others do what they want, which is a re-traumatization. Trust what your physical boundary protection needs in order to heal.)

The intellectual life sphere comprises thoughts, ideas, and beliefs, whether ours or someone else's. Healthy intellectual boundaries include how well we manage our own thoughts, whereas unhealthy or missing boundaries determine how much we give in to mind reading and making up stories about others, which ramps up anxiety and paranoia. We are in charge of our minds and what we focus on. After all, where the mind goes, energy flows.

Intellectual boundaries are violated when we mind read, when someone dismisses our thoughts or beliefs, or when we shame others for their ideas. This sphere is more in balance when we honor our thoughts, when others are genuinely interested in our ideas, and when we are interested in theirs. There is a reciprocity and acknowledgment of what is okay to discuss or not, based on social and verbal cues.

Do your insecurities get the better of you to the point that you make up stories about how others feel about you so that you feel in control? Thinking about things that are important to you, rate from one to five how well you meet the needs of your intellectual life sphere. Reflect on the boundaries you use to achieve balance in this sphere.

The sexual life sphere relates to all aspects of sexual identity and expression, intimately giving to ourselves, and sharing with another. By listening to our own needs and following respectful conversation, each party knows their consensually agreed upon sexual needs. This honest and sensitive conversation develops a mutual understanding between intimate partners for the limits of go and no-go areas. One way to establish boundaries in this sphere is to say green, yellow, or red light as a measure of comfort. Checking in with each other before, during, and after helps to keep sexual boundaries on track and intact. This also helps to normalize talking about sexual needs instead of keeping the topic in the shadows. Know that sexual attraction differs from sexual desire. Honor yourself with what feels right to give and receive for yourself first.

Sexual boundary violations occur when the trust is broken between partners because of infidelity, sharing private information with others, going against established limits, or being forceful without consent, including sexual acts or comments. Pay special attention to internal messages (boundaries) if you have a history of trauma. Trust what your physical and sexual boundary system tells you. Don't override this internal boundary just because your partner is motivated. Speak up. Your partner can't read your mind if something hurts or is uncomfortable. This sphere is more in balance when there is a conscious recognition of sexual and intimate needs. You may have no sexual desire, interest, or attraction, and that's where you are today. Honor your truth.

Do you feel safe to express yourself sexually, or do you avoid this sphere because of past traumas or an unknown fear? Rate from one to five how well you meet the needs of your sexual life sphere and the boundaries you use to achieve balance in this sphere.

The work sphere is connected to employment as well as how we occupy our time creating a sense of purpose, such as working for a company or volunteering for an organization. This effort brings income or fulfillment, or both. This sphere can get out of balance quickly because of the demands of an organization, the need to carry our load within a team environment, or the pressure to take on more responsibility to produce income.

Overcompensating in the work sphere reflects a feeling of not being worthy and wanting to overproduce to receive praise or reward from others. Work boundary violations occur when work effort is not respected, is overused, or when we make ourselves more available than needed in an effort to receive a sense of worth from others. Another boundary violation is when a partner or friend belittles or demeans our work or volunteer effort. This sphere is more in balance when our work or volunteering supports the other spheres.

What situations or people limit you from creating boundary balance in your work sphere? Rate from one to five how well you meet your needs and the boundaries you use to achieve balance in this sphere.

The time management life sphere relates to how we use our time for ourselves and give our time to others. How we allocate our time shows where we put our energy. When we give ourselves the gift of time, we do what needs doing and enjoy participating in the activities we want to do. This honoring is one of the greatest gifts we can give ourselves. When we don't manage our time well by setting boundaries, others may take over our time and use it for what they want, which creates resentment in us.

Most adults don't think they have enough time to do the things they want to do. Poor time management is often a codependent response that reflects making the needs of others more important than our own and giving our power away. If we have time to do things for others, we have time for self-care. Most of us can manage boundaries around time; it's just a matter of coming up with a list of things we want to experience and making time for them. This sphere is more in balance when we give time to ourselves and others and feel a fairness of reciprocity.

Do you make someone else's time more important than your own? Rate from one to five how well you meet the needs of your time management life sphere and the boundaries you use to achieve balance in this sphere.

The creative life sphere pertains to anything that we enjoy doing that is (usually) not connected to work. As adults, we aren't encouraged enough to play and be creative, but we are taught that we need balance—which is exactly what creativity encourages. We quiet our logical minds by anything from sports to handicrafts, from meditation to physical movement. Play brings a joy and fulfillment that recharges us so we can be productive in other spheres. Without creativity, we lose our sense of life balance and open ourselves up to anxiety and depression. Our minds need time to rest from figuring out puzzles and complex strategies.

Play boundary violations happen when our efforts are discouraged or mocked, or when something else gets in the way of the play. People who overcompensate or have low self-esteem will shut down play and creativity because it's "not productive" or they can't do it perfectly. Play and creativity boundary violations also happen for those who had to grow up too fast and take care of adult things at an early age. This parentification can lead to their creative life sphere getting neglected once they are adults. This sphere is more in balance when play is integrated into a weekly routine rather than being the rare exception.

Do you give yourself permission to play and be creative, or do you hold back and think it's not necessary? Rate from one to five how well you meet the needs of your creative life sphere and the boundaries you use to achieve balance in this sphere.

The security life sphere addresses all aspects of feeling secure in home, health, and finances and how we generate a feeling of safety in all senses of the term. We have healthy security boundaries when we design how to meet our security needs today and are clear with ourselves (and our partner, if applicable) about what we need to have in place to meet our security goals. When we have a plan and a clear path, we create an intentional energy that wraps around these ideas, helping them to manifest.

Security boundary violations occur when we sabotage our own plans or when others are not in alignment with the same goals and purposefully create distractions or roadblocks to prevent them from happening. Violations also occur when someone else thinks they know what is best for us instead of checking with us, or when we neglect our own needs because we think we are undeserving. This sphere is more in balance when we acknowledge those nagging reminders of what we know we need to do and proactively set up plans to take care of ourselves in the future.

Do you have beliefs about creating security for yourself that hold you back or sabotage your plans? Rate from one to five how well you meet the needs of your security life sphere and the boundaries you use to achieve balance in this sphere.

How did you rate your boundary balance in each sphere? As you read over these life sphere descriptions, did you give some spheres a high rating, areas where you meet your needs and are in balance? Did you rate some spheres lower, identifying areas that need boundary encouragement and fostering? We are at risk of giving our power away to others in each of the spheres, making their needs more important than our own, letting life get in the way, and not honoring our boundaries. Maintaining balance in each sphere is an ongoing process.

Perhaps you thought of some life spheres that I didn't mention, areas where you need better boundaries, such as digital or online, spiritual, or material (things and property). Look over your game board. How do you interact with everything going on in your life to achieve balance and the goals in each of your life spheres? Ask yourself, *Is this part of my life in balance today? What boundaries do I need to set to make this balance possible?* If there is an area where you need reinforcement, ask yourself why you may overlook or neglect this sphere.

Life puts a lot of demands on us, so it is hard to meet the needs of healthy boundaries in all areas all of the time. We sense when our life is out of balance, and, as you are learning, the lack of boundaries in several areas is a strong contributor to this unevenness. As long as you are working toward balance in your life spheres and your intention is to be respectful and reciprocal to yourself and others, you are headed in the right direction.

As you work through this material, come back to your life spheres and see how well you are meeting your needs once you learn more skills. Check back in with your ratings as you continue to learn more about boundaries, and see if your spheres are becoming more in balance.

Be gentle with yourself. You are a work in progress, and none of us have it all figured out. Pace yourself as you learn the tools you need to create the life you desire.

*I state my boundaries to receive and protect
what I need to fully express my authentic self.*

Clarity and Discernment

Clarity and discernment are important to develop as you learn what your boundaries are and how to express them. Clarity means being clear on what is okay and not okay with you. Discernment means being able to grasp or perceive what is not necessarily obvious, such as listening to your gut reaction to a situation. A gut-level reaction is a barometer that informs us about a boundary truth. When we grow up in a dysfunctional environment, we rarely learn the skills of clarity or discernment, as we are focused on emotional and physical safety. Our home environment greatly influences the lens through which we see the world to protect ourselves. Healing clears this fog of distortion, helping us see ourselves and others more clearly.

The more clarity and discernment you have regarding your feelings, the better you will be able to state your boundaries. Boundaries reveal your needs, opinions, and desires. When you start to set boundaries, you will quickly learn to identify those who are respectful of you and those who want you to be or do something else. Their reaction to a boundary you set is a measure of the type of relationship you have.

You will learn that your gut reaction is an early warning system for the boundaries you need to establish. For now, know that your gut reaction is what you immediately and naturally feel about a situation or something someone has done or said. This is your boundary protection system firing up. To explain this instant protection system, I sometimes use the ridiculous example of asking someone if they would want to eat asparagus ice cream. After they make a face, roll their eyes, and say no, I ask them what happened in their gut when I asked the question. They will say things like their stomach turned or that it just sounded awful. They knew immediately how they felt and what their initial thought was. This is their clarity (asparagus ice cream is not okay!) and discernment (my gut says no!) working, their boundary protection system kicking in.

The same is true with your boundary protection system when you hear a story or someone asks you if you want to do something. Your built-in system rejects or accepts, and you know immediately how you feel. The hard part is learning to pay attention to and honor this gut reaction. The more you do this, the more you will develop a clarity of what is okay and not okay. You will begin to determine what is the best choice for you in a given situation and circumstance. This is discernment. You will begin to be able to state what you need based on your awareness of this protection system. You naturally use this built-in system more than you realize.

When we know and trust ourselves, we don't need to make a boundary statement in a forceful manner. We don't need to yell to make a point; we can simply state what we would like or not like. If we feel we need to yell or justify a boundary, this means that we are not in a respectful relationship or situation. No means no, so if the other person tries to talk us out of a boundary, they are not respecting our boundary. We don't need to wait for someone to be mean, sarcastic, or abusive a second time for us to set a boundary. The first time should be the last time that they hurt us or try to make us feel small. Setting healthy boundaries can help to redefine relationships that have lost their way.

Boundaries are not a litmus test to see who should be in our lives and who we should kick out. They are not about discarding relationships but about refining and clarifying them. We are asking others to join with us when we use opening boundary statements to speak our truth and put forth our needs; we are trying to deepen and make the connection better. We are saying, respect me and I'll respect you.

It may take some people, even those you know well, a while to come around to your new boundary language. Give them a grace as they learn, and don't cut them off right away. Use your intuition and your gut reaction to see whether they are truly trying to join with you in this new boundary connection or if they just can't go there.

> *Using boundaries consistently is the greatest indicator that we are healing.*

The Goldilocks Zone is where our boundaries are neither too extreme nor too loose—they are just right, they are in context. This handling of boundaries comes with practice. Finding the Goldilocks Zone for the boundary you use with your mom, say, is different from the Goldilocks Zone for the boundary you use at work. You show up in both scenarios, but how you defend your needs and your truth is different for each. Through your boundary practice, you will begin to see how you need to represent yourself, what you need to say and not say. You will begin to determine the right engagement with life.

Sometimes a healthy opening boundary statement is followed by a request for what you want or need. The following are examples of healthy opening boundary statements:

- No. (Saying no is a complete statement.)
- I feel ignored in our relationship. I want to know what is going on and how this can change.
- I don't want to go to the movies. Can we do something else instead?
- I'm living my life the best I know how. I know what I feel, and I feel hurt when you try to tell me what to do.
- You keep telling me how I feel, and that doesn't sit well with me.
- I've noticed that you sometimes make fun of my choices. I want you to know that I feel shamed and I need you to stop.
- I want to tell you how I feel, but when I've done that in the past, you've told me that you feel worse, as if it's a contest. I feel lonely, unheard, and not emotionally safe in our relationship.
- It seems like you tell me what the rules are only after I've broken them. I feel humiliated when this happens.
- I'm confused as to why I have to keep asking you to do this for me. Is there something going on that I don't understand?
- It seems that you hear and acknowledge what I need, but there's no follow-through. This pattern is frustrating to me. Why do you think this keeps happening?

Each of these statements is an invitation for a conversation, an opening. They are examples for you to build on when you want to make a boundary statement. Have you wanted to say these or similar statements but held yourself back because you didn't want to get into it with the other person, or you've tried to have these conversations before and it didn't help? As you go through this work, you will learn how to navigate this resistance. For now, know that you will learn how to do this in a way that feels good to you. Note that if you state an opening boundary and the other person begins to disregard, minimize, ridicule, shame, or tell you that you have it all wrong, they do not respect your boundary. They hope to push you back so you relinquish your boundary and do what they want you to do.

Consistency is key when establishing and maintaining boundaries. You need to be committed to protecting your needs and your truth. If you sometimes set a boundary and sometimes don't, you send a mixed message and others won't think you are serious. Sending mixed messages about a boundary is saying that you aren't committed to it and aren't sure if the need or truth is important enough to support. This is a slippery slope back into having no boundaries and allowing others to make the rules for you to live by. (You will read more about maintaining boundaries in chapter 11, Stepping into Emotional Freedom.)

Others expect you to have clarity about what you need. When you don't, you run the risk of giving away your power and making the needs of others more important than your own. When your boundaries and consequences are repeatedly disrespected, you have to up your game and get yourself into an emotionally and physically safe space. This may mean removing yourself from the situation as a last resort and a means of self-preservation, not being retaliatory or dramatic. Only you can determine your next steps when your boundaries are disregarded, minimized, or shamed. Trust yourself, and seek counsel if you are up against someone who continues to say, in a thousand ways, that you and your boundaries are worthless.

Consider the context of a particular situation you have in your life right now. Think about how you want to express a boundary. What does your boundary statement sound like? In a private moment, practice saying this out loud. Get used to the words and their energy. Begin to feel your boundary power with your new boundary language.

The Boundary Protection System

When you just go along with what others want, they may think you are a pushover, and they like getting their way. When you set boundaries, you learn who your true friends are.

Strong, consistent boundaries come from deep within. They help us to recognize and know when someone pays attention to our needs and when they don't. We each develop a unique boundary protection system (BPS) that corresponds to our life spheres. Our BPS is a feedback mechanism that tells us what our limits are and where we are emotionally at a given moment in time within the context of a situation, and how we want to bring our boundaries forth.

Your unique BPS is an evolving dynamic. It can help you grow or hold you back, based on your healed or wounded parts. As you grow into your boundaries, it will become easier to use a core set of boundary tools no matter the person or group. Your boundaries will eventually become a part of you and how you interact with the world. The reliability of your boundaries and how you show up in life represents the integration with your authentic self. The BPS that you create will help you feel whole and complete. With this solid foundation, you will have the confidence to express yourself more fully than before. Your BPS is your internal rule book for boundaries.

An intact BPS helps us recognize when we need to use our words to either defend ourselves or retreat and take care of ourselves. We can quickly and accurately discern whether a situation is safe for us or not, whether someone is healthy for us to be around or not, when we can be vulnerable, and when we need protection. Our BPS empowers us to state, support, and protect our needs. All of this helps us to create an inner healer that is wise, patient, and strong.

*My boundary protection system helps me move
from one me to a grander version of me.*

You may be thinking that you don't want to be vulnerable and express your needs through your boundaries, but what if you learn how to develop and nurture the boundary tools that give you the courage to be vulnerable and know that you have these protection tools at the ready? This is the advantage of people who deftly navigate their relationships. They embody boundary confidence and can draw from these tools when needed. It's a quiet knowing, an unspoken strength, and a respect that is absent of demand. This confidence means being open, not guarded, feeling strong but not being a jerk. You, too, can learn how to become a conscious creator in your life instead of an impulsive reactor.

You will be learning about many types of boundaries in the coming chapters. Some will feel familiar and comfortable—your current go-to boundaries. Others will be brand new to you and may seem challenging to apply. You may have one boundary style at work, another at home, and a third with friends. You will recognize the ones you currently use and begin to see those that would be helpful to adopt and develop. Keep an open mind as you learn about the different ways to protect yourself. Give yourself permission to explore various types of boundaries to see what styles you like and which help you with connection or keep you isolated. You may decide that you want to keep using the boundary style you know because it makes life predictable, and that's okay. But you will also see that some boundaries are healthier expressions than others. You will learn how to create your unique blend of boundary expressions to suit your personality and life circumstances.

Our early foundational BPS system grew out of our childhood experiences, which shaped our relationship to our family, our friends, and our world. We developed unique tools to help us emotionally navigate new or distressing situations that were scary or confusing. For example, if you grew up in a family that argued a lot, you may have learned wounded tools of avoidance, becoming invisible, or shutting down. Or you might have become loud, a bully, or used anger as a defense. These are all wounded adapted responses to situations that feel out of a child's control. In adulthood, we continue to use the tools in our tool box, treating ourselves and others as we were once treated.

These wounded tools are essentially the boundaries we used for protection when we did not know about healthy boundaries. Using these impulsive reactions helped us to feel emotionally safer and gave us a sense of agency. They helped us feel we were making choices over what was happening in our world instead of feeling completely out of control. However, these wounded tools were developed for a unique moment in time and do not translate well into adulthood. They are timestamped for our family of origin and work against us as adults by unconsciously recreating childhood drama in our adult life.

In my book *Healing Your Lost Inner Child*, I describe the many impulsive reactions—what I call wounded tools—that helped us emotionally survive in childhood, as well as the functional tools we pick up along the way. In that book I teach the HEAL process—healing and embracing an authentic life—which walks the reader through understanding their origin story and how to heal the lost inner child who keeps showing up to try to protect us. Boundaries and structure help children feel they are being looked after, so when the adults do not reinforce boundaries, discipline, and rules, the kids don't feel safe at a deep level. Adults who grew up with parents who provided consistent structure will say, "I know my mom and dad loved me because they had rules." What they are saying is their parents modeled good boundaries, which imbued a deep feeling of safety.

I invite you to have fun exploring and learning how to make your unique BPS work for you. Even if you decide to keep your current boundary system, your newfound wisdom will help you recognize the boundary systems of others.

Dan's Story

Dan is a married father of three adult sons. His two older sons moved out of state, and he doesn't talk to them regularly. His youngest son, Jack, lives close by. Jack married a few years ago and has a two-year-old girl, who has Dan wrapped around her little finger. He often comes by unannounced to see his granddaughter. He will bring a gift that he thinks she would like or an item that he thinks would be nice for his son's house. While his unannounced visits and random gifts aren't always a problem, Jack has been annoyed by this. He has asked his dad to please text him if he wants to come by, but repeatedly saying this is hard for Jack, as he's a conflict avoider. Dan does not think stopping by or giving gifts is a problem. He rationalizes that he is helping them out and giving them things they like. Whenever Jack tries to push back, Dan digs in, becomes offended and hurt, and then argues with Jack for thirty minutes, trying to convince Jack that what Dan does is the "right" thing.

Jack's wife, Kate, also does not like these surprise visits by her father-in-law and thinks Jack gives in to his dad too easily.

Kate does not avoid conflict. She is frustrated because she wants to speak for Jack, but she respects him and does not get in between Jack and his dad. Jack admits that he tries to read his dad's moods and changes himself to appease his dad. He knows how headstrong his dad is, and remembers all the times he's tried to get him to stop showing up unannounced. When Jack invites his parents over, Dan will find fault in Jack's efforts. In Dan's mind, his criticism comes from a good place, but it wears on Jack and Kate. Jack has appealed to his mom to intervene, but all she says is, "Well, you know how your father is. I can't say anything right."

This all came to a head when Jack's parents were over one evening for dinner. Dan started telling Jack what he needed to do about something, and in a fit of frustration, Jack unleashed on his dad. He yelled at Dan to back off, that he's a grown man and can handle things on his own. He added, "Don't you understand that's why my brothers left town? Because you meddle so much in our lives!"

Deeply offended, Dan told his wife they were leaving. His granddaughter was crying for him as they packed up and left. After several weeks had passed, Jack felt bad about how things had gone. He started blaming himself and felt guilty about having said anything. Jack wanted to reach out to his dad, but Kate was enjoying the break from Dan's surprise visits. Jack had been through this before. He would apologize to his dad, but nothing would change and no apology ever came. Their daughter was crying every night for her grandpa, so Jack and Kate knew they had to do something.

Kate recommended that Jack go to counseling with his dad because trying to change things on his own hadn't gotten very far. At first, Jack refused because he could see that, once again, he would be doing the reaching out and Dan would be avoiding and playing the victim. However, he finally relented and called his dad. Dan agreed to meet with a counselor, but only one that he himself chose.

Dan and Jack met up at the counselor's office. They were cordial for the first two sessions, and then the real work began. Dan didn't see anything wrong with what he did. He was focused on his intention and behavior and how he "helps out," not on Jack's emotional experience of the events. The counselor pointed out that Jack had been working hard to try to tell his dad how he felt. The counselor observed that Dan tried to control so much in Jack's life because he felt out of control in his own. Dan essentially used Jack as a scapegoat and a coping tool for his own anxiety and need for control.

Jack said, "Dad, I know you love us and want the best for us, but when you come up with all these suggestions and then get angry when I reject them, or when you come by unannounced, I feel frustrated—like you don't trust me, like you still see me as a teenager. It reminds me of what you did to me as a kid, when you always made me leave my door open. It feels intrusive, and I need it to stop."

Dan balked at his son's boundary at first, but then, with some perspective from the counselor, he stopped resisting and heard his son for the first time. Dan said he hadn't realized this was Jack's experience. He said he was sorry. He admitted that he was concerned Jack was going to lock him out of his life like his other two sons had. Jack said he didn't want that and that his daughter really loved and missed her grandpa.

Dan no longer stops by unannounced and has reduced the gift giving, but he does still give unsolicited advice to Jack and Kate. Jack knows that his dad doesn't fully understand the "boundaries thing," as his dad calls it, but they see this as a step in the right direction. Kate married into this family dance, so she could see it all clearly. She had to work on her own boundaries and continue to respect Jack's relationship with his dad so she didn't overstep and try to control things. Jack has come a long way in speaking up. Now, when Dan says, "I wouldn't do that," Jack replies with the boundary, "Dad, I'm prepared to take the risk."

Do you have someone in your life who stops by unannounced or does things they think you'd like without asking? They may mean well, but their actions are intrusive and not respectful. They justify their behaviors and have many logical arguments (for them) about why this isn't a problem. Not saying anything in these situations enables bad behavior. Jack attempted many times to get his dad's attention, and his frustration built over time into a boundary laced with anger.

Learning the boundary language to use to express yourself in these situations can create a turning point that helps you feel more deeply connected in your relationships and in your life spheres. Boundary discussions like Jack had with his dad are hard, but they clear the air and help to develop a more heartfelt connection. Otherwise, the dance continues and hurt feelings pile up. Use Jack's story to reflect on where you can use heartfelt language so others clearly know your needs. Step forward with your truth and reshape stagnant relationships with healthy boundaries.

An imbalance in one of your life spheres is the greatest indicator that you are not maintaining your boundaries in this area. Take a breath and look at how well you create balance in many areas of your life, understanding that some areas need extra attention. That's okay. Life is about learning the art of creating balance so you can feel whole and complete.

You are learning the techniques of how to develop your BPS that will help you achieve your goals and create the life you desire. The more you trust your sense of clarity and discernment, the sturdier you are laying the foundation for a strong connection to your gut and your boundary system. Now we will move on to learning more about our interactions with others and how we sometimes give our power away for the sake of keeping the peace in our relationships.

CHAPTER THREE

Building Boundary Muscles

*When people set boundaries with you, it's their attempt to continue
the relationship with you. It's not an attempt to hurt you.*
—ELIZABETH EARNSHAW

Every time we state a boundary, our core gets stronger and we build a muscle that becomes our defender, empowering our boundary protection system, our BPS. Boundaries give us the gift of space in our connections to others. Effective boundaries help us to step back, observe, check in with our gut reaction, and assess what the heck is going on. What did she just say? What did he just do? How do I feel about it? You will learn how to do this assessment in real time, which will give you immediate feedback about the strength of your boundary muscle.

*What they said to me didn't feel good, and I need to say
something. If I don't protect myself, then who will?*

Noticing Resistance

If you are new to boundary setting, you may notice a clear resistance to setting a boundary. This is understandable. Many people think that setting boundaries is hard, but the hardest part of this work is getting out of your own way and being consistent. Perhaps you tend to avoid uncomfortable situations or people. You may put up excuses and roadblocks to avoid stating a boundary, especially if you think the other person isn't going to like what you have to say. Some statements take a lot of courage and vulnerability to express, while others are easier to state, especially when there's a built-in excuse, such as *Sorry, I can't help you out with your yard work—we are going out of town.* This limit of what you can or can't do doesn't cost much emotional capital, and while the excuse is true, it's an easy boundary to place—it is a boundary of convenience. Your gut reaction said that you didn't want to help them with the yard work, and going out of town helped you avoid stating your real feelings. The other person may be disappointed, but with the factual excuse of leaving town, you avoided a potential confrontation. Of course, we don't always have easy ways to avoid these situations, which is why learning healthy boundary language is so important.

People who are conflict avoiders like to have convenient excuses because then they don't have to state a hard no. Even if we tend to avoid difficult conversations, there are ways to bring boundaries into our relationships to protect our needs—especially when no one else can or should speak for us. Self-honoring boundaries help to manifest our heart's desires. Later on we will explore more challenging boundary statements, for when we don't have a convenient excuse and have to own our truth, not knowing how the other person will respond.

> *I feel mad at myself for not saying anything, and now she thinks that it doesn't bother me that she didn't invite me.*

Your protection is only as good as the energy, clarity, and foundation that you have built your boundary protection system upon. As you learn and develop your functional BPS from the inside out, you will gain a gentle clarity that originates from your core. Healthy boundaries lie at the intersection between your needs and your self-worth, self-trust, self-love, and self-respect. It feels powerful to stand tall in your truth, connected to your authentic self.

You can start connecting with a sense of your boundaries by answering the following questions. Write your answers in your notebook. You can review them after you've been working on your BPS for a while to see how well your skills have grown.

- How do you resist or avoid setting boundaries? What do you tend to hide behind or say that helps you avoid stating your truth?
- What are some of your main concerns about setting boundaries?
- Overall, do you feel others respect your needs, or do they try to shame you out of them?

This may all feel quite new and difficult, but with practice you will become knowledgeable about boundary language and when, where, and how to use it.

"I Don't Want to Be Mean"

If you think not having boundaries is somehow easier, you'll end up making everyone else's dream come true while yours gets dusty in the corner.

Many people don't like to set boundaries because they don't want to appear angry or mean. They tell me they know they need to set clear boundaries, but they feel that if they do state a boundary, then they will sound mean or the other person will not like them. Many of us did not see healthy boundary setting when we were growing up. Perhaps we saw others get so frustrated at a person or situation that they exploded with anger. We then developed the mistaken belief that we could only state a boundary if we were to the point of exploding; otherwise, we were to hold it in and do workarounds so as not to upset others. This dysfunctional behavior conveys, at some level, the message that we don't want others to see us as angry.

This kind of thinking originates in the "golden rule" of being nice or kind and giving to others at our own expense, even when our physical or emotional safety is at risk. Many of us have this learned selflessness (helplessness), believing we have an obligation to be nice to others even when they do not treat us kindly. This cognitive dissonance and false obligation overrides many natural boundaries. We get tangled up in how others will possibly feel and, in doing so, lose a connection to our authentic truth. Many people even stop themselves from setting a boundary because they start to feel guilty ahead of time. They protect someone else while pushing down what they need to say to look out for themselves. This codependent pattern is pervasive worldwide. The lack of boundaries from childhood obscures us from being present in our relationships because we are in a trance, repeating wounded patterns that once served us. This is the calling card of the overly empathic—the no-boundaries rescuer, fixer, caretaker.

> *The status of your boundary protection system*
> *will show up in your relationships and at work*
> *as healthy or unhealthy demonstrations.*

Most of the reasons why we don't set boundaries are rooted in our inner child wounding. This is when the events from childhood that most impacted our sense of self show up in our adult lives, affecting how we interpret events and how we see ourselves. If we have low self-esteem or low self-worth, it is harder to set boundaries because we don't feel deserving of looking out for ourselves. Or, if we are conflict avoiders because of past trauma, we are reluctant to speak up because we don't want to be seen (or hurt) again. Or, we were told to keep secrets and not say anything—pushing our sense of boundary protection further down. In most cases, we simply did not learn how to advocate for ourselves because there was so much drama in the household that our needs were lost in the swirl.

Consider a time when you wished you could have set a boundary with someone. Think about why you chose not to. What voice inside held you back? Did you shut down because of imagined negative consequences for speaking your truth? Chances are, this was the part of you that carries inner child wounding. This fear and resistance are on repeat, continuing to influence your idea of what you need and deserve.

Stating a boundary is as important for self-care as going to the gym or eating well. When you think about how you want to create your life, you are advocating for yourself and keeping your needs in mind. Every boundary you set is key to helping your inner child heal and knowing that this part of you is safe. Until you heal this wounding, your inner child will continue to step in front of you and make choices to try to protect you with impulsive responses that you have to clean up later. Consistent boundary setting shows every part of you that you can protect yourself in ways that you once could not. As you work through the boundary process, you will learn how to set limits and trust yourself, helping you claim an authentic life.

> *With the clarity of boundaries, I'm moving*
> *from feeling power-less to power-full.*
> *I'm saying "stop" or "no" when I need to.*

We don't need to explain or excuse a boundary, but we can contextualize why we don't want to do something or why something isn't okay with us. *Sorry, I can't come with you today. I'm not feeling well* gives a context to your no, but remember, no is a complete sentence all by itself. When we speak our truth with clarity, others hear it at a deep level. We can state a boundary with kindness: *Thanks for asking me to go with you, but I already have other plans.* For good friends, there's a nice way to say anything by being clear and getting our point across.

We often don't give others enough credit for being able to handle the truth. The feeling is that if we were to tell someone how we really feel, that person would crumble, break down, freak out, or get angry. The reality is that most people are resilient and able to handle news and information that may be unpleasant. They may not like what we say, but, hopefully, they will respect that we are speaking up for ourselves.

> *I know my boundaries are there when I need them because*
> *I have learned the power of being clear with myself*
> *and others about what I need in life.*

Healthy boundaries help us meet new people because we know we have the tools to look after and protect our needs. We feel more empowered to reach out and say hi to a new person because we have the confidence that comes from knowing that we have boundaries in our back pocket. This agency tells us that we have value, purpose, and meaning. When we are consistent, our lost inner child relaxes and begins to trust that we are taking care and protecting all parts of ourselves. We tell ourselves it's safe to begin to open up to another person because we realize we have the tools to use if they turn out to be a jerk.

Giving Power Away

The great risk in not setting healthy boundaries is that others will make up what they think we need or deserve. If we don't say anything to correct this falsehood, then it becomes how we are treated. People become victims of bullies, manipulators, and circumstance mainly because of fuzzy boundaries or no boundaries at all. When we don't speak up, we are complicit with the manipulator, bully, or bad situation, which in turn reinforces any inner child wounding we carry. We enable bad behavior when we go along with the dysfunction and don't try to defend ourselves in some way. The bully needs the victim to complete the cycle. They mistake kindness for weakness. By standing up to the bully, we assert a boundary, although it is true that the boundary may not do any good and the bully may still try to manipulate us. The difference is that, deep inside, we know we tried to set a boundary and tried to defend ourselves.

> *Your boundary is real and valid. Every time you state a boundary, you give others a window into your interior world. Through your actions and words, you are saying, this is how I need to be treated.*

By not speaking up, we stifle ourselves, avoid discomfort, and project that we don't think the other person has the capacity to hold or respect our truth. We make assumptions that they wouldn't understand us, but we don't even give them the option. Instead, we essentially cheat ourselves and them out of an experience that could expand the relationship and deepen the connection. We teach others how to treat us through the omission of a boundary, just as we do by setting a healthy boundary.

Others can't read our minds, as much as we may want them to. It's hard work to avoid hurting someone's feelings, but it gets even harder when we swallow our feelings to make others happy. After decades of working on myself, I am more interested in others respecting me than liking me. When we do our healing work, we become less reliant on the opinions of others to shape our ideas of self. We stand more firmly in our authenticity and know who we are. Be patient with others as you express your boundaries, as this is new language for them to hear, as well.

Tennis Match

We experience an emotional freedom when we use boundaries to navigate our relationships. Effectively using boundaries is not about control because, in actuality, we let go of expected outcomes. This confidence in letting go of the outcome is from trusting ourselves enough to use the right boundary tool needed for a given time and place. We state our boundary, put it at the other person's doorstep, and wait to see how they respond. This is where the freedom comes in. We have done our part in opening an exchange.

Think of it like a tennis match. You lob the ball to the other side of the net, but you don't know what will happen on the other side. Only when the other person sends the ball back can you determine your next steps.

We do not make boundary statements to manipulate others to do our bidding. We simply state a need, sending the ball to their side of the court. To carry this analogy further, your playing partner could just throw down their racket, leave the game, and disregard the rules. This would tell you what you need to know about their sense of play and whether or not they respect you. You could hit the ball, jump over the net, and hit the ball back to yourself, but this is overcontrol and not trusting your playing partner. Your job is to play your side of the court. Hopefully, the other person is fair and respectful and sends their best volley back to you. If they don't play fairly, then you may need to look for a new playing partner. The same is true for boundaries within relationships.

We teach others how to treat us.

Whatever boundary protection system you use at this point, know that it is helping you to feel emotionally safe in some relationships, but probably not all. Most of us still use the same boundary system that worked for us in the past. We use tools that may no longer match the job.

Observing Yourself

As I give you tips and techniques, I invite you to observe yourself in your interaction with others. See how you show up in your relationships and how you give your power away. Some people are emotional vampires or manipulators, and others couldn't care less about your needs. I will walk you through this process so that you will begin to feel comfortable as you start to set boundaries.

In the upcoming days, when you are with others, begin to notice how you feel around them, as this is your energetic system picking up on their energy. As you do this, ponder the following questions:

- How do you feel being with this person? What is your gut reaction?
- Is this a person with whom you can be open, or do you need to be on guard?
- Notice how this person talks to you. Do they use respectful language? Are they sarcastic? Do they make shameful remarks? (Note that we get used to how others talk to us. See if you can separate out what they say from how you feel when they talk to you.)
- Do you make yourself smaller when you are with this person, or do you stay "full size"?
- Have you built up tolerance for bad behavior and just put up with it?
- Do you give in to this person to make them happy or so they don't get mad?
- Do you hang around with this person even when you know they aren't good for you because you don't want to disappoint them?
- After having an interaction with this person, do you feel filled up or drained?
- Do you avoid conflict by telling this person lies and half-truths?
- If you said what you would like to say, would this person respect your needs or feelings? Or do you feel that they would disrespect, ridicule, or ignore you?

Practice in your head, in the moment or later, what you wish you could say to them. Pay attention to what your gut is telling you. Know that your feelings are your feelings. Notice if you get caught up in the codependent patterns of people pleasing and making others' needs more important than your own. Step back and ask yourself if you are honoring your boundaries or going against them. Are you the same person across your life spheres and contexts, or do you change yourself like a chameleon?

The more we change ourselves to accommodate others, the further we get from being connected to our authentic selves.

It is more important for you to speak your truth than to swallow your words. Write down your observations in your notebook. See what shows up, as this will give you a snapshot of where your life is at the moment. You will begin to see your stuck points and where you put up roadblocks to avoid getting into a boundary discussion. Be gentle with yourself as you take in all of this new knowledge. You are learning new ways to interact with yourself and others.

As you evaluate your boundaries and your connections to others, it is helpful to visually see who is in your circle of connection. The following exercise will give you a snapshot of the people who are in your life today, those who used to be in your life, and your BPS relationship to them. Include people you haven't seen in a long time, as your relationship to them and who they were will give you an idea of the type of boundary you had with them.

Exercise: Your Circle of Connection

Draw a circle about four inches in diameter in the middle of a piece of paper. Draw another circle around that one, and a third circle outside of that one, ending with three nested circles of graduating diameter.

Inner Circle

Inside the inner circle, write the names of people in your life you feel closest to. These are people you know well and who know you well. You feel safe with them, you can confide in them, and you know they respect your confidences. For the most part, they have healthy boundaries and you are able to have healthy boundaries with them. You can also add people who used to be in your life (living or dead) who fit this description. If you don't have anyone who fits in your inner circle, don't put anyone there. As a matter of perspective, most people will have only a few people in their inner circle.

Middle Circle

In the middle circle, write down the names of people in your life with whom you don't feel as comfortable for whatever reason. You may like having them in your life, but you have some reservations, which usually means you have some boundary issues with them. Some people may be on the edge of the circle—not in and not out.

Outer Circle

In the outer circle, write the names of acquaintances and those with whom you were once close but now need to keep your distance from in order to feel emotionally safe. Trust your gut, and resist the urge to put someone in the inner circle when they really belong in the middle or outer circle. Some people may belong on the absolute edge of the piece of paper. Play around with this, as it's an exercise to give you perspective. It will reveal the level of comfort (boundaries) you have with those in your life.

Sit back and look over what you put on the paper. Compare your inner, middle, and outer circles. Do you have a lot of people in one circle and not many in another? What is your reaction to seeing this diagram? Many people find a stark contrast between the inner circle and the outer circle.

If you have more people in your inner circle, you are pretty fortunate. You have cultivated friendships and relationships that are fulfilling and probably have healthy boundaries with them. Putting them in the inner circle indicates you feel safe in all aspects with these individuals. You are able to share your life more fully with them, and you probably feel a great sense of warmth for these people.

If you have people in the middle, on the edge of a circle, or in the outermost circle, observe this nonjudgmentally. With a soft gaze, see if you can feel into why you placed these people there. Be honest with yourself. Maybe some of them used to be in the inner circle but they hurt you and you no longer feel safe with them. Maybe there are those you like being friends with but don't fully trust for a known or unknown reason—it's just a feeling you have. Maybe you are just getting to know some of them and don't yet know how you feel about them. With others, maybe you've tried to set boundaries and they responded in a disrespectful or passive-aggressive way, so it's easier and safer to keep them on the outer rim. Those who are in the middle and outer circles may not respect your boundaries, or they themselves use defensive boundaries to manage their interactions.

To help you go deeper with the circle exercise, consider your friendships and relationships, then respond to the following statement prompts to see where, when, how, and why you have strong boundaries and where you have a hard time setting them.

- Being myself and setting clear boundaries is easy when I'm with:
- It is difficult to do, but I know I need to set better boundaries with:
- I get pushback when I try to set boundaries with:
- This person disrespects or violates my boundaries:
- When I try to tell this person that they are disrespecting my boundaries, they:
- I am confused when someone doesn't respect my boundaries, and I start to think this about myself:
- When someone in my family or friend group tries to talk

me out of a boundary, such as trying to change my no to a yes, I feel:

- When my boundaries are not respected by______, I do this to get my needs met:
- As a child, I learned how to set functional healthy boundaries from:
- I learned wounded defensive boundaries from:

The circle exercise gives you a snapshot of your life at the moment. It is timestamped for right now and shows you your level of connection and disconnection, revealing your BPS and the level of comfort you have with those in your life. It also shows who you trust, who you have taken in, and who you need to keep at arm's length with private or personal information.

Look over all of the names you wrote, then circle the names of the people whom you feel you need to have better boundaries with, for whatever reason. Even if you're not sure why, just trust your gut. As you learn about the different types of boundaries, you can come back to this diagram and connect a boundary type you use with each person. Then, when you are with them, you will feel equipped to set a boundary and be yourself, knowing you are protecting yourself with your words and actions. Or, you may decide to use a different type of boundary.

If you have put a lot of people in the outer circle, your boundaries—your protection—may be too rigid, as you've created walls to keep them out and you in. Examine this some more, and think about the reasons you have for keeping them out. Are some boundaries a response to situations where you were hurt or there is potential for you to be hurt, so keeping them far away is the best insurance policy? You may have put some people in the middle or outer circle simply because you don't think you have the tools to navigate getting to know them better, you feel at a loss, or you don't feel fully equipped to hold your own. They may even remind you of someone with whom you had a mixed experience, so you are guarded. Write in your notebook why you feel this way. Later, I'll ask you to come back to this.

Listen to your gut-level early warning system and discern the type of boundary you need for a person or situation. Trust what your boundary protection system is telling you.

When you have a strong sense of self and have your BPS in place, you will know the degree and measure of the boundaries you need with each person in your circles. Checking in with your gut-level early warning system will help you navigate these relationships. Beginning to speak your truth is emotional freedom, and it will help you transit through all sorts of personalities that you will encounter.

Angie's Story

Angie grew up in a big family, where she often felt outnumbered and ignored. She looked up to her older siblings for guidance, but they didn't pay much attention to her except when they snuck into her room looking to take her stuff. She retreated into books, where she lived in imaginary worlds that gave her a sense of comfort. Quiet and reserved, she wasn't like her siblings, who were always eager to give their opinions and talked over each other to see who could get the last word in.

Angie was naturally introverted, and although she knew her boundary needs, she didn't know how to express them or compete with her extroverted bully siblings. She once approached one of her more patient siblings to see if they could get the others to stop coming into her room and taking her pens and paper. She thought she had expressed herself well, but either her sibling hadn't taken this to heart or the others hadn't cared. She had asked nicely, and it hadn't made any difference. She hid her things as a way to prevent this theft, but they would rummage through her stuff anyway. Angie began to think that something was wrong with her or what she was trying to say.

Her parents were emotionally unavailable and expected Angie to sort things out for herself. Her parents thought they were helping her learn self-sufficiency and how to be strong and protect herself. Angie felt that she was on her own against these repeated personal space violations. Every time she went against the family order by setting a boundary, the pack would push against it, forcing her back into the pecking order. It's hard for a child to go against the established family system and set boundaries when there are no boundaries and everyone is in their own silo. Frustrated, Angie began to push her feelings down. She developed stomach issues and began to feel a lot of resentment toward her family. She loved them, but she didn't like how they treated her. She didn't know what she had done wrong to deserve such treatment.

At eighteen, Angie moved out to go to college. She thought moving away from her family would give her a sense of safety, but she had a hard time trusting people whom she met at school, and she was reluctant to let anyone get close to her.

Her new friends started out being nice to her, but Angie soon realized that they often asked her to help them with homework or run errands for them. She gave more to them than she received because she thought this was how to cultivate friends, but this disparity didn't feel good, and she began to feel used. She thought about bringing this up with them, but she didn't want to ruin her friendships the way she thought she had ruined her relationship with her family. She took the blame for how others treated her. This was the distorted lens that Angie was looking through, as if their actions were somehow her fault.

Angie eventually did say something to one of her friends. "I want to help you with your homework, but our friendship feels one-sided because you don't help me out when I ask you." The friend told Angie that she was making this up, that it was in her head. "Of course I help you," her friend said. Angie second-guessed herself and retreated. Just like when she was growing up, she doubted herself and wondered what she was doing wrong. Her friend's dismissal was enough to send her spiraling back into her old programming.

To help her sort this out, Angie went to see a therapist on campus. The therapist helped her see that she wasn't crazy or making things up. Angie began to understand how her family ignored her boundaries and how she had recruited the same sorts of personalities in her adult friendships at school. She understood, but she was also mad. She was mad at her family and mad at herself. All she wanted was to be nice and have healthy relationships. Her therapist helped her to see that she did, in fact, do a good job of expressing her boundaries with her siblings and friends. The problem was that they did not respect her boundaries and she kept putting up with it. She had been trained to be a victim at home, and she carried this inner child wounding into adulthood.

With this new perspective, Angie learned to not be as giving to those who abused her kind nature. She learned to firmly and clearly say no more often while recognizing the fallout of speaking her truth. She learned that she was worth protecting even when others thought that her needs were not valid or real. By applying consistent boundaries, Angie was able to see how her family and friends were gaslighting and manipulating her to get *their* needs met. She let some friendships go as a consequence, and had specific conversations around her boundaries with others.

Angie began to feel strong and whole, something that she hadn't felt in a long time. Doing this boundary work with her classmates also helped her with her siblings. Today she has what

I call a bubble boundary with her siblings—not close, but still connected, still a member of the family. She realizes she cannot change them but she can protect herself. Now she is able to have strong boundaries in more of her life spheres. She now knows more about herself and the boundary protection system she needs to interact with others. You will learn more about bubble boundaries in chapter 8, Defensive Boundaries.

What parts of Angie's story do you relate to, if any? What patterns have you carried over from childhood that impact your relationships today? Do you have any cognitive distortions like Angie had, where she mistakenly believed many falsehoods about herself? Do you have relationships in your life where you can start to set boundaries, like Angie did? The relational blueprints set in place in childhood stay with us, and in adulthood we think that this is the only way to interact with others. As you are learning, that can change.

Boundaries are about joining and connecting, but they are also about cleaning up hurt feelings. When you make declarative statements, you will remember these moments, especially when you first start to state your boundaries. In these moments, you are standing up for yourself, speaking your truth, and claiming the right for your needs to be heard, seen, and valued.

Become the person you needed when you were growing up.

CHAPTER FOUR

Inherited Boundaries

*Boundaries are the distance at which
I can love you and me simultaneously.*
—PRENTIS HEMPHILL

We began to learn boundaries in early childhood. As children, we had an intuitive boundary system, and as we grew up, we were shaped by and learned to respond to situations around us. We were corrected and shown right from wrong—but our education about boundaries was only as good as the boundaries of those who modeled these behaviors for us. The patterns of boundaries (or no boundaries) we learned were established by our parents, caregivers, teachers, coaches, and others who were influential in our lives. Some of them were necessary and vital safety boundaries, but others were based on their fears, their prejudices, and their pain.

The way we learned to protect ourselves in our families made sense for that time, but now it may cause more trouble than good.

If a parent had poor or nonexistent boundaries—they let others walk all over them, or they projected their pain onto us—then we learned this, as well. If a teacher or coach had rigid boundaries and absolutely no wiggle room, we learned the same. Or, instead, we may have rebelled against everything we were learning and broken every rule possible. If a caregiver was highly anxious and feared many things, then we learned how to be conflict avoidant and not set boundaries. Few of us had good boundary role models, as most adults have a mixed system of sometimes-on and sometimes-off boundaries, which is really confusing to a child.

In some families, there was an inherited boundary system where there were no boundaries. This type of situation is called enmeshment, where everyone is in everyone else's business. The enmeshment feels normal—that's what we do in this family—but it doesn't always feel good. People tell others what to do, step over boundaries, make decisions for others, and tell them how they feel. This overstepping is like a sweater that has shrunk and is too tight. You don't like it, but it's what you know, and you still wear it because it's familiar. We keep doing the same things because everyone else is in this drama dance and we don't know the way out of it, or we are afraid to be the one who is the truth teller and breaks the illusion. This is how intergenerational trauma gets passed down from one generation to the next. Each generation creates the same dysfunctional interactions as the one before, believing this is how we talk to and treat each other, so this is how things are. You will learn more about intergenerational trauma and boundaries in chapter 10.

This type of family has a fuzzy ambiguity toward boundary setting, so a child does not realize that they have agency and can look out for themselves; this concept is not anywhere in their vocabulary or consciousness. The child doesn't even know they can use their words to state a healthy boundary and protect themselves. Or, if they did try to say no and the no was repeatedly ignored, the child, feeling defeated and confused, stopped trying to set a boundary.

"Stranger danger" is usually taught along with the basics of staying physically safe, but the words we use to protect and look after our emotional needs in our families and relationships are rarely demonstrated.

In addition to enmeshment, most children learn what I call defensive boundaries, such as passive-aggressive behaviors, bubble boundaries, and numbing out. These are forms of avoiding something that is uncomfortable. Some family members learn to isolate and withdraw, each in their own silo, cut off from the others to stay safe and out of the way. These are examples of how we learn to compensate and bend ourselves into a pretzel so we don't have to directly deal with someone who dishonors us.

My BPS from childhood reinforced the idea that I had to stay small and quiet to survive. My adult BPS has found my voice, a strength and protection.

In emotionally unavailable households, children do not learn how to express many emotions because very few are modeled for them. Building an internal resource to protect oneself with words is not taught or even allowed. The parents don't know how to access their emotions, so they can't teach their children how to name and express theirs. This lack of strong boundary setting directly impacts a child and contributes to their sense of self-worth, identity, and agency. When a child's natural boundaries are continually disregarded, minimized, or ridiculed, this cuts deep and creates inner child wounding that influences the child's view of themselves and the world. In these households, the child learns to override their boundaries and gut instinct for the sake of harmony, but at a great cost to their sense of emotional freedom.

When a child's feeling expression is diminished or invalidated, the child is confused because feelings are a normal reaction to situations. A child might say their tummy hurts, and the parent or caregiver replies, *You're fine. Go outside and play.* What the child hears goes against how they feel, and this creates an incongruence within the child. Confusing exchanges like this are part of the reason we begin to disconnect from our gut reaction, our built-in boundary system. The child thinks they can't trust themselves, that Mom or Dad knows more than they do, that maybe their parents know how the child feels more than the child does. This simple exchange is an origin story of many childhood emotional wounds.

If you learned how to override and doubt yourself in childhood, then your authentic self probably felt deeply invalidated and unworthy by the time you were an adult. I have met with so many people over the years who look to others to determine their reality and worth. Usually, this behavior began by hearing simple comments that included doubt and shame, and by experiencing unhealthy boundaries or being disrespected at a young age. As adults, each time we go against ourselves and agree to do something we don't want to do, we lose connection with our sense of self. Our lost inner child steps in front of us and uses outdated tools to try to get to a place of safety.

Childhood wounding is not always loud and demonstrative. Adults can question children in a critical way, which can create a sense of doubt or shame in them. Sometimes children are betrayed or rejected by their friends, which creates a sense of abandonment and a fear of getting close to others. Some children grow up in unstable households where problems with addictions, money, or betrayal shape their experience, creating great anxiety over what is going to happen. In these types of households, the child takes it all in and determines the best way to emotionally navigate the situation at hand. Is the best choice to become small and quiet or loud and big? Children naturally seek emotional safety and look for the best way to achieve this goal using their wounded tools, which throws their boundary sense off course. Children may not recognize when a boundary violation has occurred, but they do know whether something feels good or not. They can also feel when they are being respected and heard, which greatly influences their ability to discern when boundaries are being honored.

As we grow into adulthood, this inner child wounding gets trapped in time and keeps spinning in the dysfunction of our childhood family. This is the lost inner child, the part of us that is frozen in time, doesn't have good boundaries, gets triggered in adult situations, and replays the poor boundaries or lack of boundaries that we learned at an early age. Children can learn healthy boundaries that adults model for them. This modeling does not need to be a grand teachable moment, simply an example of an adult living life authentically.

My Inner Child Broken Boundaries

Heal the boy and the man will appear.
—TONY ROBBINS

In my book *Healing Your Lost Inner Child*, I discuss in depth how wounded boundary patterns are established in childhood as a way for us to cope with the unique family dynamic we grew up in. For example, if you grew up in a household where there was frequent yelling, as I did, maybe you, like me, learned to be quiet, read the room, and not make waves. This was the primary wounded tool I used to feel emotionally safe.

My parents were similar to other men and women of their time, when married couples didn't talk about emotions. The relationship stress between my mom and dad was always simmering in the background of my family life and projected onto the household. Uncomfortable, unpleasant issues were avoided and pushed away, but they would usually come out in passive-aggressive behaviors or verbal explosions. There was a polarity in our home of loving, good, stable times and periods of big upsets. We had fun family gatherings and great times on the boat, but a dark cloud would descend on the house most nights, with my dad's worries and anger spilling out onto all of us.

My dad, anxious and filled with worry about work, bills, or who knows what, would drown out the noise and calm himself with alcohol. Most nights this did not work, as the normal intensity level of distress percolated and then became super-fueled by whiskey and beer. My mom responded to my dad's moods by changing herself, agreeing with him, and being quiet. Her efforts didn't have much of an effect; if she said anything at all, it gave him an opening to verbally attack her, which escalated the situation even more.

This early training taught me that I couldn't always speak my truth because if I did, there would be more yelling toward me or my mom. I knew my mom and dad loved me deeply, but I didn't understand why they were frequently upset. With my egocentric child's logic, I determined that I was the problem, so I became "perfect" and tried not to cause any problems. I was preoccupied with the state of the household and how my mom and dad were relating to each other. I became expert at reading their moods and adjusting myself to them; in other words, I paid more attention to my parents' emotions than my own. I was losing any sense of boundaries and giving my power away to their struggles. These were among my early broken boundary tools that I used to feel emotionally safe.

As I got older, I felt an overwhelming urge to help them and the family. I was totally lost in their world, trying to figure out what to do using all of my teenage logic. I only had enough emotional energy to attend to their emotions, so I ended up ignoring my own. I learned to not have any boundaries—I became needless and wantless. In this ambiguous enmeshment, I didn't know where they ended and I began. As a result of this confusion, I thought that I was the one to carry the blame when things were chaotic in the household. I became expert at reading facial movements, assessing what my parents said and didn't say, what they did and didn't do. I had an entire behavioral matrix that helped me determine what my actions should be to mitigate whatever I was anticipating in the household. I saw my job as keeping everything calm and humming along.

My mom, needing to vent, would overshare her frustrations and her pain with me. She told me how overwhelmed she was and how she didn't know what to do about my dad. I felt that she was looking to me for answers, but this was too much for me as an adolescent. Nevertheless, I took on this responsibility because I knew everything that she was going through. I wanted to help her, so I listened and gave her my limited teenage wisdom to try to reassure and comfort her. I think she saw me as being in the trenches with her; I don't think she could have shared the darker moments with her sister or her friends. It was so confusing for me and really messed with any boundaries I had left.

As a codependent-in-training, the line between me and my

parents was completely blurred, as I swam in this toxic soup every day. Now deep in enmeshment, I had lost any boundary between what was my stuff and what was theirs. I was the closest person my mom had to confide in, but as I got older and heard more than I wanted to know, I began screaming inside, *I don't want to know about this!* But I couldn't abandon her; I couldn't leave my parents in this state.

I loved them both, but I didn't know how to help them. I felt completely overwhelmed being the live-in teenage therapist. A big part of this enmeshment was my losing a sense that they were my parents. I started to feel like I was their parent. This lack of boundary structure gave me an even greater sense of responsibility, and I felt that I needed to come up with solutions like an adult would in order to solve their problems. I had become parentified at a young age.

My boundaries were nonexistent when I stepped inside that house. I worked hard to create diversions and distractions so my parents wouldn't argue in front of my sister, who is seven years younger than me. I tried to help her have a childhood that I didn't have, to somehow protect her from the chaos. As an older teenager, I was worn out, jaded, and resentful. I was immersed in my parents' pain. I was so preoccupied by what was going on at home that I was struggling in school; everything at school seemed trivial compared to the drama happening at home.

In my later teens I began to lose respect for my dad and was frustrated trying to help my mom. I had turned over so much of my power trying to make things better, but nothing ever worked, and I felt defeated. I remember saying to my mom, in frustration, that she should just divorce my dad. *Mother, just leave him. I don't know what else to tell you.* Essentially, I was setting a boundary with her—and him. I was out of ideas. I remember this scene so well, as it took a lot of my energy to say they should divorce and to suggest that boundary to her. Saying it was painful, but I was absolutely bone dry of ideas. My mom was a strong woman. Marriage was a sacrament to her, and she said she could never leave him. I respected that, but I didn't understand it because she had lost so much of herself in his pain. With my limited understanding, I couldn't make sense of why she couldn't stand up to him, why she didn't leave, why she made herself smaller to fit into his world.

When I left home for college, I felt like I was retiring from a job. I had had all I could take of their drama dance, and I wanted out of there. The distance of three hundred fifty miles gave me breathing room, but every time I visited I was thrust back into the same dysfunctional situation. Nothing changed; they were just getting older and still replaying their wounded drama. I was trying to move on. I had a unique place in the family puzzle, but I was growing and expanding in new ways—at least, I felt like I was.

As a young adult, my inner child wounding still showed up. I would shut down, withdraw, enable, try to fix or caretake others, and make everything nice. By giving my power away to others, I let them direct the course of the relationship, and I taught them how to treat me. I had created a false self apart from my authentic self. I told others, through my words and actions, that they could treat me how they wanted to and that I was okay with this no-boundaries arrangement. After all, this strategy had worked for me growing up as I tried to maintain stability in my childhood home. It became the template for my poor boundary setting and set me up for many disappointing and confusing relationships in my early twenties.

My pain and their pain was mixed together in a toxic soup.

At college, I pasted on a half-smile and entered into young adulthood with my wounded tool kit. My Catholic upbringing taught me that being selfless was a good thing and that I should strive to be this way. You know, be the nice guy and people will like you sort of thing. But this selflessness also taught me to ignore my own needs and to not ask for help, reinforcing the lack of boundaries I learned at home. I wasn't prepared for what the big world would throw at me. I didn't recognize that others around me perceived my kindness as weakness. I didn't know how to use my words to protect me. I didn't have the internal resources to recognize red flags or to stand up for myself, so I let others define my world.

My lost inner child would get activated when people would yell, get upset, or start to manipulate me. The hurting part of me would immediately go into my familiar wounded protection mode of being overwhelmed, quiet, and hypervigilant. I would "read" others to determine their degree of upset or anger. Reflexively, I would change myself to fit their mood, losing myself in the experience. In reality, they were probably expressing anger or frustration in general, but just as I did as a kid, I took the blame for their upset.

It's not surprising that the people I chose to interact with and date in my early adult life away from home were self-absorbed and emotionally needy. After all, this was the type of emotional wounding I was familiar with. I found these emotionally needy people over and over, and I would eventually feel those familiar feelings of being lost, confused, and alone. If they had a bad day, I had a bad day; whatever they needed from me, I met it. My early relationship programming and lack of boundaries had created the lens through which I saw the world, even though I was a long way from home. I had simply packed up my codependent tools and brought them out as needed.

I put others on a pedestal, wanting them to be better than who they were and molding myself to fit into their world.

I was still giving my power away, trying in earnest to feel love and connection, but now it was with a different group of people, who had more complicated adult issues. I took on their pain so they would feel better while I drowned in their wounded overflow. They would use me by dumping on me and not respecting my needs. These constant boundary violations added up over time. I felt exhausted, but I didn't dare say no.

My lack of boundaries revealed my poor relationship skills, as this was the only way I knew how to relate to people. I chose all the wrong people with my bad picker because my limited boundary system didn't alert me to any red flags. I just kept letting other people set the terms for our interactions. I didn't even know what to look for because I didn't understand the problem. I knew I wasn't happy or fulfilled, but I didn't understand the part I was playing in creating my reality.

> *When we take on someone else's pain,*
> *we lose ourselves in their wounded illusion.*

It wasn't until I began therapy in my midtwenties that I began to learn about my inner child, my codependent patterns, and my lack of boundary setting. This was a huge wake-up call, and at first I felt really stupid. I was mad at myself for not seeing this sooner and for how I gave away so much of myself for the benefit of others. I had been taking all the blame and not seeing their role in the relationship. Why had I made others more important than myself? Why did others treat me that way when they were supposed to be my friend? Why did I not honor my truth and speak up when bad things were happening to me? Why couldn't I remove myself from situations that weren't good for me even when I was being hurt physically, sexually, and emotionally? Why did I have such a bad picker? I was protecting them and beating up on myself because I had poor internal boundaries.

I began to see my parents' emotional wounding more clearly. I began to understand my dad's anxieties and how he self-medicated with alcohol, drinking because he wanted to, not because he needed to. I learned of my mom's codependent, enabling wounding and how she tried, over and over, to keep the peace. I was mad at both of them and what I came to understand as their trauma-bonded relationship. At the time, I didn't understand why my mom couldn't stand up and fight, why she let him manipulate her and walk all over her, why she chose to swallow her feelings. Why did my dad have to emotionally throw up on us at the dinner table practically every night? Why did one "wrong" move spark and ignite a rageful tirade? My parents' wounded dance played out for my entire childhood and carried on long after I moved away and went to college. I now understand this made sense to them; it was what they knew, and they used the emotional tools they had. It is an explanation—but not an excuse—for their behavior.

Anything worth having is worth working for, and as I began to heal, I realized that I had to fight for my voice, my truth, and my place in the world. I had to literally learn the words to use to set boundaries. I also had to heal big parts of myself so that I could see, hear, and feel when a boundary violation occurred. This key step took me a while to learn because I had normalized shaming language and misperceived emotions, so I couldn't always tell if someone was upset at me or someone or something else. I had to learn what my needs were and see how others would talk me into what they wanted, both subtly and directly. Once I learned what boundary violations sounded and felt like, I began to see them happening all over the place.

I had to fight for and reclaim the self-respect that I had given up to emotionally survive and make things nice. I made a commitment to myself that I was no longer going to give in to others so that they would like me. I didn't need to buy their friendship or smile through the pain anymore. I had to learn how to say no and feel the strength of an internal conviction to back it up. There was a lot that I had to unlearn to make space for all the new boundary tools I was learning.

I began setting boundaries with my parents, and as I healed, the energy between us slowly shifted. I wasn't going into problem-solving mode for my mom about her issues with my dad, and this changed our relationship. She said that she missed our talks—I missed talking with her about deeper topics as well—but I could no longer stay enmeshed with her and in their marriage. I did not miss being put in the position of the keeper of their secrets.

As I learned to respect myself, I learned to respect and hold space for my dad's journey and his pain. I didn't like his outbursts, but I now knew his journey wasn't mine, and I was able to put some cotton between me and his anger. I was protecting myself and was no longer as activated by my parents' wounding. With distance, I could see their situation for what it was. I wasn't getting lost in the drama anymore because my boundaries helped me to step back, watch, listen, feel, and then determine what I wanted to do next. I became a witness to their pain and slowly developed internal resources to end the enmeshment.

As I healed, I was able to look back through time and see myself misinterpreting this drama and taking on the blame. I learned how true the expression is that children are great observers but poor interpreters. My relationship with my parents shifted into an adult relationship once I started to set boundaries with them. I now had more tools to help me avoid getting sucked into their rinse-and-repeat drama spiral. Boundaries gave me some space so I could at least get my bearings and know where I ended and they began.

It took me a while to work through the pain, shame, and grief of this wounded dance that was left over from childhood. What I learned then, and what I teach now, is that setting strong boundaries with oneself and others is the key to reclaiming one's authentic self. I was able separate things out, let go of the wounded patterns I learned in childhood, and adopt new ways of developing and maintaining relationships. When we work on ourselves and heal our wounding, the lens through which we see life becomes clearer. As we set boundaries, we are able to see the red flags much sooner and protect ourselves. We see others' wounding so much clearer because we aren't lost in a toxic soup anymore. We are on the healed edges and see all of it for what it is.

My boundaries helped me to step into my own power, my own truth and self-respect.

When I started to set boundaries, I lost friendships and was lonely. Initially, I was devastated, thinking I had done something wrong. I didn't understand what was happening, and I felt more sad than I had felt before. I would set a boundary by saying no to something, and then the other person, whom I thought was my friend, would get mad or try to talk me into doing whatever it was. If I held my boundary, they eventually walked away or didn't talk to me anymore.

My newly minted boundaries didn't work with most of my friends. My therapist taught me that a friend who got mad at me for my boundary didn't respect me, that my friend just wanted what he wanted and would ignore and shame me into submission because that was what our relationship looked like to him. I felt mad and hurt. Why would someone whom I had given a lot of my time, friendship, and energy to hurt and disrespect me in such a way? Why would someone I had invested in be so careless with my feelings? I had thought we had a reciprocal relationship, but my prior lack of boundaries and how I enabled this pattern had prevented me from seeing this disparity. My reciprocity gauge was all off. The friendship wasn't reciprocal; they used me and I let it happen.

Through a series of examples like this, I began to see a clear pattern in what I had thought were friendships. When I began to stand back and observe, I realized that those who were in my life didn't ever call me or ask me to do things with them. These were one-way arrangements, where it all worked as long as I kept on feeding the connection by calling them, showing up, or giving gifts. I felt pretty empty and used when I recognized this stark reality.

It took me a while to admit all of this and come to terms with what I had essentially created and they had accepted. It was hard for me to admit that I had been carrying the backpack in these relationships and had made everything easy so they didn't have to do any work. I was overcompensating for my lack of self-esteem and desire to make the connection last. I felt a sense of shame about all of this and had to work through to a point of understanding that I was only doing what I had learned in childhood. In therapy, I learned that I wasn't responsible for others but that I was responsible for myself and how I showed up in relationships. I realized that my friends were more self-absorbed than they were bad actors. I learned that I had taught them how to treat me. As long as I gave in, catered to them, and ignored my needs, those relationships "worked."

I felt sad about the friendships that went away because I had enjoyed those connections, but in reality, I think I was more sad for myself. I was sad for the fact that I had not learned as a child to honor myself, my voice, my truth. I learned to take responsibility for my part and to see the other person's part. Healing is not about making excuses but about taking ownership for one's actions. It took me a while to learn how to have healthy relationships. All of the tools I am teaching you I learned on this hardscrabble path, and I still use them today.

> *I state my boundaries first for me, to hear myself say them,*
> *and then for the other person to hear.*

I learned that for my lost inner child to find his voice and reclaim himself, the adult me had to establish strong and consistent boundaries. If I started to falter and not stay consistent, my wounding would get triggered and all of those old patterns of feeling and behavior would show up to try to emotionally protect me, just like in childhood. If we aren't consistent and put forth our boundaries, we go back to behaviors that keep us stuck in toxic and wounded relationships.

As you heal and use your boundaries consistently, you may notice that you don't feel as closely connected to family or friends as you once did. There is a greater awareness of who is good for you and who is toxic or bad for you. I saw this for myself as I healed, and I began to see family and friends for who they were instead of looking through a codependent lens of who I needed them to be.

As the smokescreen clears, you can't avoid recognizing when a person isn't good for you to be around. You saw them one way before, but as you heal, you may experience a spontaneous *aha!* moment, when everything comes into sharp focus. When this happens, you may begin to wonder if they have always been this way (they have) and ask yourself why you hadn't seen it before. The more healed part of you will no longer want to be around their toxicity.

> *Changing yourself to make a relationship*
> *work is a boundary red flag.*

For a multitude of reasons, it's harder to distance ourselves from or shut out our family. We are linked to our family, which requires us to be creative and have clear and firm boundaries. Unlike in childhood, we have more options as adults to help us to feel emotionally safe within our family. We have boundary language today that helps us set the terms of our interactions. We have various boundary types and tools that we can use today, compared to the few internal resources most of us had as children.

Sometimes we put higher expectations on our family when it comes to honoring our boundaries. As adults, we want them to see and hear our boundaries in ways they didn't when we were young. But unless your family members are working on their boundaries, they may not understand yours. As you read in my story, I started speaking up while being as aware as I could be about the consequences of my boundary truth. It became more important for me to honor myself than to stay in the wounded dance of others.

Woundings of the inner child will keep recycling until we set strong, consistent, healthy boundaries. Once you claim these tools and use them consistently, the lost inner child will see that you're serious and that you will protect all of you. The lost inner child will not have to keep using the wounded tools of shutting down, avoiding, people pleasing, and so on to navigate emotionally distressing situations. You will be able to protect yourself in a functional way, and the inner child will calm, begin to heal, and eventually integrate with the functional adult self.

Sometimes it stings when the curtain is pulled back and we see a broader reality. The illusion is gone, and we see ourselves and others more clearly. I saw that my parents did the best they could with the boundary tools they had. Their boundary system was learned from their parents and the situations they experienced growing up. While I had to unlearn the poor boundary setting I learned from them, they also taught me to be kind to others, to be charitable, to help those in need, and to be inclusive. This worked out well in a lot of my friendships, and I'm grateful for these lifelong connections. It's an easy cheat to blame our parents or others for how we see the world, but when we accept that they were doing their best with the tools they had, we can move on, be responsible for ourselves, and not be stuck in victimhood.

It is too easy and simplistic to make my dad the villain in this story, as he's not. He was a good man who had undiagnosed anxieties, and he used alcohol and passive-aggressive avoidant boundaries to deal with this pain. I don't see my mom as the victim in this story because she had a strong internal sense of self; she made choices for herself and my sister and me to stay in this wounded relationship. They both would have been sad to know how much their arguing, oversharing, and turmoil had affected my sister and me. They would have never wished or wanted that for us; they always wanted the best for us and showed us this in small and big ways throughout their lives. I healed, and I love and respect my mom and dad for everything they did and everything they were. I wouldn't want it any other way because if it were different, I wouldn't be the man I am today or have my life as I know it.

My sister sees our childhood from a different perspective, since she wasn't on the front lines as I was. She saw our parents' back-and-forth arguing as ridiculous, and she didn't buy into the drama. Now we both see how I protected her; when I went off to college, she had to learn a whole new skill set that I had shielded her from having to know. Using my wounded tool kit, I had created a buffer from the blast of our parents' pain. She could see our parents as though she were looking from the outside in, like looking into a fishbowl. She learned to speak up, she pushed back, and she found her voice much earlier than I did. She left home and went to college, determined to be independent and self-reliant. She and I both went on to heal this childhood wounding, and through our individual work, we each learned how to set strong boundaries in adulthood.

I feel such tenderness, love, and respect for my parents today. But this is after years of therapy work, learning and using healthy boundaries with them, and watching them grow and heal. I see and feel how much they loved me unconditionally and how I received pride and encouragement from them for the positive small and big things in my life. They were deeply loving people who were loved by their family and friends, but like all of us, they had their secret pain and struggles. My parents remained married until they died, and they truly loved each other. Their wounded dance with poor boundaries continued up to the very end. This is what they knew, this is what made sense to them, and I guess it was too hard or painful for them to disrupt the wounded dance they had for more than fifty years. I hope they are at peace now.

People look at me today and imagine that I've always had good boundaries, but as you've learned through my battle scars, that's not the way it unfolded. Maybe you experienced something similar in your childhood. These early emotional blueprints come to us through many examples, but the resulting pattern is the same: we honor others more than ourselves. The playbook for a codependent person is to set boundaries to protect others but not necessarily for themselves.

Trauma is always relative, and you may have had it worse. Trauma recycles inside of us until we heal it. Know that if you have siblings, you each grew up in a different household, where one sibling felt things were okay and another felt things were awful. You were together, but you were all different ages. Your experiences were similar, but you each looked through a different lens. You each received a different version of your parents based on what was happening at the time.

If you relate to parts of my story, know there are ways to unlearn a poor boundary system and ways to recognize when others violate your boundaries. There are many ways to heal. There are many ways to reconnect with your authentic self, your voice, and your truth to develop a strong and consistent BPS. A strong part of you is still in there waiting to speak up. Through this unfolding process, I will help you to reconnect with those parts of yourself that you've kept under wraps for safekeeping.

Be gentle with yourself as you evaluate yourself and those around you. I encourage you to observe, feel, and assess. Resist the urge to make quick decisions. Sit with your new knowledge, and let it marinate into a new understanding of who you are and what you need. You will develop the specific boundary language you need for your life.

There is a wonderful part of you that is waiting to come out and claim a sense of emotional safety in your relationships. This is the beginning of your journey toward emotional freedom.

Red Flags

When we grow up in a dysfunctional environment with poor boundaries, we don't learn how to recognize boundary violations. In other words, we miss the social cueing and red flags that signal someone else is disrespecting us. Our BPS is clouded from repeated emotional trauma wounding. For instance, as a result of a wounded boundary system, we hear someone's sarcasm as their being funny; we make excuses for an inappropriate touch; and if someone yells at us we say, well, they had a bad day. These are examples of how we overlook red flags and make up stories so others' behavior fits into our narrative. We normalize the abnormal, go along to get along, and avoid making waves. We are looking through a wounded lens, so we don't recognize boundary violations and don't know when others have poor boundaries. We also project onto them who we need them to be instead of seeing who they really are.

We subconsciously choose people who match our level of being healed or wounded. Hurt people find other hurt people, and we end up choosing those who match our healthy or unhealthy boundary type. In our relationships and friendships, our boundary type fits hand in glove with another's boundary type. These unconscious pairings perpetuate our inherited poor boundary drama from childhood into adulthood. Our unique skill set interacts well with their unique skill set, but unfortunately, there are also a lot of boundary violations that manifest in this wounded pairing. This lack of boundary setting will show up in all aspects of their life, just as it does with ours. People reveal themselves over time if we are patient and open to seeing them accurately, through an unclouded lens.

> *If your friends tell you someone isn't good for you, believe them. If your boundary system is wobbly, you may see this person as who you need them to be instead of who they are. Hurt people find other hurt people.*

These repeated codependent behaviors and boundary violations reinforce our mistaken belief that another's needs are more important than our own. We override our intuitive gut feeling, which is why we bring in and keep hurtful people in our lives; it just doesn't register that they are being hurtful. My theory is that, at a subconscious level, our gut registers their bad behavior and we know they are being hurtful, but we also know that it would be really uncomfortable to set a boundary with them, so we make up a story that "it isn't so bad." I often hear people say that they tried to set a boundary but the other person didn't like it and pushed back, so they gave up. It's a rinse-and-repeat of a pattern that is all too familiar.

An example of how someone disrespects you in a relationship is when you find the courage to speak your truth and the other person gets defensive or offended and flips this back on you, making you the bad guy. This person, for whatever reason, is not ready to hear your truth and is not respecting your needs. They don't want your healthy boundaries messing up their wounded dance; more specifically, they don't want to change.

When our boundary is rejected, we may shut down and maybe even learn that there is a cost to setting a boundary with that person. We don't know how they will react in the future, how things will change, or if they will get mad and leave us. We give more power to the outcome and their reaction than we give to the fact that we are being hurt by their disrespect of our boundary. This learned helplessness repeats our early childhood programming whether we were bullied, ignored, neglected, or disrespected. We tell ourselves that someone being mad at us isn't worth standing up for ourselves. Through this wounded lens, we discount and minimize our hurting self.

In my book *Healing Your Wounded Relationship*, I discuss these wounded relationship pairings, how our unresolved inner child wounding keeps showing up, attracting and meshing with another's codependent parts in a wounded dance, and how this can be healed through better communication skills and healthy boundaries.

If you wonder why you don't see red flags, it's because your BPS has holes in it.

If you feel your BPS is off and you don't recognize the red flags, tell someone who has an intact boundary protection system about a recent interaction you had and see what they say about it. In most cases, they will see through the drama and clearly see how you are not being respected. We can't rely on others all of the time to determine whether something isn't good for us, but when we are just learning how to set boundaries, they can give some perspective. The Boundary Violations section in chapter 6 will help you to better understand what red flags look like.

Throughout your life, you may have noticed that it's much harder to set boundaries in relationships that have meaning to you. We know those close to us as well as they know us. We have more invested in these relationships, and there's more to lose compared to, for example, saying no to a stranger. Any relationship worth having and developing will have a healthy boundary exchange. Most of us are trying our best with the tools we have.

Setting Boundaries Can Be Difficult

People usually understand the concept of boundary setting intellectually but find it hard to put into practice. This reluctance comes about for many reasons. If you recognize that you need to set better boundaries, answering the following questions may help you to discern what is holding you back. Remember, this work is just for you (unless you want to share it), so you may want to write your answers in a notebook to get a bigger picture of where your BPS is today.

- Do I have a good sense of whether people are good for me or toxic?
- Is it hard for me to see this good/bad distinction in my long-term relationships?
- Am I concerned that if I set boundaries, some people will not want to be my friend or be in a relationship with me because I don't cater to them?
- Have I tried to set boundaries and assert some power in my relationships but gave up when it didn't work?
- Have I been honest with myself and examined if I play the victim role in my relationships?

- Do I recognize what is important to me, or do I just follow the leader and those whom I think are better than me?
- Do I just want everyone to be happy, get along, and not get into a lot of drama?
- Have I created a list of my wants and needs?
- Am I more focused on someone else's life and their choices than in taking care of myself?

Your answers to these questions will help you further examine the patterns and themes that keep showing up in your life. You may have a resistance to setting boundaries because of past interactions with people who were not respectful. That's okay. Start out slowly. You may want to choose a safe person with whom to set boundaries so you can get a better feel for what this is like.

We all step up to the life that we are ready to receive. We embrace a reality that we are ready to manifest and hold. We are all spiritual beings having a human experience. You have a set of boundaries from your childhood that may or may not serve you now. Know that with practice you will be able to set boundaries with yourself and others in ways that you've only imagined. With a newfound clarity, you will be able to recognize the red flags in your relationships and come up with appropriate responses.

It would be great if we could just say no and people would take our no for an answer. But others don't respect our boundaries most of the time, so we think that our boundaries are the problem, when, in fact, we are not being respected.

When we have a strong BPS, we know that we have the tools we need for the many different types of interactions we have with others. We feel confident enough to stay strong in our clarity.

Others pick up this new strength, which we carry in subtle ways by our behaviors. They won't quite be able to put their finger on it, but they will know that we seem more like ourselves, more relaxed and confident. Trust yourself. You know more than you realize.

CHAPTER FIVE

Healthy Boundaries

Healthy boundaries are important, but you may be building a brick wall when a picket fence would do.
—AMY DICKINSON

Healthy boundaries are meant to help us have happy, reciprocal, respectful, inclusive relationships, where each person feels they have a voice. We honor our needs and the needs of others, and hold these in high regard. When our boundaries are supported, honored, and encouraged, our authentic self comes forward and we feel strong and safe in expressing our convictions. We stay strong when we have clarity in our words, in our truth, and in ourselves. The following are examples of how to start a boundary conversation:

- Would you be able to help me with this project? I can tell it's too much for me right now.
- I feel like you talk down to me when you point out my mistakes. I need you to be more respectful when you talk to me.

- Thank you for asking. I still need to figure out what I'm going to do. What ideas do you have?
- I'm hurt that you keep ignoring my emotional need for intimacy.
- I'm trying to stay strong in my recovery, so I'm not going out clubbing tonight.
- I need a minute to think about this. I don't know what I'm feeling right now.
- I'm grateful for your help, but I'm going in another direction than what we talked about.
- I'm going to be nicer to myself today and not put myself down when I make a mistake.
- I appreciate the offer, but I think I have this under control.
- I need to take some time for me today and rest. I've been giving a lot to others lately.

When we open conversations in this way we set healthy functional boundaries. We help to reinforce and heal the part of us that carries emotional wounding. We tell ourselves that we are worth protecting and loving by putting these opening statements out there. After all, the biggest reason we have this wounding is because our boundaries were violated or ignored a long time ago, or maybe even recently. Boundaries form the bridge for the wounded self to heal and grow up emotionally. Once healthy boundaries are established, the wounded part can set down all of the wounded responses of defensive avoidance.

If you have trouble imagining how to begin a boundary conversation, look to others in your life whom you think have healthy boundary practices. These people can be your resource mentors, and they probably have some tips that helped them create a BPS that works for them. Take what they say, hold it, and see if it would work for you. This is one way to gather information to add to your BPS for each of your life spheres.

The concept of boundaries as protection is easy to understand. The hard part is understanding the types of boundaries we need to establish in our life spheres and then following through with setting them. In order for us to set effective and consistent boundaries, we need to know ourselves and our needs as clearly as we can. In other words, we need to know what we like and don't like, what feels good and what feels bad. We can begin to regularly check in and pay attention to ourselves and our needs. When we have this connection with ourselves, we can recognize when we need to set boundaries and, most importantly, when our boundaries are being violated.

> *Boundaries are not about being selfish;*
> *boundaries are about self-honoring.*

What resources do you have that will help support you as you learn how to set boundaries? Connect with people you trust, as they will help keep you balanced as you learn to speak your truth. For now, avoid sharing this part of yourself with those who may not be accepting or respectful of your boundaries. Often, our core group of friends knows us best and can be there for us in ways that family cannot. Boundaries give us a sense of emotional freedom in our relationships as we develop clarity about what is good and not good for us, what we need and don't need, who is respectful and who is disrespectful. When we have a clear sense of boundaries, we can more easily find the words to speak our truth so others know where we stand. When we own our truth, others don't have to wonder how we feel or make up stories about us. *I don't want to go to that restaurant for dinner* is a clear and direct statement. Some people may not like or understand our boundaries, but this is what we need to employ to help us feel emotionally safe and strong.

I know that as I have healed, my boundaries have gotten stronger and clearer, and I have a sense of emotional freedom. But even with all my years of practice, I still have to work on them by reinforcing what I need, recognizing when people honor me and when my boundaries are violated. Every day I work on speaking my truth because if I don't, I am at risk of sliding back into my old codependent behaviors of giving my power away, explaining my boundaries, and dishonoring myself. I consider myself a codependent in recovery.

Listening to Your Gut

As you have learned, an easy way to access your boundaries is by paying attention to your gut reaction to a person, place, or situation. Your gut is your first responder, your intuition—a hunch or a feeling that you can't quite name, that visceral reaction to a situation. Your natural gut boundaries come from the part of you that immediately and instinctively knows whether you like something or not. It is an internal source of truth, your built-in energy feedback system. Your gut is a wise part of you that you pull from to discern what is good for you or not.

If our boundaries are poor or nonexistent and our gut starts churning in fear, we may disregard this reaction and excuse others' toxic behaviors, overriding what we are telling ourselves. Then we go against this internal wisdom and stay in such relationships and friendships way past their expiration dates, for example.

> *We override our gut because we want something*
> *to happen or we want to make others happy.*
> *This is the ego talking, mistaking a want for a need.*

As you learned in chapter 4, when we were babies we had a heightened, natural, intact physical boundary system, and our gut reactions were immediate and transparent. Babies set boundaries all the time. They naturally spit out food they don't like, they cry when a loud or new noise scares them, they kick off blankets when they are hot, and they cling to caregivers when they want comfort.

When you were a baby, your physical needs boundary system was intact, and you instinctively set physical needs boundaries every day. Your energy feedback system was aligned.

As a small child, you knew when something wasn't right, such as a touch or something someone said, but you didn't have the boundary language to fight back. This was your built-in gut reaction, but you didn't have many resources to call on to protect yourself. Your gut was reading the situation, but as a small child with no real means to protect yourself, you had to push the feeling down, yell out the feeling, dissociate, or learn to stay out of the firing range. You protected yourself with the boundaries you had. Sadly, when boundaries are repeatedly ignored, such situations often create rage, which is a combination of anger and a feeling of helplessness or hopelessness. As you matured, you were socialized away from this instinctual gut boundary system pushing down your feelings and intuitions. You learned to disconnect from your gut reaction—your inner wisdom—which created a separation from this natural system. You learned to put others first, for example, discounting your own needs. The good news is, you can relearn how to pay attention to it again, now joined with your new boundary language.

What is your gut, your energy system, telling you?
What is the best way to express your needs at this time?

An easy way to know when your boundaries are violated is when, for example, you feel angry, rageful, frustrated, jealous, exhausted from trying, resentful, or spiteful in your gut. These feelings are an indication that you are not being seen or heard at some level. Just like when you were young, this is your early warning boundary protection system alerting you that there's been a boundary violation and your needs are not being met. The more you heal and listen to yourself, the more clearly you will hear your gut reaction to a person or situation. This will often give you the most accurate read.

I believe that listening to our gut can be better understood by learning a little bit about how gut reactions play an important part in our health and behavior. Dr. Stephen Porges developed a theory that looks at how the nervous system (specifically the vagus nerve), including a gut reaction, responds to social factors and cues of safety or danger. Through this process, which Dr. Porges calls "neuroception," we automatically scan other people and our environment for what is likely safe and what could be a problem. This body connection is a useful filter that helps alert us when it can matter most. I believe Dr. Porges's theory aligns with having a gut-level intuition about a person or situation.[1]

Many reactions, such as turning the steering wheel or hitting the brakes, are so automatic that we don't even think about them. Trauma and other impactful experiences can layer in with gut responses that we don't consciously think about but may need to untangle as we begin to set healthy boundaries. We process a deep level of information in seconds, which informs our BPS as to the next appropriate step to take.[2]

Sometimes we need to inform our nervous system that we are safe, especially when past traumas are triggered and we are not in present danger. We can do this by reassuring ourselves that things are okay and that what happened then is not happening now. We can take deep belly breaths, which calm down the nervous system, instead of shallow breaths, which keep us in a state of hypervigilance. Repeat and reassure: I am safe now.

1 *The Pocket Guide to the Polyvagal Theory: The Transformative Power of Feeling Safe*, by Stephen W Porges, PhD, W. W. Norton & Company, Sept. 5, 2017.
2 *Polyvagal Theory: How Our Vagus Nerve Controls Responses to Our Environment*, by Jodi Clarke, MA, LPC/MHSP, www.verywellmind.com/polyvagal-theory-4588049, last updated Oct. 25, 2023.

An early blueprint of behavior shapes our sense of boundary and informs our nervous system as to how, when, and where we need to protect ourselves. For myself, growing up in a household where random yelling happened, I learned to be hypervigilant, read other people's moods, and always made their needs more important and valuable than my own. My BPS was rooted in trauma and became a way for me to feel emotionally safe. As a child I trained myself to read faces, behaviors, and moods and to change my behavior instantly. Unknowingly, I was training my neuroception system (my gut) to anticipate and react to changes in others, which then helped me feel more in control and emotionally safer.

When we grow up in a traumatic environment, we learn the unspoken household rules. This learned traumatic response from childhood is why it's hard for many of us to speak our boundaries, or we were told to stay silent or to keep a secret. In many cases, we wanted to be invisible and hide to stay safe. When we begin to heal with the help of our boundaries, we learn that it's okay to be seen by safe people and speak our truth. The healed part of us says, *I'm not going to hide my whole life. I can be myself and hold a sense of freedom and agency. I can trust myself and others whom I know are safe.*

If you've been traumatized at a deep level, the emotionally wounded part of you deeply wants your voice heard. To be heard and seen is a recognition of self and opens a pathway for healing your trauma. You can practice speaking your truth with no one else around. Become used to saying those words that your hurting self has held on to for so long. Right now, this expression is just for you to get used to hearing your truth: *I'm mad. I'm hurt. Why did you do this to me?* With this voice comes freedom from the pain of the core trauma wounding. Be gentle as you bring this dormant energy from your shadows. Speaking your truth that was once forbidden takes great courage and is a pathway to establish the strong boundaries you wished you always had.

Exercise: Trust Your Gut

In your mind's eye, picture a situation that is unresolved, where you keep recycling the situation and the emotions around it, such as a time when someone wronged you and you are still hanging on to resentment. Hold this situation in your mind, then follow these prompts to create an "I feel" opening boundaries statement:

- Breathe into the experience as you remember the situation and what was said.
- As you recall this situation, notice what is happening in your gut. Does your gut feel a churning sensation, yucky, rumbly, flipping, dropping, tightening, queasy, warm, cold, or neutral?
- If it's hard to name a specific sensation, just check in with yourself and ask, does this feel good or bad? Ask the question, then feel for the answer. Go to an internal place of neutral discernment and get out of your own way.
- See if you can put a feeling to the sensation. If this sensation could talk, what feeling word would it use? For example, do you feel hurt, repulsed, offended, joyful, excited, dismayed? (See Appendix: Feelings Inventory for help with these words.)
- Finish this sentence: I feel ______________.
- The feeling word you find is your boundary word for this situation. Use "I feel" language to create your opening boundary statement. For example: *I feel hurt when you continue to shame my choices.*
- Now say your "I feel" statement out loud. Get used to your opening boundary statement and own it.
- Boom—opening boundary statement created.

This newfound clarity will empower you to formulate a message that is aligned with how you feel. With this clarity, you will feel stronger and know that you have discerned what you want to do or say. The ensuing conversation with the other person will then lead you to having a deeper discussion about the underlying or ongoing issue.

Look over the following list of things to say to help you find your words.

- What's going on with me right now? How does my gut feel? Am I agitated, confused, depressed, or hurt?
- Am I having my own feelings, or is this how someone else feels and I'm being empathetic?
- Have I felt this way before with the same person or situation?
- Am I shutting down my gut reaction because I know someone else won't like me talking about my feelings?
- Am I afraid to admit how I really feel because this is a truth I cannot unsee?

Pay attention to what you need rather than the energy you may be picking up from those around you and what *they* want. When others want to go on the roller coaster and you absolutely do not, you do not need to push yourself through this experience so that they are satisfied. It's important to first recognize what you feel, then put it into the best possible language that fully expresses this feeling. You are simply putting this message at their doorstep for them to pick up and examine. Remember that when you state your boundary, you are not in charge of how others receive it. You can deliver it in the best way possible, and they may still interpret it as criticism or control. Remember that if the other person doesn't have good boundaries, they will probably not respect your boundaries. They disrespect themselves as they disrespect you. Discern what feels like the truth and what feels like a falsehood—trust yourself.

Start with a Small No

I feel proud and anxious.
I just set my boundaries for the first time.

A good way to begin setting new opening boundary statements is to say a small no and see how it feels. Stating a small no is a quick way to see how respectful others are of your boundaries. Notice how they react when you speak your truth, as this will tell you a lot about the relationship and them as a person. For example, you want to go out for Mexican food and they want Italian. State your preference and observe their response. If you say no to Italian food but your choice is overridden and you are pressured to say yes, that tells you a lot about their level of respect for you. I teach this to people who are starting to date and getting to know someone else because it's a quick demonstration of how the other person will respond to your request (your boundary).

Let's begin to exercise your "no" muscle. Recall a situation when you said yes instead of honoring your no. Suspend any self-judgment and ask yourself why you made that choice. What were you avoiding or afraid of? You will probably come up with some good reasons why you agreed to say yes and didn't use your "no" muscle. Our analytical minds become used to justifying our choices and play tricks with our emotional selves, our authentic selves, because we have had a lifetime of training our minds to override our gut, our authentic selves, and our boundaries. We have been socialized to believe that we should say yes.

> *If we can't be ourselves, then we are at risk of*
> *playing a role in someone else's movie.*

Recall again the situation when you said yes instead of no. Check in with your gut, and see if you still think it was the best choice for you. You may still say yes for all sorts of reasons, and that's okay. This exercise helps us to remember to listen to our gut and determine the best next steps.

When you state your boundary and someone respects your no, check in with yourself and see how you feel. Having someone actually see and hear your needs may be a new experience. I've had people come in to see me and excitedly tell me that boundaries actually work. When this happens for you, just take in that feeling and hold it for a while. It's nice when our needs are honored and seen.

Fill in the blanks based on what you are learning:

It's easy to state a small no boundary with ______________ (name) because ______________.

It's hard to set a small no boundary with ______________ (name) because ______________.

My guess is that the person with whom you have difficulty setting boundaries has either ignored or dismissed your boundary in the past, and you feel a greater level of trust in the person with whom it is easy to set boundaries, knowing they respect who you are. Your boundary statements are rarely the problem in the discussion; it is the other person's lack of respect and their dismissal that shuts down your BPS when you are first learning to set boundaries. People who love and respect you care about your well-being and don't try to make you smaller for having needs.

Start your boundary practice by saying no to someone with whom it is easy to do so. Don't go right away to the person you have the most conflict with to practice your new boundary skills.

As you learn to use your "no" muscle, you will begin to get the hang of when you need more power for various types of situations. For example, if you think a new friend doesn't realize that you don't like being called by a nickname, you can gently correct them. It is probably an honest mistake, and they aren't trying to offend you. But if they still call you by that name after you have told them, that's a different story. Some people go overboard when they are learning boundaries and jump all over another person for a boundary violation, but this reaction is akin to using a firehose to put out a birthday candle. A little goes a long way, and you don't need to yell or scream a boundary. Simply stating it is a good start.

You have learned about inherited and broken boundaries, and you have learned about how those around you helped create your BPS when you were a child, and how the wounding inside of you shaped your current boundary protection system. As you looked back over your interactions with others, you saw your boundary journey from childhood into adulthood and how some people respected your boundaries and needs while others disregarded them. You can see how you developed one way of relating to people and thought this was the best way. You have learned that what you thought was helping was, in reality, working against you.

As you do this work, observe yourself in a nonjudgmental way. Try to practice what is called a "loving detachment" from your parents or caregivers, and be more objective. I believe they were doing the best they could with the tools they had, but this doesn't excuse responsibility for abuse or trauma. Recognize your inherited boundaries and how they may have once helped you but now work against you.

Think back on the boundaries you learned in childhood, who modeled good boundaries and who didn't. Then complete the following sentences in your notebook, based on what you know so far. You've answered similar questions already; see if the same people show up in your answers:

- I learned healthy boundaries primarily from my _______________.
- I learned to have poor or no boundaries primarily from my _______________.
- Today my go-to boundary response is usually _______________. I saw _______________ use this response.
- I have difficulty setting healthy boundaries because I _______________.
- I often get in my own way and don't set healthy boundaries because _______________.
- Even though I know they're not the best, I keep using the boundaries I learned from my family because _______________.

This work is not about assigning blame, as that would keep you in a victim space. It is about recognizing who owns what part of your emotional development so you can have clarity and not get lost in someone else's story. This is intergenerational wounding, and I believe you can break this chain if you recognize what is happening instead of being lost in a blurry daydream of doing what you have always done because it's familiar and easier.

Inherited boundaries may be your go-to boundaries, but they are not always the best choice for every situation. You have come a long way with the BPS system you are developing, and now you can refine these tools to work even better for you. As you build a healthy BPS and reassure and heal the part of you that carries the inner child wounding, you will begin to feel whole again.

When you are learning about boundaries and how to make them, it is helpful to keep them simple. As you develop the fundamental boundaries, you can begin to identify and refine them for the boundaries in your life spheres. Understanding boundary violations, how to make "I" statements, and learning what your needs are will help you develop a strong foundation for building your boundary protection system.

Philip's Story

Philip and Julie have been married for seven years and have three small children. With so much going on, the two of them rarely have time to themselves to talk about things that come up or to enjoy doing things together without the children. They have gotten into the habit of talking about plans and schedules when they are in the car or in bed late at night. Julie hadn't realized that Philip has difficulty driving and talking about schedules at the same time and has a hard time keeping track of things late at night, when he's tired. He would try to remember dates and scheduling changes when she told him, but the information would quickly fly out of his head. Then, when he would forget something, Julie would get mad at him and think he was doing it on purpose. She was making up a story based on Philip's behavior, and he was confused about why she would get angry with him for what he saw as an honest mistake.

Philip realized that Julie was getting upset with his inability to be present during these conversations. He wanted to explain to her that he was not able to track information or write anything down in his calendar while he was driving or when he was very tired.

Philip set a time for them to talk, and he was able to state his boundary. *I want to follow through on the things we talk about, but I'm frustrated when you bring them up to me while I'm driving or tired. Is there another way we can do this?* Julie did not even imagine that Philip couldn't remember everything because *she was* able to keep track of dates and times in her head.

Julie thanked Philip for telling her that he was struggling because she had no idea what his experience had been. The two of them now set a dedicated time for when Philip could be present to talk about schedules. Julie broke down her extensive list into bite-sized chunks and slowed down her delivery so she didn't overwhelm him. Once Philip was clear with his needs, they came together and felt more connected. A simple boundary solution to a nagging problem is often what it takes to clear up frustrations in our relationships.

This is an example of a relatable story I hear from couples who come into my office. The conversation isn't earth-shattering, but talking through things and gaining clarity will bring boundaries and a smoothness to this relationship.

Internal and External Boundaries

A straightforward way to think of boundaries is to put them into two categories: internal and external. Both of these boundary types are ways we look out for ourselves. In her book *Facing Codependence: What It Is, Where It Comes From, How It Sabotages Our Lives*, international authority on codependence Pia Mellody goes into great detail about internal and external boundaries and how they are shaped by our childhood family. She describes boundary protection systems and "invisible and symbolic 'force fields' that have three purposes: (1) to keep people from coming into our space and abusing us, (2) to keep us from going into the space of others and abusing them, and (3) to give each of us a way to embody our sense of 'who we are.'"[3]* Internal and external boundary statements are not always about saying no. They can also state what you will do or agree to.

Boundaries are needs expressed.

Let's look more deeply at internal and external boundaries and how to set them.

Setting Internal Boundaries

Internal boundaries are promises or commitments we make to ourselves so that we feel good about how we are living our lives. We make these silent "I am" statements regarding multiple issues throughout each day. This is how we judge what is acceptable and unacceptable, what we want and need. Internal boundaries are silent, self-regulating decisions we make about small things and big things that we usually keep to ourselves. This is how we shape our internal relationships to situations, people, places, and things. We form an inward opinion and then determine how we want to internally interact with this dynamic.

Internal boundaries are when we make a promise to ourselves to work toward what we desire or want to achieve; when we intentionally direct our minds toward what we want to focus on instead of leaving it up to a wandering mind (this is especially true for anxious or intrusive thoughts); when we follow through with something to honor ourselves; and when we note how we want to interact with someone.

---

3 *Facing Codependence: What It Is, Where It Comes From, How It Sabotages Our Lives,* by Pia Mellody, HarperCollins, New York, 2003.

The following are examples of internal boundary statements:

- I am going to maintain strong boundaries with others and say no when I need to.
- I am going to smile more and practice finding the good in myself and others.
- I am going to keep my recovery on track and not drink or use today.
- I am being honest with myself and have realized my party friends aren't good for me.
- I am going to find a therapist to help me with my depression and anxiety.
- I will use positive self-talk more often instead of sabotaging myself.
- I am going to keep my commitment to myself and go to the gym at least twice this week.
- I am not going to make up stories in my head when I feel nervous about my relationship.
- I am not going to take in criticism from others; that's their reality, not mine.
- I am not going to demean or shame others.

These are examples of making commitments to oneself. People who know themselves have a strong internal BPS that they have cultivated over time. They rely on this system to help them reach their goals and maintain healthy relationships. What do you say to the voice in your head that is your internal boundary dialogue? If that voice puts you down, a healthy internal boundary response is, *That's not true, and it's never been true!*

Setting External Boundaries

External boundaries are often "I" statements or positions we establish with another person or situation. This is when we express to others what we want and don't want, what we need and don't need. External boundaries are verbal or physical demonstrations, and by these actions, others know how we think and feel about a particular situation or request. An example is when someone asks if you would like to do something, yes or no. Your response is the boundary. Or you state your opinion about a situation and how you think something should be done. This is a boundary statement. External boundaries define our space in our relationships and give us a sense of power, safety, and confidence. They are outward behaviors.

External boundaries are when you clearly state what you need by word or deed; when you make a choice to remove yourself from a situation that is not good for you; when you make a choice to bring into your life a person or situation that is good for you; when you use feeling words to let others know what is going on inside of you; and when you use different boundaries for different people and situations. When you use external boundaries, you are always honest with yourself and don't lose sight of your authenticity.

The following are examples of external boundary statements:

- I feel hurt because you continually talk down to me.
- I feel trusting and safe in our relationship. Thank you for your kindness.
- I feel excited that we are going on this trip together.
- I don't like it when you stand so close to me. I feel that my personal space is being disrespected. Can you step back?
- This is hard for me to say, but I don't want to go on the trip with you.
- I feel frustrated and shamed when you tell me how I should raise my kids.
- I feel lonely and would really like a hug from you.
- After a lot of careful thought, I want you to know that this relationship is no longer working for me.

- I will respect you when you say no, and I ask you to respect me when I say no.

External boundaries create the guardrails in our relationships with ourselves and others. Without strong and clear boundaries, we open ourselves up to doing what others want, not what we want. We swallow our truth and do not express ourselves, which gives an opening for others to shape our reality. The more we push down our truth and don't set boundaries, the more we contribute to our depression and anxiety.

Our word or behavior is the boundary, and we do not need to defend, justify, or explain how or why we feel the way we do. If you need someone to hear a message from you, be as clear as you can be in expressing it. Remember, this is important to you, so you don't need to be vague just because telling them the truth might sound blunt. Think about how can you say what you need to say in a grounded, respectful, and honoring way. Honor your words, your truth.

Boundaries are the guardrails in our relationships.

It's one thing to think about missed opportunities to set a boundary, but the reality is that your stifled, unexpressed boundary words are getting thrown into an emotional bucket. As unexpressed feelings fill up the bucket, they accumulate energy. If you keep stuffing them down, they will manifest as depression or anxiety. These feelings then come out sideways, often as passive-aggressive behavior or anger. When you state a boundary, you let these feelings out, which leads to emotional freedom.

Think of boundary setting like a sliding scale: one end of the scale is where you need to be concrete and spell things out in order to be in relationship with certain people, where they need to know what is and is not allowed based on their past behavior.

On the other end is where you have a feeling of mutual respect in a relationship, where you trust them and they have your back. Where someone falls on the scale determines how often you need to set boundaries, as boundaries are dynamic and based on the person, place, and situation in a given moment.

Boundary setting is the main tool we use to determine the shape, feel, interaction, and energy between ourselves and others. Without boundaries, the shape is determined by circumstance, chance, and other people. As you examine your own boundary shapes, you will see how others may have stepped in and made boundary choices for you in the past.

"I" Statements

Statements that begin with the word "I" followed by a feeling or a need are called "I" statements. The concept of "I" statements was first developed by psychologist Thomas Gordon as a way to help children connect emotions with behavior.[4] "I" statements are essential building blocks for expressing boundaries and a quick-start way to get into the habit of expressing your needs. Learning how to use "I" statements is an important part of advocating for, owning, and defending your needs and expressing your boundaries. An "I" statement is meant to express your feelings in a way that others can hear and know what is important to you without their becoming defensive or feeling blamed, accused, or guilty. Remember, though, that you can't control other people's feelings or reactions.

Speaking in "I" statements is different from using "you" statements, such as *Why do you always do this?*, or, *You make me so angry when you . . . .* "I" statements are not about blaming and shaming; those are conversation enders, and you won't be heard.

---

4 *Origins of the Gordon Model*, Thomas Gordon, https://www.gordontraining.com/thomas-gordon/origins-of-the-gordon-model/, last accessed July 27, 2024.

When you use "you" statements, the argument, disagreement, or misunderstanding just keeps spinning in place until the next blowup happens. "I" statements are focused primarily on your own feelings when you talk about a situation or behavior that the other person does that causes distress.

Our conversations are more productive when we can start by saying statements such as *I need you to know that I feel frustrated because I keep asking when we can talk,* or, *I feel that I'm being put off, and this feels dismissive. When can we set up a time to talk?,* or, *I feel upset that I keep asking you to put your boots in the closet and you don't do it,* or, *I feel worried when you don't call if you're going to be late. Can we come to an agreement on phone calls like this?* We connect our feelings to an issue and give constructive feedback that then carries forward and creates an action plan. This is direct, to the point, and expresses a frustration with an ongoing issue. The "I" statement is a call to action for the other person. You are saying, *This is important to me. I need you to hear me, and we need to talk about this.*

A caution is to avoid using an "I" statement to attack. An example of an attack is, *I feel like you aren't paying any attention to me and are ignoring me.* Initially, this sounds like an "I" statement, but it accuses the other person and doesn't state the speaker's feeling. Saying, *I feel lonely and not seen when you are on your phone when we are with each other* is more specific and emphasizes the speaker's feelings while linking those feelings to the other person's behavior.

When you start making "I" statements, you may notice that the receiver might see it as an opportunity to attack you. *Well, you always do this . . . ,* or, *You never listen to me, either.* This defensive posture is meant to distract and divert the conversation. Your response here is key. Calmly restate your "I" statement: *I hear you, but can we please focus on my feelings of being left out and lonely?* Resist the urge to refute or challenge whatever they bring up, as this will derail your communication. When the other person uses this diversion response, they are essentially saying that the conversation is unnerving and scary to them and they don't know how to navigate. You may need to come back to your feelings several times before they drop their defensiveness. At best, the other person may finally say, *Okay, I get it, you're lonely. I'm sorry. Can we just move on?*

For most people, this is a new way of communicating feelings, and the natural inclination is to defend oneself and not address the underlying feelings. Be patient with each other, as you will probably need to express your feelings again at another time. Stereotypically, men can process emotional language only in small doses before they get flooded and overwhelmed. This is an unfolding exchange where you both are learning a new communication style.

> *When in doubt about how to begin a boundary statement, simply begin with an "I" statement to get you started, and the rest will follow.*

Starting to use "I" statements in your conversations may be difficult, as this doesn't come easily for most, and some people say it sounds like "therapy-speak." The process sounds simple on the surface, but recognizing and then verbally naming a feeling will probably be new to you. Pick a feeling word that first comes to mind related to the behavior that disrespects your boundary, then start with small efforts as you slowly introduce "I" statements into your everyday life. It gets easier with practice, and others will get used to your new way of expressing yourself.

"I" Statements and Your Needs

Needs are an essential part of our lives. They are different from wants, which are fleeting desires that do not have lasting value. Needs fulfill our sense of self-worth and esteem at a fundamental level. Identifying your needs will help you understand yourself better, and you will be able to communicate your needs (boundaries) to others more clearly when using your "I" statements. Expressing needs is akin to expressing feelings but in a deeper, more emotionally available and connected way. *I need to feel loved* is a heartfelt, deeply personal expression of a need.

Following is a Needs Inventory from the Center for Nonviolent Communication. The words are generic, but the way you interpret them is specific to you. For example, when you read the word "affection," you may get an immediate impression of how you miss affection in your life and how you'd like to receive more of it. Take a moment to practice using this word right now: translate the need for affection into an "I" statement in boundary language. For example, *I need to feel closer to you, and I miss our intimacy. I realize I need more affection. What are some things that we can do to create this feeling in our relationship?* By using this sort of language, your communication will immediately go to a deeper level. The receiver will feel the truth and your earnest desire in your needs statement. (What was your reaction when you read this?)

These "needs" words coordinate well with the life spheres. Look over the Needs Inventory and identify the needs that are being met right now and those you want to manifest. Circle or highlight the needs you need more of in your life.

Needs Inventory

CONNECTION	CONNECTION	HONESTY	MEANING
acceptance	safety	authenticity	awareness
affection	security	integrity	celebration of life
appreciation	stability	presence	challenge
belonging	support		clarity
cooperation	to know and be known	**PLAY**	competence
communication	to see and be seen	joy	consciousness
closeness	to understand and be understood	humor	contribution
community	trust	**PEACE**	creativity
companionship	warmth	beauty	discovery
compassion		communion	efficacy
consideration	**PHYSICAL WELL-BEING**	ease	effectiveness
consistency	air	equality	growth
empathy	food	harmony	hope
inclusion	movement/exercise	inspiration	learning
intimacy	rest/sleep	order	mourning
love	sexual expression		participation
mutuality	safety	**AUTONOMY**	purpose
nurturing	shelter	choice	self-expression
respect/self-respect	touch	freedom	stimulation
	water	independence	to matter
		space	understanding
		spontaneity	

As you looked over these words, were you able to recognize where your needs are being met in your life spheres? How about where your needs are not being met? Consider that you may not be expressing your needs as boundaries to protect and receive what you want. How might you limit others from giving to you by not expressing your boundaries? Do you avoid being specific about your needs so as not to offend someone? Where do you shy away from stating your needs because it feels too vulnerable? Have you tried to express your needs in the past but dropped them because they were not acknowledged? Practice now with an "I" statement, just to yourself, to see how it feels. In the upcoming chapters I will give you many examples of "I" statements to help you craft yours as needed. (See also Appendix: Feelings Inventory for a list of feeling words.)

When we are able to be calm and listen to ourselves, it is easy to identify needs; the hard part is expressing those needs because we are unsure of how others will feel about or respond to them. We might think, *I don't want to make them feel bad*, or, *I don't want them to think they aren't doing this for me already.* Remember that you don't have any idea what others think, just as they don't know your thoughts. Discern what you are feeling rather than what you think you are getting from someone else. Stand strong in your word, and express your needs and your truth in the best way possible.

Do you have any other advice? asked the boy. Don't measure how valuable you are by the way you are treated, said the horse.
—CHARLIE MACKESY

Post-Boundary Feelings

As you practice setting boundaries, you may occasionally regret having done so. You thought deeply about what you wanted to say and how to say it. You rolled this dialogue around, carefully crafted the message, and imagined how the other person will accept your truth. When the moment came, you put it out there: *I don't want to go with you to the concert because crowds overwhelm me.* Instinctively you held your breath, realizing you just went against all of your old programming of *don't speak up, just go along with things, don't make waves.* No matter how prepared you feel to state a boundary, you may immediately regret doing so.

When boundary setting is new, you may experience a strange, uneasy feeling as you float in uncharted territory. When you pierce the air with your boundary statement, you feel as if time stops. You have no idea what their reaction will be. Breathe, and settle in to this feeling. It's just a feeling. You are standing in a new place of owning and declaring what is important to you. The world is still spinning, and no one freaked out.

You may sometimes state your boundaries too forcefully or defensively. This overcorrection will happen as you learn and practice your new boundary language, especially when you are moving from no boundaries to healthy boundaries. Be a patient teacher for yourself, as each time you state a boundary you are reinforcing this muscle.

When we use boundaries, we weigh the convenience of an excuse with the power of standing firm in our convictions.

In this new post-boundary world, you no longer say things just to make others happy or to meet their needs. Now you hold and honor your truth. Still, uncomfortable feelings will come up that need to be acknowledged. Here are some common feelings you may experience after you've stated your truth and set a boundary:

- Fear that others now know how you feel; you feel exposed
- Immediate regret—you want to take it back or apologize
- Fear that they will leave you after hearing your boundary truth
- A sense of relief
- Heavy feelings of shame or sadness
- Surprise that you actually did it
- Anxiety about what others think about you now

- Concern that someone will use your truth against you
- A feeling of freedom
- A sense of ease

You may feel more than one of these feelings—some of which are also mind reading—in post-boundary moments. Know that you can breathe and calm yourself as you settle into the fact that you have honored yourself. The only thing that has changed is that someone else knows what has been inside of you for a long time. Their reaction will tell you a lot about them and your relationship. Trust what you see and hear from them because they will show you who they are. Give yourself a pat on the back. Say: *I'm proud of myself for saying that and honoring myself!*

Suppose you regret something you said, then overcorrected, and now you want to take it back. You can't unring a bell, but you can go back and say, *You know what I told you the other day? Well, I have reconsidered*, or, *I need to make sure that is just between us.* True friends and trusted people honor this. Resist the urge to second-guess your boundary truth by going back into people-pleasing mode and scrambling to repair what you think you messed up just because you feel exposed. See if you can discern where the feeling of regret is coming from. Are you freaked out because you spoke your truth or that they now know how you feel? We are not perfect and sometimes life is messy, feelings are messy. Work with these feelings, and see what you settle on. You may experience some post-boundary sadness—though not necessarily regret—after stating your boundary. That's okay. You have spoken your truth. Trust yourself and your feelings.

If someone doesn't like a truth you've stated, talk with them to see why. Remember to not explain or try to teach them why you have your boundary, as it's not a negotiation—you know what your needs are. Talking is for helping you understand each other better. There will be wins and losses as you learn this new skill. Some people will respect you, and others will not. Give your friends some credit, as they probably can handle your truth. Have faith in yourself. When you are consistent, your friends will hopefully see you are serious, but if they don't, that's on them. Stay strong in expressing your needs one statement at a time as you build your boundary power. Remember that boundaries are about connection and joining.

Jane's Story

Jane has worked at her company for five years. She likes her job and has close friends whom she met at work. Two of her friends, Amber and Lola, work in her department, and another friend, Crystal, works in a different area. They meet up for lunch at work and play on different teams in a bowling league.

Jane likes her friends but has had some run-ins with Amber in the past, when Amber was negative and complained about things that Jane does. Jane has said things like, "Can we talk about positive things instead of all of this negativity, as it really bums me out?" Amber says she just tells it like it is. She brazenly makes comments about their other friends, as well. Jane figures that Amber thinks of herself as the ringleader of the friend group and expects the other women to follow her lead. The others try to stay on her good side because if they don't, she will say mean things about them. When Jane took this job five years ago, she didn't see this behavior. She was just glad to have friends at work.

One day, as she walked past the breakroom, Jane heard Amber make mean comments about Jane's weight. Jane stopped in her tracks, out of view. Her stomach sank and she teared up. Amber knew Jane was acutely self-conscious about her weight. Jane kept to herself the rest of the day. She knew what she had overheard but didn't know anything else about the conversation. Triggered by her insecurities, she made up a story that none of the women wanted to be friends with her anymore. They were no longer going to bowl with her or sit with her at lunch. She got herself spun up in this fiction.

The next day, Jane got in early and went straight to her desk, hoping to avoid everyone. When Lola stopped by to say hi, Jane hurriedly said hi back and put her head down. Lola could tell Jane was upset and asked if she was okay. Finding some courage, Jane said, "No, I'm not okay. I heard what you all were talking about at lunch yesterday. I couldn't sleep at all last night." Lola didn't understand what Jane meant and asked for clarification. Jane said she had heard them talking in the breakroom about her weight and that she was really upset about it. Lola had to think hard because she didn't remember the conversation. Eventually, she recalled Amber talking about Jane's appearance, but the others did not support what Amber said and moved on to a different topic. Lola reassured Jane that her friends hadn't said anything to support what Amber said and had, in fact, defended Jane. Lola apologized and reinforced that only Amber had talked about Jane's weight.

Jane was somewhat reassured but was still mad at Amber. As if on cue, Amber walked up to drop off some paperwork. She saw Jane, red-faced, and Lola, who looked guilty. Amber asked what was going on. Jane knew how Amber was when she was confronted—she became even more passive-aggressive and made sneak attacks later. Jane hesitated, as she didn't want to get into this at work. But she used her anger to find her courage and blurted out a boundary statement: "I heard you talking about me in the breakroom, and I'm really upset." Flustered, Amber said, "Well, it's true. You have put on weight." Humiliated, Jane was beside herself. She got up from her desk, went to the ladies' room, then took the rest of the day off.

After she spent some time thinking about what had happened,

Jane realized that it was Amber she needed to talk to, not her other friends. This conversation was a long time coming. She wrote out what she wanted to say first, then texted Amber to ask if they could meet outside of work to talk, which they did. Having thought about her boundary statement, Jane said, "Amber, I need you to know that what you said about me was very hurtful, and I don't appreciate it. For us to be friends, please don't talk behind my back anymore." Amber became visibly defensive, and all she could say was, "Okay." Jane wanted an apology, but she knew Amber wasn't going to give her that, so she took what she got. At least Amber acknowledged her.

Jane clearly saw that Amber had been a bully the entire time she'd known her; she just hadn't wanted to face this reality before. She had been projecting onto Amber who she needed her to be rather than who she really is. Jane now has much clearer and stronger boundaries with Amber. Jane also has a clear consequence of not being friends with her anymore if she continues this behavior. She sees Amber for who she is and knows she cannot trust her like she does her other friends.

Sometimes when we speak our truth, the other person is not able to respond in the way that we hope for. The best that some can do is acknowledge that they heard us. Jane made a big step in confronting Amber and speaking her truth. Her courage established a benchmark for behavior that she expects from Amber going forward. She didn't hold out for Amber to apologize, as that may never happen. Jane's story is a great example of why we set boundaries for ourselves to hear first. We can't control the other person's response, but we can develop the courage to state our boundaries.

What parts of this story did you relate to? Have you ever had to confront a bully? Have you ever made up a story based on only a few facts?

Think about a time when you chose not to speak your truth. What did this omission cost you? Do you think you were better off by not saying anything? If you had said something, do you think the outcome would have been better or worse? Only you can determine this within the context of the situation and your relationship to the person. Be gentle with yourself as you do this examination. You are learning so much about yourself and your relationships.

> *Everything you think you have lost will probably be replaced with something even better than you could imagine, if you just let it happen.*

CHAPTER SIX

Boundary Violations

Boundaries are basically about providing structure, and structure is essential in building anything that thrives.
—HENRY CLOUD

As you have learned, a boundary violation is when our stated internal and external boundaries are not honored, respected, or acknowledged by ourselves or someone else. Boundary violations occur when someone touches us without our permission, speaks for us, tells us how we feel, or goes against what we want. Boundary setting is also about ownership, so we can violate our own internal boundaries by not following through on something that's important to us. In this chapter we will go deeper into what boundary violations look and feel like so you can have clarity about when you or someone else violates a boundary you have set.

Internal boundaries are violated when we disregard or contradict ourselves, creating cognitive dissonance—the state of holding contradictory thoughts and feelings. We don't listen to our own feelings and ignore our gut reaction, overriding our BPS. These violations occur when we go against a promise or commitment we made to ourselves, when we make up and believe stories about others that aren't true, when we repeatedly deny ourselves self-care even though we know it would be good for us, and when we over-commit ourselves, giving more than we told ourselves we would.

We have all been in a situation where a friend asked us to do something we didn't want to do. We didn't want to disappoint our friend so we said yes, but inside we were screaming, *No, I don't want to do that!* The moment we said yes instead of no, we ignored our internal boundary and denied what we authentically wanted. Our friend got what they wanted at the sacrifice of our own needs. We violated our own boundary.

Saying yes instead of no is a short-lived, temporary relief because we know in our gut what we want, and when we say yes instead of no, we start a resentment cycle against ourselves and our friend, and we may, in fact, start dreading doing the activity at all. If we go with our friend anyway, we may start to feel angry, then afterward beat up on ourselves for having taken the time and spent the money to do an activity with them we didn't want to do. It creates a vicious cycle because we didn't honor ourselves and took the easy way out instead. We pay for this quick yes long after the event. The price we pay for the temporary avoidance of a disappointed friend turns into a lingering resentment that we recycle inside and beat ourselves up for. Resentment is a heavy emotion that is difficult to reconcile.

External boundary violations happen when others take from us without permission, tell us how we feel, do things for us without asking, get into our personal space, or ignore our requests when we ask them to stop. An external boundary violation can happen because someone does not pay attention to our needs, whether intentionally or absentmindedly. They say things like,

You don't really feel that way, or, *This is what you want to do*, or, *I know what you're thinking*, or try to shame us into submission. When our boundaries are repeatedly violated, the codependent part of us gets used to the violations, like when we stop hearing the slow drip of a leaky faucet. We don't like it, but we go along with it because, even though we've told the other person to stop, they continue to disrespect our boundaries. We mistakenly stay in a wounded position of either thinking that our boundaries are wrong or that the other person knows better and is right. We also do this to avoid getting into an argument or making the other person mad, which would create more drama.

Certainly, there are times we make a value judgment and, out of reciprocity and kindness, go along with what someone else wants or accept what they have done for us without asking. When I do this, I consciously acknowledge that I'm going against my BPS. I say to myself something like, *I know I don't want to do this, but I love her and want to help her out, and I know she really wants me to go with her*. So I go against my internal boundary, but I consciously override it to help my friend. I don't do this all the time, though, as I would be dishonoring myself.

It's important to recognize when boundary violations happen, as many people with codependent patterns learned early on how to disregard their gut feeling and make an excuse for the other person's behavior. In other words, we learned to override our early warning boundary protection system, to "be nice" and not make waves. Work on recognizing when this is happening. Don't minimize the other person's behavior or your reaction. How you feel is real, and boundary violations are real. Practice checking in with yourself and recognizing the programming you picked up to deny or ignore your gut reaction. Remember that you do not need to explain why you want or need a boundary, but you will need to defend your boundaries in other ways. You will learn more about how to defend boundaries in a later section.

The following are several examples of different boundary violations. See if you can identify why each violation is internal, external, or both.

Internal boundary violations include being open and vulnerable too soon, too fast; overcommitting to others to make them happy; going through the motions or numbing out; and giving to others at the expense of self.

External boundary violations include sharing intimate details about a partner with friends or family; being shamed by others, overtly and covertly; others deflecting blame onto us for something they did; telling someone what to do when they have not asked for our advice; and someone hugging us or otherwise getting into our personal space without permission.

Boundary violations that are both internal and external include saying yes but feeling no; making ourselves smaller to fit into someone else's world; making excuses for others; and taking on the responsibilities of others (e.g., doing their work for them) so we don't have to deal with uncertainty.

These are all examples of how, when others disrespect us, we override our internal boundaries and do something that does not honor ourselves. When we continue to give others the benefit of the doubt instead of honoring ourselves, we are saying to ourselves that their opinion is more valuable or that their needs are more important than ours.

As you're learning, there is a temporary relief when we avoid speaking our boundary truth, but we eventually have to pay a price for not honoring ourselves. If you don't want to do something but continue to go along with it, ask yourself why. Are you doing it for yourself or someone else? There is a price to pay no matter what. We pay on the front end when we put our boundary statement out there, or we pay on the back end with regret and resentment when we swallow our words and do something we don't want to do.

You don't need to explain a boundary;
it is just your boundary.

Boundary violations can sneak up on us before we realize what's going on. The more you know what these violations sound like, the better you can recognize in the moment when someone violates your boundary. See if you can identify the boundary violation in each of these statements:

- You're fine; let's just go.
- I know what you're feeling. You're mad at me right now.
- I'm giving you a hug right now whether you like it or not.
- Why do you always keep doing the wrong thing?
- I know I didn't ask, but I went to your house today and moved your furniture. I hope you like it.
- I went ahead and told her what you didn't want me to say because she needed to know.
- You made me do this because you get me so frustrated.

What is your gut reaction to reading these boundary violations? Have you heard someone say something similar to you? Notice how most of the statements are coated in a layer of shame. It doesn't feel great when someone disrespects our boundary and talks over us, talks down to us, or shames us. They are projecting their own pain onto us. If someone is repeatedly mean to us and we continue to take it, we are effectively telling them that this treatment is okay, and we become part of the problem. The solution is to learn to set boundaries and defend them.

Learning to recognize boundary violations takes practice, especially if you've never consciously thought about boundaries. So far, I've given you examples of internal and external boundary violation situations and what violations sound like coming from someone else. Another way to learn to identify boundary violations is to ask yourself the following questions. If you answer yes to any of them, see if you can identify them as internal or external boundary violations, or both.

- Are you being shamed or ridiculed by someone's words or behaviors?
- Are you being touched without your consent? (For example, someone repeatedly touches your back or shoulders without consent.)
- Do others make decisions for you because they say they know what is best? Do others try to turn your no into a maybe or a yes?
- Do others try to engage you in arguments so they can go into a victim space?
- Do others shame you by saying things like, "Stop being so sensitive," or, "Just get over it"?
- Do others gaslight you into questioning your own reality, that you said or did something you didn't?
- Do others tell you what to do in a controlling or directing way instead of collaboratively?
- Do you come into someone else's space and start moving things around or "helping" because you think you know what needs to be done?

Take a moment to write out some boundary violations that come to mind. Is it primarily one person who violates your boundaries, or many people? Is the same kind of issue repeated, or are there different types of situations? Look for patterns to determine what their responsibility is for the boundary violations and what your responsibility is for not setting boundaries. Try not to be judgmental, just observant. See these exchanges for what they are. In your head or on paper, begin to formulate healthy boundary statements for each violation. Sit with these boundary statements and feel how it would be to take back your power from someone who did something without your knowledge or permission.

Sometimes we are too close to a situation, give too much benefit of the doubt, or are just used to how someone talks to us even though we know it's wrong. If you have trouble determining whether someone has violated your boundary, check in with a trusted friend or therapist to see what they think. They may be able to see through this language to help you determine whether there is a boundary violation or not. With their input, you can check in with your gut reaction to see if you need to assess the situation differently. Try not to over-rely on someone else's opinion too much, though. Trust your gut.

There is no deadline for when you can and can't state boundaries. If you keep recycling something that someone did or said and you didn't state a boundary at the time, you can always go back and make your boundary statement. You know, I'm feeling hurt by what you said last week.

There are clearly many types of boundary violations. I have noticed, however, that most people don't recognize them as violations; they just see them as a behavior and not as a pattern. Over time, repeated violations create a tolerance for bad behavior. We tend to minimize boundary violations with excuses such as *That's just how they talk*, or, *They don't mean anything by that*. We become so used to how others treat us that we override our gut reaction to something that would be upsetting if it were coming from a total stranger.

Gaslighting is when someone uses all manner of declarative statements to get you to question your own reality. Gaslighting sounds like, *You don't feel that way*; *That's not how it happened*; *You are so sensitive*; *Everyone thinks you're crazy*. People who do this are usually very persuasive and consistent, and their manipulations impact how you think about and interpret a situation. This boundary violation technique is meant to get you off base so they can manipulate you into doing what they want and get you off topic. Check in with yourself to see if someone is gaslighting you to get their needs met. With this knowledge, you are now developing the skills to recognize these violations and how to defend yourself. You will learn more about manipulators in chapter 9.

A word of caution: If you feel someone gaslights you, don't weaponize this term back at them during a heated moment. Use your boundary statements to express yourself clearly instead of labeling what you think they are doing. Often this labeling creates distraction when what you want to do is state your boundaries clearly and stay on topic.

As you're learning, boundary violations can come upon you quickly. Let's say you drop off your car for service and the technician starts hitting on you by complimenting you or asking how often you work out. At first it feels like a compliment and you're flattered. If you are in a vulnerable state, it might be hard to turn away from this attention. But then they keep it up, and you start to feel uncomfortable. It's too much, it's creepy, it's weird and off-putting, and you just want to get away as soon as possible. In that moment you can choose to ignore the queasy feeling in your gut or you can stop the conversation. Simply say, *I need to get going*, or, *What you're saying doesn't feel right to me, and I don't appreciate how you are talking to me*, or you can talk to the manager.

Pay attention to your gut reaction, and remember to focus on your truth, not on their response or how they might feel. Don't try to create the perfect boundary statement; just get something out there to protect yourself. The point is to honor what's going on inside of you instead of going back to old behaviors and ignoring your feelings. Keep yourself safe, and know that you can process this boundary on your own without talking to the person if that feels safer to you.

These interactions happen so quickly that we often overlook them, but notice that it is this sort of exchange that keeps recycling inside of you and is off-putting. If you find yourself replaying the scene and feeling the emotion, this probably means that a boundary violation of some sort occurred. If you don't feel comfortable saying something in the moment, check in with yourself and acknowledge what happened. Say to yourself, *That was really weird. I didn't like how they were talking to me. I'm glad I got out of there. I'm going to avoid that place (or person) in the future. I am taking care of myself.*

The traumatized part of us impulsively freezes, fawns, fights, or wants to flee. Use your newfound boundary language to protect yourself.

As you practice checking in with yourself and being more aware of how others treat you, you will begin to recognize boundary violations as they happen in the moment. You will also be able to hear violations that happen around you all the time. Years ago I was at the zoo with friends. I overheard parents talking with their kids using shaming language, such as *I can't believe you did this again*, or, *How many times do I have to tell you?* Over time we get used to hearing this kind of correction, and it doesn't register as shame-based language. We normalize the boundary violations as everyday speech. What boundary violations have you become numb to?

Ask yourself how you might open a door for boundary violations to happen. Are you inconsistent in your boundary presentation? Are you noncommittal when someone asks your opinion or if you want to do something? As you are learning, we curate the environment for our relationships, and our boundary inconsistencies open doors for others to do what they want rather than what we need.

Consequences of Boundary Violations

As you've learned, boundaries without consequences are not boundaries; they are requests. There needs to be consequences when our boundaries are ignored or disrespected. We make opening boundary statements when we want to have a conversation with someone about our needs. When these statements are not respected, we level up and bring forth the consequences. Simply put, consequences are about getting someone's attention if they do not honor our opening boundary statement. When there are no consequences, we inadvertently enable and encourage disrespectful behavior. Without consequences, we run the risk of being stuck in a conflict-avoidant loop, staying in a victim mode, and blaming others for not listening to us and violating our boundaries. Meaningful consequences give backbone to our boundaries when we have been continually ignored, shamed, neglected, or disrespected.

We need to enforce a consequence when we state our truth and our boundary is not respected. Not every boundary declaration needs to have a consequence as, hopefully, most people will respect your boundary statement and you will not need to enforce a consequence. Consequences are for those who don't respect your word. This is your boundary enforcement and the ramification of their bad behavior or choices. Know that you are protecting yourself, as they are not looking out for your best interest in these situations.

Consequences need to be direct, clear, and able to be carried through. They are not meant to punish, manipulate, or be weaponized, but to send a clear message that you are protecting your boundary. Consequences need to have meaning for the other person. It's best if you start with the least impactful because that will give you somewhere to go if they don't respond to your initial consequence. Consequences are most effective when you take away something that the other person values. This could be your time, access to something they want, or your presence. Consequences are meant to put someone on notice that you recognize that their behavior or choices don't work for you and that it needs to change. The language to use is, *If you continue to do this, I will need to . . . .*

Not every boundary needs to have a consequence. For example, *I'm feeling adventurous and I want to go hiking with you today. Would that be okay?* This is a request. If the other person acknowledges and joins you, wonderful. Conversely, if they say, *What if we do something else that I've been thinking about?*, then that leads to a bigger discussion where you can meet in the middle. If the other person *always* overrides your idea, then this is when to bring in a consequence. *It seems that every time I want to do something, you will bring up what you want and talk over me until you get your way. If this continues, I won't ask you to do things with me anymore, as I don't feel heard or seen.* This is a simple example of how a request can graduate into a boundary statement with consequences. These situations come up in everyday conversation. Each exchange feels different, so you will need to evaluate your gut reaction when you bring up your ideas to determine whether you feel respected or not. Look for respect and reciprocity in the relationship, as this will tell you if you need to up your game with consequences.

Here are more examples of boundary violations with consequences:

> I really want to have an open and vulnerable connection with you, but I feel offended by how you talk to me. If you continue to invalidate and shame me for my feelings, I will need to rethink if this is the best relationship for me.

> I feel violated because you continue to go into my personal space and use my things without asking after I've asked

you not to. If you continue this behavior, I will put a lock on the door and you will need to ask for permission to go in there.

I don't feel heard or seen in this relationship. I want us to have a conversation where we both feel validated, but if you continue to yell and talk over me, it's not going to work. I'm going to do some laundry, and I'll come back later. Then we can restart this conversation in a respectful way.

As an exercise, take a moment to think about a situation in your life where there is a boundary violation. Now create your own boundary violation consequence language using this formula: I feel _____. If you continue _____, then I will _____.

Don't worry about getting it perfect. The important part is naming how you feel, stating the offensive behavior, and clearly saying what you are going to do because of it.

Sometimes people make mistakes and are clumsy with their words. Life is not about perfection. If this is their first time violating your boundary, then use your "I feel" language to point out the boundary violation. Most people will notice this and either apologize or make a note of it and won't do it again. First offenders of boundary violations do not want to dishonor you; they value the connection they have with you. You are asking that they respect you. Some people are repeat boundary violators and do not listen to your ask or regard your needs. This is when you need to look out for yourself and state the consequences for their repeated boundary violation behavior, as they don't have your best interest in mind.

Consequences are my boundary reinforcements.

Symbolic Letter Writing

Symbolic letters are a great way to put your feelings into words and help you create a boundary statement that reflects your mood. As you're learning, the more you can clearly state your feelings when a boundary violation occurs, the deeper you honor yourself. Once we name a feeling, a part of us that carries the hurt or frustration feels acknowledged and quiets, and when we are ready, others can better hear our truth.

Symbolic letters are written in a stream-of-consciousness style; that is, rapidly and without editing or self-criticism. Symbolic letters are meant just for you, even when you address them to a person or situation. They are not a diary or record for anyone else to read, and you don't give the other person your symbolic letter. They are meant to help you face your emotions as you learn to hold space for others in a new way. They are a great resource to use when you don't want to engage with someone else, or you are not ready to talk with them about a boundary violation and want to clarify how you feel.

The time to write a symbolic letter is when you can't move past an issue, when you are unsure of your feelings, or when a boundary violation keeps nagging you and you want it to go away. This writing process diffuses a lot of the energy punch so that when you are ready, you feel grounded and can clearly state how you feel. In some situations, if you launch into your boundary statement without examining your feelings first, you may let the raw emotion come blasting out, coating everyone with your wounded pain. They walk away thinking, *Jeez, he was really angry* instead of hearing what you're angry about.

As an exercise, think of a boundary violation that you have been recycling in your mind. Then, without hesitating or pre-thinking, write out what you'd say to that person if you could say anything. Once you connect to this stuck energy, it will feel like a dam breaking, letting loose how you really feel. Suddenly, all of the thoughts and feelings you've had are staring back at you. You are giving yourself permission to fully and freely express emotions that have been bottled up and unexpressed for a long time. This creates the movement that leads to healing.

Putting pen to paper (or typing it out) helps us to access a deep part of ourselves that reacts to a boundary violation. We know this information intellectually, but writing it out gives us room to explore from a feeling aspect. The kinetic movement of writing forms a bridge between the conscious and the subconscious. For example, you may discover that what you thought of as anger or frustration is actually hurt or betrayal. I know from my own experience that once I write out the feeling word that most accurately reflects what is going on inside, a part of me settles down because I've named my pain. (See Appendix: Feelings Inventory for a list of feeling words.)

When we name our pain we can claim it, we can own it,
and it is ours to choose what to do with it.

You may need to write several symbolic letters to relieve some of the pressure that's been inside of you and for you to have a clear idea of your feelings. See how far you can get on your own to come to terms with what happened before you consider talking it through with the other person. If you want to talk to the other person, your letter writing will help to clarify what you feel and what you want to say. The letter is for your process, so you will not give them the letter. Be sure to manage your expectations before you talk about your feelings. Remember, they probably haven't been working on being as intentional with their emotions as you have, and they may not be in a grounded place. In fact, they may not even realize (or care) that what they said or did violated your boundaries.

If you've tried to talk with someone about their boundary violations in the past and you felt worse afterward, this is an indication that it will be more useful for you to work through these feelings on your own. (You will read more about this in the section on boundaries with manipulators.)

When you are ready to write, I suggest that you don't pre-think what you are going to say; just sit down and start writing. Give a voice to the part of yourself that is recycling the pain. Once you've written out your feelings, read what you wrote, then tear up the paper or delete the file. You may even want to shred or burn the letter as a way to move into a place of solace with this issue. This is a private process. See what emotions start pouring out of you. You may be surprised at all the heaviness you've been carrying and how freeing it is to let it go.

Symbolic letters don't fix or solve an issue, but you do free up space inside so you can more easily access your authenticity and agency. You let go of pent-up energy that no longer serves you and gain a new perspective on the situation, opening yourself up to the possibility of healing. Symbolic letters are a healing gift we give to ourselves. We move this jagged energy out of us to make way for feelings of contentment, safety, and stability.

David's Story

David works in sales and reports to his manager, Jenn, who is fair but firm. David struggles to meet his monthly goals and doesn't like giving Jenn his sales figures. It was mid-month, and three of David's big clients told him they were not going to sign their contracts. David had been counting on these deals and felt angry about losing them. He complained to Jenn about the leads he was getting and said that his clients were the worst. Yelling, he then blamed Jenn, saying she wasn't managing him well or this wouldn't have happened.

Jenn heard David out and realized he was going into a "poor me" victim state, which was his pattern when he was in a difficult spot.

She wasn't going to let David put the blame on her. Remaining calm, she set a boundary by saying, "It seems that you want me to take on the responsibility of your not making your goals, and then to find a solution. I feel like I'm being set up as a scapegoat here, and I don't like how you're speaking to me." David squirmed and continued to yell, saying he was doing everything he knew to do, but it wasn't his fault the clients weren't signing. Jenn again asked David to speak respectfully. She asked if there was anything he thought he needed to do differently. With this boundary, Jenn didn't take on the responsibility for David not doing his job, and asked him to self-regulate his emotions. She said she would help him help himself by encouraging him to be creative with his sales approach. Jenn knew she had to talk with David about his disrespect once he cooled down. She stayed professional, encouraged him to find an answer within, and, wanting David to build an internal resource, she did not go into fix-it mode.

David's inner child backstory is that he was the middle child in his family. He was always overlooked, felt like his voice was never heard, and felt that everyone was out to get him. He replays this wounded drama in his adult life by wanting attention and projecting onto people in authority the role of the parent who overlooks him.

This conversation between Jenn and David could have gone in a different direction if Jenn had not stayed grounded and firm in her boundaries. This is an example of clarity in boundary setting paying off by not getting lost in someone else's drama. Jenn knew this wasn't about her, and she didn't take the bait. This work relationship is imbalanced and needs better communication to create better cohesion. Boundaries give us a solid advantage of strength and clear vision.

⁓

You are learning how to express yourself more clearly so that others are not in the dark about how you feel or what your needs are. You are learning how to take care of yourself in situations where others violate your boundaries and are disrespectful. Along the way, you are developing a sense for when others speak in a shaming way. You are learning how to acknowledge your feelings, protecting all of you in a new, affirming manner.

Observe the situations in your life where you can begin to bring in your boundary statements. Consider those situations where you have tried to set boundaries and they have been ignored. Ask yourself if you need to bring in consequences to enforce your boundaries. You are worth protecting, and your words are your greatest defense.

CHAPTER SEVEN

Stretching into Boundaries

The only people who get upset when you set boundaries are the ones who benefited from you having none.
—EMMA GANNON

So far you have learned how to discern what is okay and not okay with you, how your boundary protection system was influenced by your childhood, what internal and external boundaries are, the importance of learning and setting boundaries, and how to begin recognizing boundary violations, to name a few. In this chapter we will explore how reciprocity is an important indicator of healthy boundaries, look at specific boundary types, discuss how to deal with complicated and toxic relationships, and more. As we stretch and grow in our relationships, our boundaries help us on this path by taking us to deeper heartfelt levels of connection and healing.

Reciprocity

In chapter 1 you learned that the fundamentals of respect and reciprocity are the bedrock of a strong relationship and the foundation that helps our boundary system to flourish. Reciprocity is when both parties in an exchange feel heard, seen, respected, and understood without judgment. In other words, the interaction feels balanced, and there's a back and forth where each person gives and receives, helping the relationship to thrive. Understanding the degree of reciprocity in your relationships will help you to determine whether you have healthy boundaries and if your needs are honored.

Understanding reciprocity is necessary for a healthy relationship because without it, one person is at risk of making the relationship work in a codependent way while the other sits back and reaps the benefits. An unfair and disrespectful imbalance is created when one person carries more responsibility for maintaining the relationship than the other. Most people freely give and help others out without looking for something in exchange, which builds and enriches relationships. Reciprocity is not about a one-for-one exchange; it is about unspoken agreements with others, where you know they have your best interest in mind and would help you as you help them. Over time, we know at a deep level if there is a fair exchange in our relationships or not.

An exchange of respect and reciprocity establishes a balance within the relationship. Without a fair exchange, resentment and misunderstanding may result.

Each of us has what I call a built-in internal reciprocity gauge—gut reactions to situations that come up in our relationships that help us recognize when an exchange is reciprocal. An example of imbalance is when you go out of your way to help a friend but they are never able to help you when you need it. They are nice when you see them and you enjoy meeting up, but something doesn't feel right between the two of you. Chances are, your gut is telling you that there is an imbalance (unexpressed boundaries) in the relationship, and you are doing more of the work. This lack of reciprocity, where one person feels they are doing the heavy lifting, is often a subtle feeling and hard to describe to others without sounding petty. Recognizing the degree of reciprocity will help you clearly see when, where, and how boundary violations occur in your relationships.

Reciprocity is a hallmark of a mutually respectful friendship. Without reciprocity the relationship gets wobbly, like a three-wheeled wagon: sometimes it's upright, and sometimes it tips over. Reciprocity is easy to identify when, say, you've given a gift and receive a gift in return. But this internal reciprocity gauge is not about one-for-one exchanges. Instead, it subconsciously measures the give-and-take—the flow—in the relationship. It is the feeling of being honored and seen, and you honoring and seeing others.

To accurately assess your internal reciprocity gauge in a particular dynamic, you will need to look at the arc of the whole relationship. Over time, has the other person shown an intention, good faith, and a desire to see and honor your needs, and you have done the same? If so, then the relationship is in balance. But when respect and honoring are not mutual over time, then the relationship becomes imbalanced. If the imbalance is chronic, it's time to make a boundary statement such as, *I'm confused. I feel like I help you a lot, but when I ask for help, you're not there for me.* Look over your relationships and assess the degree of healthy reciprocity. What does your inner reciprocity gauge tell you? Are your relationships in balance? Do you tolerate someone who doesn't reciprocate? Have you enabled an inequality by not speaking up?

Exercise: Your Internal Reciprocity Gauge

For this exercise, turn to your notes from the circle exercise in chapter 3. Consider the people you placed in your inner circle. For each person, check in with your internal reciprocity gauge, then use the following prompts to see how healthy the reciprocity and boundaries are. Then do the same for people in the middle and outer circles.

- Do I feel good about this relationship, or do I feel resentment?
- Do I feel this person honors me as I honor them?
- Do I feel this person gives something of value to support the connection?
- Do I feel this person has contributed in kind over time as I have?
- Do I feel that I carry a heavier load and they take advantage of it?
- Do I put up with an imbalance because I haven't set a boundary or spoken my truth?
- What would I like to say to this person because I feel our relationship is not reciprocal?
- If I have tried to talk with this person about this imbalance, what was their answer?

Are you beginning to see how reciprocity is an indicator of healthy boundaries? Do you notice anything new about these relationships or within yourself? Sometimes the codependent, wounded part of us wants to overproduce, overgive, and overcontrol relationships and not let the other person reciprocate. If you have a hard time receiving, you may not open yourself up to being vulnerable and letting others give you gifts or help you out. This often comes from wanting to be in control and not wanting to look as if you need help or assistance, or from not wanting to feel that you owe anyone. The root of this uneven exchange is usually a broken trust issue rooted in childhood. Know that this can be healed and that, over time, you can open yourself up to receive.

A lack of reciprocity in either direction, if chronic, is a boundary violation. If the other person does not reciprocate your participation in the relationship, then this is an external boundary violation of your kind gestures being taken for granted. An internal boundary violation occurs when the codependent, wounded part of you continually gives while overlooking the lack of reciprocity. This imbalance often leads to feelings of lingering resentment.

I'm taking care of my side of the street.

Here is another exercise: On a piece of paper, draw a vertical line down the middle. Label the left side "None" for no reciprocity, and the right with "Too much" for relationships where one of you gives too much. Write in the names or initials of the people from your circles you feel you have an imbalance with (none or too much). What is your impression of the root cause of each imbalance? What does this diagram reveal about you? Who do you overdo it with? Why? Whose lack of reciprocity do you ignore? Why? Do you feel that if you don't give to them, they won't like you? Is there someone in your life who showers you with gifts and gestures? How do you feel being on the receiving end of this largess (or love bombing)? Do you have a lot of friends who give you very little or too much? Remember, reciprocity is not a one-for-one exchange but how the reciprocity feels over time. What does this exercise show you about your relationships and reciprocity?

Reciprocity means that we acknowledge the other person in the relationship and they see us. When there is a back-and-forth exchange, this steadies and builds the relationship over time based on shared experiences and being honored.

Honoring Those Who Reciprocate

When people in our lives respect our boundaries, it creates a win-win. They tell us they trust and respect us. We are seen, and our needs and truth are being held. This enhances and deepens our relationships, helping us to feel more connected. It's important to recognize when others reciprocate by telling them that you recognize their effort in joining with you in the relationship and connection.

We can honor others directly or indirectly, depending on the type of relationship it is. For example, honoring can be a direct statement, such as *I really appreciate how you listen to me. I feel seen by you, which hasn't always been the case in my life,* or, *You do a great job of doing things that I'm interested in, and I feel really lucky to have you in my life.*

You honor someone by showing up for them. They honor you in return by showing up for you. This consistent reciprocity over time solidifies the relationship and imbues a deep sense of loyalty and nonverbal honoring. Women are usually better at directly honoring reciprocity with feeling words. Men honor in nonverbal ways when they physically show up to help out.

Honoring is recognizing how each person in the relationship works hard to create a mutually respectful and reciprocal connection. Showing appreciation for this reinforces the strong boundaries that relationships are built on. When you say thank you in your own way, you give others something we rarely hear as adults—praise. Opening ourselves up is a gift we give in friendship, and when others do this for us, it creates a mutually beneficial, reciprocal deepening of the connection.

Grieving Toxic Relationships

Today I will not give toxic people any more space in my life.

As we heal, we begin to look at life through a new lens. We give ourselves permission to see how others disrespect us and our boundaries. We start to see relationships that we thought were okay, but we now see that they were not reciprocal or respectful. We begin to realize the power we have given away and the time we lost investing in someone who was not able to give back to us.

No matter how consistently you state your boundaries, some people will ignore these efforts as if nothing was said. The more you state your boundaries, the more they resist the change. They are being themselves, but you are changing and expanding your language. Now you know too much, and you can't unsee the fact that they are repeatedly disrespectful and ignore your needs. You see, and now feel, this boundary violation. In my past, I would hold on to these unhealthy relationships for far too long out of a sense of misplaced loyalty or false obligation. I didn't want to let go of the dream that I had about our connection, idealizing them instead of seeing reality. I think I didn't want to feel the pain of the loss, but in the end, I was better off once I was able to let these toxic relationships go.

If someone does not treat you well on social media, or calls you only when they need something, you are not aligned with them and they are not healthy for you. Release this connection and move on.

As we heal and set stronger boundaries, we grieve for the ending of a connection that we once wrapped in stardust and put so much emotional capital into. We grieve the loss of the journey we thought we would take with them. We grieve the relationship we thought we had. It's akin to looking at a deflated balloon on the ground and remembering when it was light and lofty. As much as we may want to undo our new knowledge and understanding and go back to the before time, we can't. The toothpaste is out of the tube. The connection no longer fits us. We can no longer make ourselves smaller to fit into this outdated version of ourselves.

As you heal and set boundaries, you will expand your idea of yourself and recognize who is good for you and who is bad or even toxic. You will hear what people say in a different light and feel a drop in your gut when someone uses shaming language. As I grew into understanding and healing myself, I began to see others for who they were instead of who I needed them to be to complete my dysfunctional drama. Parts of me began to heal, and I could now recognize how they treated me, how they talked to me, and that they were not honoring or respectful. I saw how some people would push their anger onto me even though I wasn't the cause of it. They wanted me to go back to how I was before I learned boundaries, but I could no longer make myself smaller to fit into their world. Looking back, I was also struggling with not fully understanding my new role, as I primarily knew how to be the people pleaser but not the boundary setter. People pleasing and changing myself for others was familiar to me, so stepping into this new world with healthy boundaries was scary at first. It is normal and healthy to grieve the end of these dysfunctional relationships and how we used to be, but it's not easy.

This aspect of healing and creating definition in your relationships may be hard for you, as a part of you wants the dance to continue, especially if you've had these connections for a long time. But as the smokescreen clears, you cannot avoid realizing that some people aren't good for you or that you don't feel good when you are around them. You thought you knew who they were, but as you healed, you saw them clearly for the first time. You begin to feel they aren't reciprocal or respectful. Observe and see them for who they really are. You may wonder if they were always this way (they were) and how you didn't see it. Your wounded part chose dysfunctional friends or relationship partners because doing so made sense to the hurting part of you. This wounded part meshed with their wounded part, so you thought it was a functional match. You needed those toxic friends to complete your wounding story, but the healed part of you doesn't want anything to do with this drama dance anymore. Hurting people look at life through a wounded lens. It's only after we begin to heal that we see how we filled our lives with other hurting people because we didn't know the difference. As we grow and heal there is a natural ending to some relationships. Be gentle with yourself in the unfolding process.

A dull ache may sit in your gut as you feel the grief of an ending. It's okay. You're just holding space for the tenderness of the connection you thought you had. Over time, your sense of self-respect and feeling of being emotionally free are going to dissolve this aching grief. This void can be filled with healthy connections and fulfilling relationships.

Be gentle with yourself as these revelations come to light, as they can be jarring and searingly bright. Don't blame yourself for being in a relationship that was unkind or volatile. The smaller, wounded version of you that put up with those boundary violations before is now growing, healing, and moving on. Your boundaries tools are only as good as the ones you know, and now you are learning how to use healthy tools. You're learning so much about yourself, and the fact that you can look back and recognize the wounded patterns and see the healthy patterns is absolutely huge. Being able to see our emotional wounding means that we are healing.

Grieve the loss of what you thought you had because, in reality, it was a projected illusion of pain. Healing begins the moment you honor and respect your boundaries and do what you need to do for yourself, to see what you don't want to see but what's always been there. Forgive yourself for what you didn't know. Celebrate yourself for what you are learning, and know you will find a new groove to relate to others with your healthy boundaries. You are moving mountains inside of you as you expand and grow.

Healing can be a double-edged sword, yet we have to transform dysfunction in order to grow. We cannot carry a weighted, wounded pain while we hope to soar into healthy new relationships.

Don't confuse the legitimacy of your boundary with the other person's lack of respect or response.

Boundaries and Addictions

Many situations in life will probably never change—as much as we would like them to—and this challenges our BPS. One of the more challenging parts of life is when we or someone we love is going through a situation that cannot be easily controlled, changed, or fixed. This conundrum brings up a lot of emotions: anger, worry, frustration, bewilderment, resentment, and grief, to name a few. Some examples of things not easily fixed or changed are having a chronic illness, watching a loved one's ongoing addiction, being estranged from family, and having crushing debt. These are situations where we feel we have no control, where we can't see a light at the end of the tunnel and there is no easy solution. These situations test our good nature and stretch us beyond where we thought we could go, often leaving us feeling helpless and hopeless because we don't have the tools to process the emotions or find a resolution. The best thing we can do is to not lose ourselves in the fear of the uncertainty and to use our strong internal and external boundary system to help guide us through this experience. Our boundaries become the guideposts that help us walk this path.

Such situations are a great challenge because our natural instinct is to try to control outcomes. When we are in a place of fear, we want to control so we feel safe. But some situations are out of our control, so we have to find a way to hold this out-of-control feeling. Setting a strong internal boundary will create a safe container to hold this fear and anchor you. Saying things to yourself such as *Things are going to work out; I'm going to be okay; I know I am loved* will create a sense of calm and reassurance that will help you to take things one step at a time. There is not one word, phrase, or solution that is going to make the situation all better, so you need to use your creativity and wisdom to anchor you in your truth.

Loving Detachment Boundaries

When someone in your life is going through a challenge or an issue, it's important to take care of yourself first, then help them. An effective way to do this is to develop "loving detachment" boundaries. This is when you love and want to help the person, but you clearly see where you end and they begin. Loving detachment does not mean closing yourself off to the other person. You are saying, *I love you, but I'm not going to get pulled down into your pain or let you destroy my life as you are destroying yours.* It's being compassionate and available, understanding limits, and holding space for their journey while being a witness to their healing.

In situations where there is ongoing untreated addictions, what I often find is that the addicted person doesn't experience emotions or consequences as deeply as those around them because they are lost in the fog of their addiction. In other words, the one who is at the center of the storm is often in denial of the situation while everyone else is reeling from the chaos that their unstable, addicted self creates. When this happens, we may take on and "carry" their feelings, try to fix their leaky ship, get lost in their drama, and project ourselves into their story. We feel all the raw feelings and consequences as if they are happening to us because we aren't self-medicating with drugs or alcohol.

We think we can assert some control over the situation to stop the spinning, but the addicted person will often sabotage our best efforts to help. Very quickly we can lose ourselves in this maze because our empathy, fears, guilt, or compassion drowns out any boundaries that we thought we had. In most cases we cannot make things better no matter how much money or resources we throw at the problem. They don't want the illusion to end because then they would have to face a reality they have become expert at avoiding. Sometimes there must be consequences or a rock bottom for the person to face their addiction. If we don't bring in consequences for these situations, our boundaries become enabling phrases shouted into the wind.

If you are dealing with someone in this situation, one way to stay grounded is to state your boundaries as a reminder for yourself to stay focused. A boundary statement for this example would be, *I feel very uncomfortable and don't like to be around you when you are drinking. If this is what you choose to do when I'm with you, then I will leave.* This is an example of a boundary and consequence. You could go on to say as a reinforcing consequence, *If this becomes a pattern when I'm with you, then I'm not going to come over to see you and will only communicate by phone as needed to protect myself.* If boundary violations continue, then you would need to evaluate whether or not this relationship is good for you. *If you continue to dishonor me, I will need to evaluate if this relationship is good for me.* With this example you can see the build of boundaries and consequences that are needed to protect yourself.

When someone you love is in the throes of addiction, your boundary statements themselves are rarely enough to get through their thick web of denial. You're learning to state your boundaries first for yourself to hear and then for the other person. This is especially true in these cases, as the addicted person is in an altered state and cannot clearly hear or process what you are saying.

If we continually enable through fixing, smoothing the path, paying for, or cleaning things up for the addicted person, we remove consequences from their life so they don't experience the pain of their choices. Those who are addicted often go into a victim space, which may tug at our heartstrings and want to make it all better. We think we are helping, but in many cases this enabling behavior only makes ourselves feel better, while the addicted person is just waiting for the next chance to use and undo what we have "fixed." By removing consequences, we remove the opportunity for them to learn a lesson of sobriety and the hope of recovery. Letting them fall, crash, be evicted, lose their license— this is where tough love comes in, and it is the hardest part. When we enable and do more than the addicted person, we compromise our boundaries and feed into this wounded cycle. We need to practice loving detachment boundaries with the addicted person, where we stay in our lane while loving but not enabling them. *I love you, but I can't save you from yourself.* Our boundaries keep us steady on our course, while the addicted person does whatever it is they do.

The goal is to learn coping skills to help us stay grounded by having strong internal and external boundaries and not getting lost in their drama, addiction, fear, and pain. For us to stay solid, we must learn to express ourselves clearly and manage our expectations, as unrealistic expectations will lead to disappointment. The hard boundary lesson is learning we can't walk the path for them; it's up to them to make better choices. Love them, point them to resources, set boundaries, and get out of the business of monitoring their sobriety. A good resource for family and friends is your local Al-Anon meeting, which will help give you support and encourage your boundaries.

If there is someone in your life who has a chronic issue that is not likely to change, start setting internal boundaries to protect yourself from taking on pain or fear that doesn't belong to you. You love them but carrying their burden doesn't help them; it will just make you feel overwhelmed and exhausted. Offer them resources, and maybe drive them to appointments, but they need to have a sense of ownership in their recovery. Loving detachment is not about being uncaring or unloving; it is about setting clear boundaries so that your interactions are the healthiest they can be.

Here are some internal boundary ideas to help keep you steady with loving detachment:

- Make a list of positive statements that reinforce what you know to be true about yourself. This will help you ground yourself before engaging.
- Control what you can of the situation, and be honest about what is out of your control. Say to yourself, *I can do what I can do and no more. These are their life choices, not mine.*
- Create a place inside for this situation to live, sort of like a treasure box you can fill with all of the emotions that swirl around this situation. *With love and kindness, I put this away so it doesn't take over my life every day.*
- With loving detachment, separate from the choices someone else has made. Let them carry the impact and responsibility of their choices. If you carry their issue or pain out of love, you will get pulled down and won't be good for anyone. You can "give" them back their choices through a symbolic letter writing exercise.
- Say to yourself, *This is their story, not mine. These were their choices, not mine. This outcome is for them to hold, not me.* It's about clarity, not about being unfeeling.
- Stay focused on the things you can control. Join support groups for boundary reinforcement. Surround yourself

with positive and forward-thinking individuals, and do those things you enjoy.

These practices will reinforce a strong internal boundary, maintaining a sense of where you end and they begin. *Their life, their choices.* Often, holding space for this reality is about taking life one day at a time. Stay connected, but don't walk their path for them. Be gentle with yourself, as these circumstances can take a great toll on you. Learn to become an observer rather than a participant in the drama. The greater clarity you have with your internal boundaries, the better you will be able to stay strong and focused, and not lost in the fear or pain.

If you are in recovery, congratulations. Every day that you work hard to set strong internal and external boundaries to keep you on a sober path, you give yourself a priceless gift. Those around you who are not in recovery do not understand this hard daily journey, and they may harbor feelings of hurt, resentment, and anger from the choices you made when you were using. It is hard for them to trust this new version of you that is emerging. Be patient and work the twelve steps or the recovery program that suits you best to create strong boundaries between your experience and someone else's emotional experience of your addiction and recovery journey. In time, when you are ready, you can talk about your experiences from a healed place.

Bringing recovery into your life will unfold over time. Know that each day is the most important day of your recovery, for today you are choosing a sober life. Your new boundaries will help you to anchor new sober behaviors.

> *Loving detachment is not about loving them less;*
> *it's about loving yourself more so that you*
> *are available for yourself and for them.*

Whatever ongoing issues you have in your life, apply this boundary language you are learning to help you navigate complex problems. What sort of boundaries with consequences do you need to use to help yourself feel strong and not spun around by someone else's situation? Know that with loving detachment you can still love a person and set strong boundaries.

Picket Fence Boundaries

Healthy boundaries are not meant to be huge walls to keep others out and you in. They are not fuzzy and wobbly with no definition. Healthy boundaries draw a line between where you end and others begin. The image of a picket fence is one of the better metaphors to help define a healthy boundary.

Think of a healthy boundary as being like a picket fence, where you can see over and through the slats. You know what is on their side and what's on your side. This picket fence metaphor reinforces the idea that boundary setting is not about keeping people out of your life but about defining how, when, and where you want to interact with a person or situation. You can reach over the picket fence and shake hands or even hug them, but you are still on your side. To carry the example further, if the person on the other side of the fence is in trouble, you could jump over the fence and help them out, but afterward you would come back to your side of the fence.

The picket fence metaphor is a reminder that you are on your journey and the other person is on theirs. Respecting someone else's journey reminds us to stay on our side of the fence. It helps us to remember the need to heal the codependent, wounded part of us that wants to caretake, fix, rescue, or control, and to remind ourselves that it's not our job to run other people's lives or give suggestions when not asked.

> *I can connect on a deeper level with others when*
> *I have strong boundaries. I know where I stand,*
> *and others have a better sense of who I am.*

The contrast to this metaphor is having no fence, no barrier at all. The lack of boundary is where most of us get into trouble because we are too joined with the troubles of others and overidentify with their pain. We tell them what to do, and they meddle in our lives. This is the enmeshment you learned about earlier, where everyone is melted together in a soup and things get very confusing very fast.

On the surface, making a boundary statement seems pretty straightforward. Most of us have some boundaries whether we realize it or not. You have learned a lot about your own boundaries so far. The following exercise is a boundary self-assessment using the picket fence metaphor. Take a moment to think about your interactions and determine how well your boundary protection system is functioning.

Exercise: Picket Fence Boundaries

For this exercise, sit quietly in a place where you can take a few moments to yourself. Have your notebook handy.

Picture yourself with someone you know, either someone with whom you have a good relationship or someone with whom you have a challenging time or feel resentment toward. Now picture a picket fence between the two of you. You can see them on the other side. Notice how you feel with the fence there. Take away the fence and see how you feel. Put the fence back and answer the following questions:

- With the picket fence in place, does the relationship between you and this other person feel different from how it usually feels?

- Do you feel safer within yourself when the fence is in place?
- Do you feel safer with that person when the fence is in place?
- Do you feel a separation or disconnection from them because of the fence?
- Would it be easier to speak your truth with the fence there or not there?
- With the fence in place, what is a boundary statement you would like to make to this person?
- Are you tempted to tear the fence down and be closer to them?
- Are you tempted to reinforce the fence, make it taller or solid?
- Is it easier for you to feel more like yourself (authentic and whole) with the fence in place?

Now sit with your gut feeling after this exercise. What is happening inside of you right now? Do you feel stronger and better equipped with the picket fence boundary in place? Does it help you feel safer in this relationship?

Your reaction to this picket fence boundary reflects your boundary status with this person and whether you need to adjust your boundaries with them. If you want the fence to be higher or more solid, ask yourself what is happening emotionally. What reactions do you have that you feel the need for a stronger wall instead of creating healthier boundaries?

Often we feel the need for a stronger boundary when others talk over us or don't listen to us. If you haven't had good boundaries with this person, the picket fence metaphor will help you feel emotionally safer, as you probably need to stand up for yourself more with them. Give yourself permission to say no or to respectfully speak your mind. On the other hand, if you want to tear the fence down or jump over it because you can't stand the separation, ask yourself if this is a relationship with healthy boundaries.

Does the fence make you feel cold or unfeeling? Do you feel it prevents you from loving and caring for the other person? These reactions are normal as you learn to set boundaries. Just hold those feelings for now. As you go through this work you will have greater clarity of what the right boundary type is for a given relationship.

How did this exercise feel different from the circle exercise? What did you learn from the fence between you and the other person that is different from putting them in a circle? Just hold space for this knowledge, as all of this is building a strong boundary muscle within you.

Repeat this exercise to assess your current boundary status for anyone with whom you have some relationship snags. If this exercise has been helpful, remember this image of the picket fence when you interact with others as you practice setting boundaries.

Carol's Story

Carol agreed to go on an overseas trip with her friend Natalie. She felt nervous about it but ignored her gut feeling, not wanting to upset the plans. Natalie was an experienced traveler and had been all over the world, while Carol had only traveled to a few US states, and never out of the country.

The minute they landed Carol knew she had made a mistake, as she felt overwhelmed by the foreign language and different customs she had not anticipated. As they got in the rental car and Natalie started driving, Carol felt even more nervous. They drove through narrow roads and small villages before arriving at their hotel, which didn't look friendly to Carol. Her stomach tightened even more. Once in the room, Carol noticed that the door didn't lock well, but she stifled her feelings. She didn't sleep at all that night because she was watching the door like a hawk.

They went sightseeing the next morning, but Carol was exhausted. She just wanted to be somewhere familiar and safe. Natalie wanted to see a play that evening, so they went and then had dinner afterward. Carol kept quiet and went along. After dinner, they drove on dark, winding streets back to the hotel. Carol gripped the dashboard, her stomach reeling. Natalie asked if she was okay. Carol said no, not really, but Natalie jokingly replied, "Oh, this is fun. Just relax and hang on." Carol was confused. Maybe this *was* fun, as she liked being with her friend, but she also knew the gut reaction she was having to all of this.

When they got back to their room, Carol burst out crying. Natalie didn't know what was happening. Through tears, Carol admitted that she was scared and had been white-knuckling it ever since they landed because she didn't want to disappoint her friend. Natalie was still confused because she was having a fun adventure and it seemed Carol was smiling all the time. Carol said she was trying hard to smile but her stomach was in knots, and she knew Natalie wasn't being mean to her. Carol was using her inner child wounding of people pleasing and giving up her power to avoid disappointing Natalie. She was pushing herself beyond her limits for her friend, ignoring her true needs.

Natalie heard Carol say that she was hurting, but she asked Carol to let her know what was going on because she can't read her mind. Carol admitted this was something she was working on and she would try to speak up. They agreed that they would only do things they both wanted to do from then on.

Once we understand how necessary it is to express our needs and to have respect and reciprocity in our relationships, the idea of boundaries becomes much clearer. This helps us to recognize when, where, and how our relationships got off track as a result of what we allowed and did not correct. Respect and reciprocity help us know where we need to reinforce and state our boundaries to look out for ourselves.

There is an art to using loving detachment when others make self-sabotaging life choices. Being a witness to someone else's pain and their journey is a boundary skill that takes time to learn and to know what the right setting is for you. Be patient with yourself, as it is much harder to not step in and take control. You are learning masterful boundary skills that will help you in many life situations.

You've come a long way since learning about the fundamentals of boundary setting. You have a visual of the picket fence, a boundary tool to visualize in your relationships to determine your boundary status with others. Now we move on to the different types of boundaries that most of us learned at a young age and that we continue to use in our day-to-day lives. You are developing a strong boundary toolkit that will help you with a variety of personalities and situations.

CHAPTER EIGHT

Defensive Boundaries

Walls keep everybody out. Boundaries teach people where the door is.
—MARK GROVES

Being defensive is a natural boundary; we have all needed to defend ourselves physically, emotionally, sexually, and mentally at some time. Acting defensively is both an instinctive and a learned boundary skill, yet we want to be able to stand up for ourselves in an emotionally healthy manner, not in an emotionally defensive way. Defensive boundaries have a place and a purpose based on context and circumstances, but in general, they are avoidant and keep us from being direct and feeling emotionally free. Some of the defensive boundaries we will discuss in this chapter include fuzzy, angry, passive-aggressive, extreme or no-contact, numbing-out, bubble, and walls of boundaries. There are more, and we will address them all in turn.

People have asked me if we should use defensive boundaries. The short answer is no, as they don't always get us the results we want, but some types of defensive boundaries are useful within certain situations. We use defensive boundaries as we learn to develop healthier boundary patterns, and we learned most of these wounded boundary patterns in our childhood families.

We all have used a combination of defensive boundaries at some point in our lives. What is important to remember is that being defensively guarded is useful and helps us in times of pain and trauma. These boundaries create separation when it is needed to help us get through a tough time, to keep us safe in all senses of the term, and to protect ourselves. What can happen is that sometimes defensive boundaries become the default boundary setting and are overused even when there is no need to be so guarded. It is akin to wearing a life jacket all of the time because you were once on a boat during rough weather.

The common theme of most defensive boundaries types is that they use nonverbal or behavioral responses as the main form of expression instead of using healthy boundary language. It's the idea that others should magically know how we feel instead of being upfront and clear with a boundary message. Defensive boundaries are avoidant strategies that we use when there isn't a better healthy boundary choice or we don't know of one. Before I did my healing work, and depending on the situation, I used a combination of angry, passive-aggressive, mixed, and no boundaries. All of these felt normal and natural to me because I didn't know any differently. These defensive boundaries helped me feel emotionally safe before I developed my healthy BPS.

Relationships and life situations are dynamic, and we need to assess what boundary to use based on context and where we are emotionally at the time. For example, if you use a bubble boundary or a numbing-out boundary to feel emotionally safe in your relationships, then that's the one you need to use for that purpose. Once you heal and feel safer, you can introduce healthier and more functional boundaries.

Learning which boundary types you use will help you to recognize what works for you and not against you. You will find the types that help you feel closer to another person and assess which types keep you isolated. The goal of boundaries is to help you feel a sense of personal safety deep within all spheres of your life.

The boundaries we use are a barometer that measures our wounded and healed parts.

Defensive boundaries help us to avoid conflict, buy us time, and help us feel safe from trauma, but if they are overused, they will hold us back from healing. As you read about the different defensive boundaries, see if you recognize a boundary type you have used in the past or one that you use now. You will also see the stark contrast between defensive boundaries and the healthy boundary expressions you've been learning about. I will describe how each type of defensive boundary may have served your needs at one time but now works against you by inhibiting a healthy boundary expression. Each description includes an explanation of what it's like to use that defensive boundary. You may find that you use a combination of defensive boundary types. Your go-to defensive boundary is a familiar wounded part of you that protects you because you feel threatened in a situation or have felt threatened in the past. This is a normal response to trauma if we do not have knowledge of healthy boundary expressions.

Bubble Boundaries

Many people feel that they need to have defensive boundaries and be guarded all of the time by sealing themselves inside of a protective bubble, what I call a bubble boundary. Adaptable and flexible, strong but not set in stone, this bubble boundary is ever-present, even when the situation is over. It is an invisible suit of armor people put on every day to keep others at arm's length and protect themselves from outside risk or peril. People with bubble boundaries are wary of trusting or getting too close to others, further reinforcing their need to stay inside the bubble. Bubble boundaries let them develop connections based on their terms and comfort level. *I see you, and I'm going to let you in only so far.*

Children who grow up in emotionally unavailable families, where feelings and boundaries are not discussed, often develop a bubble boundary. The bubble gives them a sense of safety and containment in their dysfunctional household, yet allows them to still feel connected to family and friends. They are present but not emotionally available or vulnerable. The child in such a household often learns to mind read, taking a kernel of truth and then making up a story about their world to feel a sense of control. The basics of food, shelter, and clothing are met, but emotional nourishment is at a deficit. The child retreats to the bubble and works hard to develop an interior world that fills this emotional void in an attempt to feel whole. This reaction not only creates the boundary but also enables isolation, escapism, and withdrawal.

The emotionally undernourished child rarely receives praise or compliments. Dejected, they stop looking to the parent to supply emotional reinforcement. They give up and stay firmly in their bubble, which is safe and known. The bubble provides them protection in a sense that the parent could not, but it is not a healthy long-term solution because it was created by and grew out of a wounded place.

Bubble boundaries can also develop in households where there is a lot of reactivity and emotional overstimulation. If the household is emotionally overwhelming, the need for the child to have some protection increases so they don't get swallowed up by the emotion that coats all of these interactions. The bubble becomes a safe escape pod from an emotional storm.

> *I need to keep my guard up because you never know what may happen.*

In adulthood, those who utilize their wounded bubble boundary do so in various situations and across relationships, but the bubble still functions in the same way. Their defensive boundary patterns are brought forth unconsciously. They want closeness but don't know how to achieve it. Inside they yearn to be seen, but they have spent years cultivating this bubble, hiding and being guarded. People with bubble boundaries literally don't know how to easily connect to others because their fears hold them back and they lack practice.

I have noticed in my practice that a high percentage of people who use bubble boundaries are also naturally introverted. Introverts are thoughtful, resourceful, and creative people who gravitate toward intimate, quiet surroundings and relationships compared to extroverts. It takes a lot of energy for an introvert to interact with others, which is why they typically avoid relationships or big groups—it's exhausting. Sometimes introverts use their bubble boundary because it's easier than trying to explain themselves or their needs.

If you identify as an introvert, know that you have unique skills and contribute to life and relationships in your own way. Ask yourself if you use a bubble boundary as a way to avoid people because you don't know how to interact with them and stay safe. See if you can develop opening boundary language around joining, such as saying, *I'm pretty shy at first, but I'd like to meet up to play a game sometime,* or, *It's hard for me to reach out, but you seem friendly, and I'd like to get together again if that would be okay with you.*

Sometimes a bubble boundary person will overshare too quickly. Telling everything about themselves is an attempt to get the messy part over with and leap into a relationship. But this oversharing is too much too soon for most people to receive. It is an overwhelming data dump that can derail even the best beginning of a hopeful relationship.

Sometimes bubble boundary people overshare to test others' reactions. It's hard for them to sit with their shame and insecurities, so they blurt out their secrets, testing the other person to see their reaction. If the other person can hold their trauma dump, then they pass the test; if they can't, then the bubble boundary person determines that they aren't right for them. This is wildly unnecessary and self-sabotaging, and ultimately drives the other person away. The bubble boundary person doesn't have the tools to reveal their personal information over time. They think they are being brave to step outside of the bubble, but they aren't prepared. Afterward, feeling worse, they slink back into their bubble with less-than messages of *I'm not good enough,* or, *See, things never work out for me.*

Bubble boundary statements are meant to distract, deflect, and redirect the conversation. As you read over the following bubble boundary statements, notice how they are designed to be noncommittal and keep others at arm's length.

- Thanks for asking. Yes, it's been a tough time. How are you?
- I'm still working out what I want to do. What's new with you?
- Thanks for the suggestion. I'll have to think on that for a while.
- I haven't decided the direction I want to go in, but I'll figure something out.

- I know I haven't been around, but I'm here now.

These statements work well when others are concerned about you and want to help, but you don't want to go into detail, you are tired of talking about an ongoing issue, or you don't want them close to you at the moment. Others pick up on these blunted deflecting statements, and at some point they may not try as hard to engage with you—they have gotten the message: *Don't get too close to me. I don't want to be in the spotlight.*

If you use bubble boundaries, then intimacy and being close to others may be challenging. If you tend to be introverted, you may use bubble boundaries more than other boundary types. Keeping others at arm's length gives you a sense of control and privacy, but you may also block people who are important to you from getting close. This behavior sends a mixed message, so it's important to recognize this pattern and let key individuals know that you are challenged by being close and that you are working on letting them in.

As you are learning, bubble boundaries can help you in certain situations and work against you in others. Try not to use them in every situation, as that will cut a lot of people out of your life, and you may regret losing them. If you want to join and connect with others, there are ways to move out of the safety of your bubble and into a safe place where you will not feel as isolated. You don't need to keep up this defensive boundary in order to feel safe. To feel more whole in the future, it will help you to first understand the emotional messages you give to yourself that keep your bubble boundary up and running.

Exercise: Evaluating Your Bubble

If you think you use a bubble boundary, then this exercise will help you evaluate your internal and external boundaries, see how you keep yourself safe inside your bubble, and see how you keep others out. As you go through this exercise, you will look at when, where, and why you want connection with others and when you shut them out.

No one else should determine my value.

In your notebook, draw a large circle in the center of the page that represents your bubble boundary. Leave space above and below the circle. The inside of the bubble is how you feel and what you say to yourself, and the outside is your interactions with others, what you say and how you behave. Your bubble has a window in it that opens to your outside world. You can connect with others through this window, but it is also how you lock them out.

On the inside of your bubble, list the feelings you have about yourself and about life that keep the window closed and the bubble in place. These are typically fearful or insecure feelings, such as lonely, confused, hurt, or scared. Include self-limiting beliefs, such as *I'm never enough; I'm never going to find someone; I'm not a good person.* You might write that deeply connecting with another is too risky, you are tired of being vulnerable, you feel victimized, or you are scared of rejection. You can also write feeling words or expressions that you say to yourself over and over. (See Appendix: Feelings Inventory for a list of feeling words.)

Outside of the bubble at the top, write down what your interactions look like when the window is open and you want to connect and join with others. What do you say to them? For example, *I'm so glad to see you. I miss you. Let's meet up again.* You can say these words when you feel safe and trusting enough to reach outside of your bubble. Think about statements of trust and connection: *I can be myself around my good friends,* or, *I feel safe when I go to this person's house or this kind of gathering.* These are the statements that open you up to allowing others into your life and help you move out of always being in your bubble.

Next, outside of the bubble at the bottom, write down what your interactions look like when your window is closed. These are the actions and words you use to keep others at arm's length when you don't want to connect or join with them. This is how you reinforce your bubble, keep others out, and create a push-pull in a relationship. *Let me get back to you. I don't know, I'm very busy. Not now, maybe in a few weeks.* Do you avoid situations where you have to talk to others? Do you talk only to "safe" people? Do you give people mixed messages? Are you noncommittal by using phrases such as *I don't know if I can, let me see*, or *maybe*? Do you say you will do something and then back out at the last minute? How does your wounding and bubble boundary manifest in your relationships? You can also write down people, places, and situations you avoid because they are too much work, they are exhausting, or they scare you. These are words or actions that contract you and reinforce to others that they should stay away, keeping you isolated.

Once you have identified what you say to yourself and those outside and inside your bubble, answer the following questions to determine whether you still need this boundary or if you'd like to consider another way of connecting with people. Write down your answers in your notebook.

- Do I want to join with other people but don't have the words or know what to do?
- Do I keep people out because I am afraid and don't want to be hurt again?
- When others genuinely try to connect with me, am I scared to accept because I don't know what to do next?
- Are the reasons that I created the bubble in the first place still happening?
- What purpose does my bubble serve?

- Do I keep my bubble out of habit?
- Are all of the people in my life unsafe? Do I overgeneralize this fear to make sure I never get hurt?
- What do I think will happen if I set healthy boundaries and let others in?
- What are the types of boundaries I need to set with others so I can let them in?
- What are the things I need to say to myself (internal boundaries) so I can find the courage to relax my bubble?

Look over your answers and see if you notice any trends or patterns. We are creatures of habit, so we often keep doing things long after they serve us. Do you feel you are in a routine that no longer serves you? You may have developed your bubble boundary system for an entirely different time in your life and haven't replaced it with a healthier boundary expression. Gently observe yourself and see where you want to make some changes in your interactions with others.

Understanding why and how you keep others out when you want to feel close will help you discern what to do with your bubble boundary. You don't have to stay defensively guarded in all situations. You have a choice in how you interact with yourself and life. This is not about popping your bubble and losing all of your protection; rather, it is about learning to set healthy, functional boundaries that can replace a homegrown bubble boundary and help you feel authentically whole. Is your desire to connect and not feel lonely greater than your need to stay guarded?

You are learning so much about yourself and how you interact with others. When we understand ourselves better, we can make conscious choices with our internal and external boundaries.

*Each day, in every way, I'm learning new ways of
protecting myself and speaking my truth. I am giving
myself permission to be connected to others and
show more of myself in my relationships.*

A Wall of Boundaries

A wall of boundaries is a rigid boundary system we create because we feel threatened and unsure of things. It's easy to put up a wall and shut others out, but it takes energy to maintain and leads to a lot of repair work with others if we take our wall down later. A wall of boundaries is different from a bubble boundary in that it is akin to a reinforced brick wall rather than a bubble. This wall often results from having experienced a traumatic event and a need to limit whom we talk to. We may also use a wall of boundaries when we are going through a stressful time and need to lock down whom we talk to, when, and about what. It's important to remember that putting up a wall is making a statement that you feel threatened and you don't know any other way to keep yourself safe.

*Holding on to grudges and resentments means
there's boundary work to do. It's a hologram
wall that isn't real except in the mind.*

The walled-off person is highly defensively guarded. Feeling hurt and traumatized, they are behind a wall for a reason. They probably have unexamined anxiety and resentments, and a reinforced wall becomes a coping skill for these feelings. By creating a wall of boundaries, they are trying to manage and control outcomes. This black-and-white reality is all about control, and for the fearful person, control equals safety. People who create a wall of boundaries are deeply protective of their time, self, and personal information. In relationships, they can come across as quite prickly and keep others at a distance to avoid the possibility of rejection. They have justified their wall and don't see themselves as being standoffish. For them, just looking over the wall and saying hello is a big effort. They feel that physically showing up for others is enough because it took so much energy to find the courage to be there.

The learned response of building a wall of boundaries reassures the walled-off person but confuses others. Often, friends or family will try to get them to loosen up, interact, and discard the wall, but the defensive person may see this well-meaning gesture as a threat and retreat even further.

There are many types of walls that we build for any number of reasons, and all of them create a containment. Those who feel that a boundary wall is the only boundary that works for them need this solid reinforcement to know they will be safe. We develop walls through our words and the lens we look through at ourselves and others.

Walls protect us, but repeated overuse will make us lonely, isolated, bitter, and angry.

Here are some examples of walls and rigidity:

- Saying no to everything all of the time.
- Creating a wall of words so others can't speak or make their point.
- Stubbornly clinging to resentment and grudges to avoid moving forward.
- Describing in detail how others should behave so they will be "acceptable."

- Staying detached so as not to get hurt.
- Having few close friendships, as being alone feels safer.
- Feeling victimized by life and not understood.
- Avoiding situations that may lead to rejection.
- Being anti-dependent, never asking for help of any kind.
- Being unwilling to discuss a lack of intimacy (emotionally, physically, sexually).

Sometimes people overuse a wall of boundaries and overgeneralize the need to maintain it long after the threat or stress has passed. They feel that if they were to relax their boundaries, they would get hurt again. I believe that people who use a wall of boundaries don't know how to have a strong, healthy BPS that would enable them to be close to others and know when, where, and how to set boundaries when they need to. Doing this requires vulnerability, and this is exactly what the wall is guarding.

If you feel you use a rigid, wall-building BPS, see if you can determine when this behavior started. What event(s) happened that caused you to have this sort of reaction? Are those things happening today? Do you still need to create this type of boundary with everyone in your life? Do others try to connect and get close to you but you shut them out? If this behavior is the result of trauma, please begin working with a therapist, as there are many modalities to help you heal and move beyond trauma.

If you experienced trauma in your early life, you probably play a "trauma movie" in your head. This is a natural response to trauma, but in doing so you keep scaring yourself by playing the trauma movie on rinse-and-repeat. You can begin to gently stop the trauma movie by saying to yourself, *I know this movie. I know what happens next. I don't need to watch this today.* Then gently distract yourself and move on. Trauma is layered and takes a while to unpack, so be gentle with yourself. Know that your wall may be a response to the trauma and that it can be healed. You will learn more in chapter 9 about how trauma wounding impacts your ability to set boundaries.

It's hard to give up a boundary behavior that served you well in the past. It's hard to know when it's safe to become emotionally open with others and share yourself. Know that you can find safe people with whom you can open up and show some vulnerability. You may want to start with a trauma therapist. Know that you can learn how to share more of yourself through the examples and exercises I am giving you.

See if you can determine the origins of your wall of boundaries by answering the following questions in your notebook:

- Did something happen that was traumatic or frightening and no one helped to put it into context or explain it to you? See if you can write it out in your notebook to help you understand this better.

- Do you play a trauma movie over and over in your mind trying to understand what happened? Work with a trained professional to heal this trauma before dismantling your wall. What would it be like to go outside the wall and share your very private pain with someone else?

- If you were taught to ignore your feelings, to push down and push through, what would happen if you found the courage to really look at and hold your feelings?

- If you have resentments that you can't or don't want to move past because then the other person would "win," how might your relationship with them improve if you could release your grip on the resentment?

- If you paste on a smile to keep people from asking if you're okay, what do you think would happen if you were honest and let a little of your real feelings show?

- If you learned in the past that others would get mad at you or reject you when you expressed how you felt, how strong is your desire to bring forth your truth? How would you like to express your feelings?

- If you continue to have a wall of boundaries because it's easier than learning how to open yourself up to others, what would happen if you lowered that wall just a bit? How would you feel?
- If you wish someone could really see your pain and show you the path through and out of the darkness, how would you lower your wall a bit so that could happen?
- If you secretly yearn for connection because you feel lonely, isolated, and sometimes even not wanting to live, what are you willing to do to start dismantling your wall of boundaries?

Rigid boundaries can easily become the default setting even when they are no longer needed. If you recognize this within yourself, take a moment to imagine what your life would be like if you felt safer and had a connection with others.

> *I don't need to put on a happy face just so everyone around me feels more comfortable.*

I realize that your initial reaction may be hesitation and resistance to taking some bricks out of your wall. Know that this is your programmed response; it served you well in the past, but it doesn't help you all of the time. Picture in your mind's eye someone in your life today whom you could open up to and let in a little bit. I'm talking about a small crack, not opening up all the way. It could be as small as saying something to show them you would like to connect. For example, you could say to your safe person, *Hey, did you see the game last night? That was an exciting final quarter.* This comment isn't earth-shattering; you are peeking over your wall and connecting by asking a question. Hopefully, they will respond in a reciprocal manner and say they watched the game and then share their thoughts about it. Your question and their response could be the entire conversation, but you will have given yourself permission to take a brick out of your wall of boundaries and see that you are indeed safe to share more of yourself with that person. It's a beginning, and we all have to start somewhere.

Walls of Belief

What we believe creates the reality that we manifest, both internally and externally. If we believe that we are bad, unworthy, or undeserving, this self-limiting belief will lead us to build a defensive wall and possibly sabotage opportunities. Conversely, if we believe that we are deserving and worthy, we will be open to manifesting opportunities of growth and expansion. A wall of belief can create an internal defensive boundary that limits how we see ourselves and our world.

In their book *The Energy of Belief*, Mary Sise and Dr. Sheila Bender describe beliefs this way: "Beliefs, whether negative or positive, are thoughts that act as filters for your experiences and may be compared to tinted glasses that influence the color of all you see. Beliefs not only influence all you perceive and respond to in the outside world, they also affect how you view yourself. For example, if you have the belief *I deserve good things*, you stand tall and reach for a far-off possibility, but if your belief is *I don't deserve good things*, the energy of that belief keeps even the closest of opportunities out of reach."[5]

Walls, physical or imagined, are designed to keep us in and others out. As you have learned, this is often in response to

---

5 *The Energy of Belief: Simple Proven Techniques to Release Limiting Beliefs & Transform Your Life*, Mary T. Sise, LCSW & Sheila Sidney Bender, PhD, Capucia, LLC, York, PA, 2022 (p. 13).

dysfunction or repetitive outer trauma. Negative beliefs we have about ourselves can also be a repeating trauma. The negative messages we received from others when we were young are essentially curses, especially when absolutes are used, such as *you always, you will never*, or, *you're nothing*. The walls of belief we build around these messages are defensive boundaries that lock us inside with our false narrative. They become part of the stilted story upon which we build our sense of self and our self-esteem.

When we are told negative things about ourselves as children, these messages soak into the deepest, darkest places inside of us. They root in and hide out. This is why these wounded messages so often feel like a part of us and become a belief that this is who we really are. They are well camouflaged as truisms and feel real because someone whom we trusted told us these falsehoods. These wounded messages came from outside of us; they are aliens to the authentic self. Know that if this wall of belief came from others, if it doesn't fit who you truly are and how you want to feel, then it can be released and torn down. A wall of belief can become an internal boundary that greatly influences our sense of self-worth and the narrative we carry.

> *Projections are beliefs or fears others have about themselves that they project or push onto us. They unconsciously slime others with their wounded pain.*

Take a moment now to identify a wall of belief that keeps you from feeling connected to yourself or others. It could be a cognitive distortion, such as, *I'm always messing up my life and can't do anything right*. Write down this belief in your notebook. Now think of a positive affirmation with a forward-thinking view, such as, *Every day I am doing the best I know how. I am learning to trust and love myself with kindness*. Write this one down, too. Read them both, then feel the difference between the two statements. It certainly feels better to have an internal boundary of wanting to speak nicer to yourself. Note that the affirmation doesn't reference what you don't like about yourself. This is purposeful so that you don't give the false narrative any more power. You are future-focused and positive. See how you are already changing your internal wall of belief—you are opening yourself up to a more expanded and healed version of yourself.

I know you may not be there right now, but it is something you can move toward. Don't worry if it is hard for you to believe these positive messages about yourself. Those negative messages are sticky, and at one point they gave you the illusion of consistency while keeping you stuck. They have been recycling for a long time and won't give up easily. Remember that where your mind goes, energy flows. Know that you are rewriting and reprogramming yourself into a new, healthy boundary protection system built on your authentic self. The intentions you are creating right now are establishing a positive and affirming internal boundary of how you want to feel about yourself.

Curated Walls

We build walls of many kinds to keep people away so we feel safe. Most or all of these walls come from a place of trauma or shame, but sometimes we build a wall just to feel safe from the world in general. We curate, or handpick, these specific walls to serve a unique boundary purpose for a unique experience or time. Each of these walls is a reflection of the need for a healthier internal boundary system and better communication.

Read over the following descriptions of these curated walls of boundaries and see if any of them apply to you. If they do, just note them and remember that you are learning to build strong, healthy boundaries that allow for safe, healthy relationships. You have options.

- Wall of anger—to push others away; protects vulnerability and disguises shame.
- Wall of physical weight—to physically keep others away; especially true for sexual abuse survivors or those who are afraid of intimacy.
- Wall of words—so others don't overtake you; also, using a sharp tongue as a weapon.
- Wall of sleep and isolation—to block out what you don't want to see or feel going on in your world.
- Wall of silence—used as a method of control so others don't know how you feel.
- Wall of smiles—*I'm okay, go away. Don't get too close.*
- Wall of things—physical objects that feel familiar but keep you tied down so you can't move forward; when possessions possess you.
- Wall of overidentifying with illness—used so others don't see the deeper emotional pain; *I have this chronic illness. This is who I am. Don't look any deeper.*
- Wall of overwork—used as a distraction to avoid intimacy and connection; overcompensation and work itself reinforce the wall.
- Wall of muscles and strength—used to fight back because at one time you were victimized or felt powerless or defenseless.

We use these various walls of boundaries when we don't think any other way is going to work to protect ourselves. We become deeply attached to these beliefs about ourselves and our world, and we can become defensive when others point them out. We guard them because at one time they served as an important BPS.

We may not realize we use these different types of walls, but at a deep level they help the wounded part of us to feel safe.

If you are in a relationship with someone who uses one of these walls, know that this is what they know to do; it is their defense system. Use your boundary language to express your feelings about their walls and your need to feel more connected.

Your wall of defensive boundaries has played an important role in helping you feel safe. But consider how much energy it takes to keep this wall up and running now. If you still need your walls to feel safe, ask yourself if they help you or hold you back and keep others away. If you didn't see them as walls before, maybe now you can see how they keep you separate from others. Hold space inside of yourself for a different reality, one that doesn't have such extreme walls. Know that you can learn to use healthy internal boundaries and positive affirmations to slowly take some bricks out of your wall, letting you out and others in. Take it one step at a time. There's no rush.

Fuzzy Boundaries

Fuzzy boundaries are inconsistent and wobbly. They arise when we are not clear about what we want, and we come across as indecisive. A fuzzy boundaries person is all over the place, neither in nor out, and this ambiguity creates confusion for others, as these boundaries are extremely fluid. They may have strong, immovable boundaries about some things and be completely loose about other things. A person with fuzzy boundaries is confused about their boundary style, and those around them are confused because the dial is always moving and isn't predictable. In general, their default boundary setting is loose or no boundaries. They don't like the idea of being held accountable so they stay "fuzzy." They don't know where they end and others begin, and would prefer it if others made decisions for them. This ambiguity reinforces the avoidance of consistent boundaries.

The fuzzy boundaries person will say things like, *I might want to buy your car,* or, *I will hopefully—maybe—buy your car.* This messaging is not direct. It is tentative and almost apologetic. If the person wants the car, then that should be clearly expressed: *I want to buy your car. How much do you want for it?* This is clear and direct.

It can be hard for the person with fuzzy boundaries to be direct, as they would feel accountable, vulnerable, and exposed. They enjoy the wiggle room in their fuzziness. They have a greater desire to be liked or loved than they do to be clear and direct and thereby risk the friendship. It is important for them to know what others think about them, and if they don't know directly, they will make up a story that fits their narrative. In general, the fuzzy boundaries person feels vulnerable to other people exploiting their insecurities. They fear that if they do speak up, they will open themselves up to abuse or neglect. They give their power away to gain acceptance.

Manipulators sometimes use fuzzy boundaries in order to be noncommittal or to play both sides. The manipulator will be intentionally vague to keep others guessing, to remain in control, and to covertly manipulate others. They will use strategies such as deflection and shaming language to turn things back on the other person when the other person is just setting a boundary (as in, *Stop telling me what to do*).

Here are some examples of fuzzy boundaries:

- Saying "maybe" to things you don't want to do.
- Saying "I'm sorry" a lot.
- Being indirect and apologetic when asking for what you need.

- Reading other people's moods and changing yourself to fit.
- Allowing others to insert themselves into your life and try to run the show.
- Overidentifying with other people's emotions or problems and feeling like you need to carry their pain.
- Worrying about a situation as if the outcome depended on your worry.
- Having expectations that are either too high or too low.

If you recognize that you have fuzzy boundaries, know that you developed this style for a reason. Maybe you grew up in a family where you felt uncertainty and were filled with anxiety about outcomes. Maybe you tried to set boundaries in the past but realized that others did what they wanted to anyway, so you just gave up and gave in. You may be confused because you know what healthy boundaries are but it's easier to not state them.

Ask yourself if you are feeling someone else's pain more than is appropriate, known as "carried feelings." We do this in an effort to connect with and have empathy for others, but we run the risk of being in the deep end of the pool with them instead of helping them to the edge. This fuzzy boundary blurs the line between us and them and makes us enmeshed, or lost in the weeds with them.

Most people take a long time to say the thing that hurt them the most. Take care not to dismiss another's feelings, as you don't know how long they have held on to these feelings and were too scared to speak up.

To strengthen your boundaries and create a healthy BPS, think about how you can bring healthier boundaries into all of your relationships. You may want to start by practicing clear boundaries with someone you feel safe with.

Mixed Boundaries

Mixed boundaries happen when we give mixed messages about our needs. The mixed boundaries person uses healthy boundaries and defensive boundaries with different people. This inconsistency across people and groups is confusing to others. The clear boundaries they have in one life sphere do not translate into all spheres. People with mixed boundaries respect others' boundaries only as needed; otherwise, this is an effort for them.

Mixed boundaries are different from fuzzy boundaries in that the person with mixed boundaries may, for example, have rock-solid boundaries at work but not in their home life, and are not consistent in their boundaries for each life sphere. It's usually easier for us to have strong boundaries at work because work has defined rules and codes of conduct, and most of us observe and reinforce the rules. Coworkers see the mixed boundaries person as being respectful, attentive, and observant, while at home the person can relax and say what they want, which may come across as being inattentive, lazy, disrespectful, careless, or absent. Of course, we don't have the same relationship with our work colleagues as we do our families. I'm not talking about someone who is just being themselves at home, joking and having fun. This is not about being off the clock. Specifically, the mixed boundaries person's presentation of themselves is different for each sphere, and others don't know which version of them is going to show up. They will treat others, even strangers, better than their own family. They have kind words for people outside the home and mean, dismissive, or uncaring words for the family. They tell others how much they love their kids, but never tell their kids they are loved.

The mixed boundaries person can also play the martyr by saying that they do everything for everyone else but nothing for themselves. Then they impulsively gamble or spend a lot of money on new clothes—which they do for themselves, but they don't see it that way. They see this incongruous behavior as something they are due. They give and give, make others feel bad about it, and then indulge themselves. Their boundary system across their life spheres is all out of whack. In general, the more comfortable the mixed boundary person feels with someone, the more likely it is that they will have inconsistent boundaries with that person.

Manipulators use mixed boundaries like a shell game to control others and get their needs met. They are chameleons, always keeping others guessing and showing up differently.

Here are some examples of mixed boundaries:

- Having poor boundaries with family and friends because it feels too much like being at work.
- Being inconsistent; others have a hard time understanding your boundaries because of the inconsistency.
- Showing your nice side only to people outside of the house.
- Setting clear boundaries only when you want to, rather than when you need to.
- Using your words and actions to manipulate relationships because it feels easier.
- Using mixed boundaries to be unpredictable or to get away with bad behaviors.

If you recognize that you have mixed boundaries, ask yourself why you use strong and consistent boundaries with some people and not others. Why might you be intentional with your language at work and then shame and dismiss your family? Have others said to you that you are not consistent in how you express yourself or that your behavior is unpredictable? As you heal you will be able to use consistent boundaries across all of your life spheres.

Sometimes a mixed boundary system develops in an alcoholic household, where inside the house it is a dysfunctional mess, but the person presents to the outside world as having a happy family. This is confusing for children, who then learn how to change themselves for different people and situations, and become mistrustful of what is real and what is fake. In other words, the child disconnects from their authentic self, becomes a chameleon, and learns that certain boundaries apply to some groups but not others. This is how intergenerational trauma persists.

Growing up in an alcoholic household, I learned this mixed boundary system. It was confusing to see how my dad treated me when he was spun up and agitated, and then see him treat friends and strangers kindly. I had confused perceptions of myself and my dad. I had to do a lot of work to understand these mixed boundaries origins so I could heal the confusion around my own boundaries and learn how to express myself in an integrated, consistent manner across all of my life spheres.

If this is part of your history as an adult child of an alcoholic, begin to work on connecting with your authentic self by being true to your gut reaction and what you need. Speak your truth to others, and develop consistent boundaries that will help you have healthier relationships. Be patient with yourself as you unpack the boundaries you learned from your family of origin.

Angry Boundaries

Like a lion with a thorn in its paw, anger is a defense that protects a vulnerable part we don't want others to see. It is known as a secondary emotion because it is fueled by tender, buried emotions such as fear, hurt, sadness, or shame. Many people have trouble giving themselves permission to state a boundary, and they learn to rely on anger to express themselves. The anger gives them a sense of justification to express feelings that would otherwise be stifled. *You made me so mad, so now I'm going to tell you how I really feel.*

Anger can also be a go-to response instead of using better words to accurately express specific feelings. An angry person may feel that by using this indirect way of expressing themselves, others will see the loudness of their anger and get the underlying message. They see the angry boundary as an excuse, saying that they wouldn't have put the boundary forth if the other person hadn't "made" them angry. We can't make someone else feel a certain way, but they can react to what we do or say.

As you learn to express boundaries, you may find that using anger will push your boundary language to the forefront. Angry boundaries are not ideal, as they often lead to more pain and disconnection. Anger is normal, but the goal is to take the time to connect with what is making you angry and put this into a healthy boundary statement.

> *My anger keeps people out but keeps me feeling isolated and lonely.*

In simple terms, angry boundaries are both instinctual *and* learned behavior. For example, when someone does something we don't like, we naturally get angry. When boundary violations happen, a conflict-avoidant person with angry boundaries pushes down their feelings over and over until these feelings build up to a toxic level inside and the person explodes. This explosion of anger is stating a boundary but in a negative and often aggressive manner. This "you made me so mad" response is their way of blaming another person for the cause of their blowup. They hide behind this excuse and don't own their tender feelings. Angry boundaries are a smokescreen, so the real issues are never addressed. The blowup happens, chaos ensues, doors slam, and nothing gets resolved.

Anger is a language of boundary violations. Aggressive anger is yelling and attacking and can include physical boundary violations. Assertive anger is clear and direct. It uses feeling language that does not shame another. Everyone knows you're upset, but you own your feelings while stating what upset you.

Angry boundaries are usually learned in a home environment where the expression of feelings is discouraged. A child is told by the parent to be quiet, don't be angry, be nice. The child then gets confused when the parent reaches their own limit and explodes with anger. The child learns, ahh, that's how we do it in this house; we hold on to things and "don't be angry" until we can't hold it in any longer, then we blow up. The child is taught to deny the existence and value of anger. The core hurts are lost in the cacophony of the anger.

Some children will lash out in anger to say, *No, I don't want to do this,* using the language tools they have to set a boundary. A child's (or adolescent's) acting-out is often seen as being disruptive and disrespectful, but they are trying to assert a boundary using a child's logic and language. The child is showing their dislike or fear about what is happening, but their message gets lost in the delivery as others focus on the disrespectful behavior or loudness instead of trying to understand what the child's fear or dislike is. In fairness, a lot of times children can't say what or why, and then the parents or caregivers have to take a breath and ask for patience.

When a parent or caregiver says, *I'm so mad at you* in frustration, the child may hear that they aren't loved. The child may internalize that they are bad rather than that the behavior is bad. Boundaries get crossed and cognitive distortions can happen quickly in these sorts of exchanges. When they happen over time, this shaming language can become a false narrative the child carries into adulthood.

When parents and caregivers model boundaries and how to express feelings in an appropriate way, the child learns how to access deeper emotions and use feeling words rather than anger. For yourself, were there adults who disregarded your feelings? Or were there adults in your childhood who respected, saw, and heard you and helped you create a boundary sense? Being seen and heard is exactly what most children (and adults) yearn for. When parents focus only on behaviors, the opportunity for connection is lost and the child can feel shame.

I used angry boundaries as a kid but only when I was pushed to the edge because I learned to be a conflict avoider by being nice and pushing down my feelings. I didn't learn how to express any sort of boundary when something was bothering me. I needed the intense feeling of anger to justify expressing myself. My anger would come out defensively, indirectly, usually in the form of sarcasm or passive-aggressive behavior. I had to get super angry to go against the family dance and express myself. I didn't have the words to express my tender emotions. When I was upset, my go-to feeling words were sad, lonely, or angry. I didn't learn how to state my feelings so others could hear them, so I would get super quiet, shut down, or blow up. I also didn't want to show anger because I saw my dad primarily using aggressive forms of anger and did not want to express myself in that way. I equated anger with being out of control, and I wasn't an angry kid. I was hurt, confused, and disappointed, but I didn't have these feeling words. I didn't have any boundary language other than blowing up when I was fed up.

Boys and men receive confusing, mixed messages about emotions: don't be angry; boys don't cry; tell me how you feel because I can't read your mind; you need to be stronger; don't get into fights at school; stand up for yourself; you're the man of the house now; man up. Girls and women are told: don't be so emotional or dramatic; why are you so quiet?; tell me how you feel; you are too sensitive; you need to be strong to be taken seriously; why are you so mean? They are under pressure to conform to societal standards and make themselves smaller for the convenience of others while being told to *just be yourself* and *we love you for you.* These mixed messages join the boundary type we learned from our childhood family, creating an intersection of emotions and explosive reactivity or stifled anger.

> *The only way my feelings were ever heard or acknowledged as a child was when I yelled. This doesn't work very well in my adult relationships.*

When the angry person explodes and yells, the house often shakes and everyone becomes frozen in fear. The anger forms the boundary of *stand back!* The angry person coats their household with their word vomit. A heaviness lingers in the air, and their words echo. The family quietly shuffles with tentative movements and tries to resume normal activities. The person who got upset feels a sense of relief; they had been holding on to their anger for a long time, and now they have let it go. Everyone else in the house feels traumatized and blindsided. It takes a while for them to recover, but the once-angry person feels relief. If you've experienced this type of situation, you know that it's very hard to be on the receiving end of this built-up toxic release. Through their blowups, the angry boundaries person keeps others away and ends the conversation, essentially saying, *Don't talk to me about anything because I don't know what to do with my feelings other than explode.*

Angry boundaries people will often threaten with their anger: *If you keep talking, I'm going to get mad.* This is a warning, their way of setting a defensive boundary. Their message is, *Stay back or I'm going to yell at you to stay away.* They are indirectly saying, *I'm not in control of my emotions, and I'm feeling overwhelmed.* Sometimes the angry person antagonizes others, wanting them to fight back. Engaging in this behavior reinforces and validates the angry person: if someone joins in anger, they don't feel alone. To the angry person, it feels good to yell and have others yell. There's an adrenaline hit that comes with rageful anger, and many people say they get a rush from it. They feel alive when they are angry, and if someone else is angry with them, they feel connected to the other person. Some couples equate yelling to a form of intimacy, and some people will try to make another person angry because if the other person becomes angry and starts yelling, the originator can then go into a victim space. This mixed-up logic doesn't make sense to a non-angry person. It feels disruptive, violent, and unnecessary.

Some people defensively hold on to anger or grudges as an insurance policy for future offenses. They will not let go of something that made them mad because they don't want to forget it and risk getting hurt again. This grudge becomes an anger scorecard that protects them from the outside threat—but this wall isn't a functional boundary, and it takes a lot of energy to maintain. Others can feel their anger; it's like standing next to a big humming machine that is building up steam and is about to blow. They will say things like, *Why are you so angry? Why can't you let that go?* This is a message to the angry person that they are being stubborn to a fault and fighting a losing battle with no one but themselves. They don't work through their pain. Instead, they harbor, stew, and spin in this compacted feeling.

The natural emotion of anger is projected as a boundary in many ways. Here are some examples of angry defensive boundaries:

- Sitting on your feelings until you can't take it any longer and then explode.
- Weaponizing your anger and holding the household hostage: *If you don't do what I say, I'm going to get angry.*
- Believing that stifling anger and keeping the peace is more valuable than expressing your feelings.
- Yelling as a way to push others away and keep them from seeing your true feelings.
- Holding on to a grudge as insurance that this won't happen again.
- Shutting down communication and blocking people out of your life.
- Feeling a lot of shame, not knowing what to do, and projecting it onto others.
- Justifying setting boundaries with your anger.
- Ignoring someone else's needs because your needs aren't being met.
- Being passive-aggressive and sarcastic in the hope that other people will read between the lines and get your message.

If you hold on to grudges or resentments, writing symbolic letters is a good way to move through these feelings. Know that your forgiveness of another is not an absence of consequence; they still hurt you, and they are responsible for that. Forgiveness doesn't enable their bad behavior; it sets you free. You don't need to forgive someone to move on, but it certainly does help.

If you have angry boundaries, know that you don't need to blow up, store your anger for a better time, or hope that it just goes away. There are better ways to express your feelings in real time, as things are happening. Your anger shows up to defend you from someone or something. I'm not saying don't be angry; my message is to honor those feelings and express them in a healthier way. We need anger as a functional emotion to help us protect ourselves.

You are learning how to express your fears, disappointments, and concerns in healthier and clearer ways from the examples in this book. Know that you learned from someone else how to stuff down or yell out your anger, or you thought it was the best way to keep the peace. Know that today you don't need to do that anymore, as it is destructive to your relationships and others feel terrorized by it.

Sometimes the hardest part of expressing emotion is finding the right word or words to describe your feeling. Once you have the right word, then you can clearly express yourself (see Appendix: Feelings Inventory for a list of feeling words). If you can't find the right word but you are feeling some emotion, just say, *I don't know how I feel; I just know I'm upset.* This will let others know what is going on because chances are they can feel you getting angry.

Honor your feelings. Give them a voice or talk them out with a therapist. With practice, you will be able to match up feeling words to what's going on inside of you. You will see that you have subtle emotions under the anger that can be described by using the right words. Do yourself a favor and talk about your feelings; they are real and valid.

The following are examples of healthy opening boundary statements (instead of *You made me so mad*) that are clear, direct, and assertive when feeling anger or hurt:

- I feel really upset right now because the setup directions weren't followed.
- I am hurt that you keep yelling at me. Please tell me how you feel using more words instead of cursing at me.
- I'm confused as to what you want me to do because you keep giving me different answers.
- Help me understand this because I'm getting frustrated.

Know that you can set boundaries with your words or actions; you just need to determine what the best approach is, given the circumstances. If you use angry boundaries, you probably feel more feelings than you know how to express. Use more feeling words to express yourself, and you will eventually get to the root of the issue.

If you are in a domestic violence household with an angry person, please talk with a counselor about how you can set boundaries for your particular situation, as confronting the violence-prone angry person may not be advised.

Bryan's Story

Bryan was a complicated, angry man who struggled to keep a lid on his explosive reactions. His family and everyone who worked for him knew when he was getting upset, and they would avoid him. He would brood around the house or office, and everyone would scatter. He would see things going wrong at work, and when he couldn't hold it in anymore he would blow up. When he got to the point of expressing his anger, he would cut off friendships or fire people if they didn't agree or see things his way. If someone from work challenged a decision, he would yell louder to intimidate them into doing what he wanted. Blasting his feelings was how he established boundaries instead of using conversational language that would help people understand why he was upset. He had built the company up from nothing, so he knew every job that needed to be done. He was hard on himself and everyone around him.

When Bryan was growing up, his father would beat him and not let him talk about his problems, calling him names and shaming him into silence. Bryan harbored this rage, and it would come out sideways. After an outburst he would feel ashamed and sheepishly half apologize, but the damage was done.

Bryan would walk over to his employees, stand behind their chair, look at their work, second-guess what they were doing, and walk away, shaking his head. He would perceive an honest mistake that an employee had made as a personal attack. He felt people should just know what to do, like he knew. In his mind, he was being helpful when he pointed out something that was going to create more problems for the company. His intentions were good, but how he went about giving feedback was all wrong. Like a trapped animal, he would get anxious about mistakes he found. When he couldn't contain this feeling, he would find someone to take his anger out on, and then slump back to his office in a shame spiral. He owned the company and wasn't going anywhere, so the good workers never stayed long because of his behavior. His angry outbursts were his way of setting boundaries as a protection for things he felt were out of control.

Bryan felt justified in his anger because he thought he was protecting everyone's livelihood. His mind was a steel trap when it came to people not doing what he wanted them to do, and he never let go of grudges. When someone tried to challenge or reason with him, he would say mean things to them to shut the conversation down and maintain his authority (just like his father did to him). He didn't see that his overprotection and overly defensive boundaries were destroying what he wanted so much to protect. In addition to protecting his company, his displaced anger was a spikey boundary to keep others from not getting too close.

People like Bryan have a lot of trauma, shame, self-criticism, and self-judgment. They have a lot of healing and internal boundary work to do, as it is rare that anyone can reach through this pain to get them to hear that they are their own worst enemy. They are deeply passionate about things and have a lot to say, but they don't know how to speak in a way that others can hear. They push their feelings down until they explode, and then use this energy punch of anger as a way of giving themselves permission to say all the things they have been withholding.

After some key employees quit, citing Bryan's anger as the reason, Bryan's good friend encouraged him to get some help for his anger. Going forward, he is trying not to blast out his feelings and instead goes back to his office and writes down what he feels. He still has angry outbursts, but now he understands more about the cause and effect of what he feels. The hurt, sadness, and confusion he feels when he perceives people not listening to him is a shadow reflection of his father not acknowledging him. He understands now that he used his anger as a shield to keep people out because he didn't feel worthy of their love, friendship, and attention. Bryan does what a lot of us do: he treats others as he was once treated. He is slowly learning how to have compassion for himself as he honors his feelings. He is learning how to respect the boundaries of others as he respects his own.

Passive-Aggressive Boundaries

Passive-aggressive boundaries are similar to angry boundaries but are sly, sarcastic, and indirect. Many people feel that they cannot be direct with their boundaries but still want to express themselves and hope the other person will just get the roundabout hint. This is a form of conflict avoidance. It buys time, but because nothing is said directly, there is often misinterpretation and frustration about the issue.

Typically, people with passive-aggressive boundaries will say or do things indirectly or make snide or sarcastic remarks to make their point. *Oh, so you're doing that thing you do again* sort of thing.

They feel they are being clever and stating a boundary, but all they are doing is setting up the relationship for hurt and confusion. They passive-aggressively try to control someone else because they feel that person is trying to control them. They do this to feel a sense of safety, but they do it in all the wrong ways by being sneaky.

Years ago I worked with someone who made it a consistent practice to avoid anything unpleasant. If he was asked to do something he didn't want to, he just wouldn't respond or would hang up the phone. If he didn't get along with a neighbor, he would move. His defensive conflict-avoidance system worked overtime. He thought he was sending boundary messages to others that they would understand, but his messages were often misinterpreted. Being a single man, he could accommodate his need to avoid anything unpleasant even though it cost him a lot of money and relationships. This broken system worked for him until he married and he couldn't avoid unpleasant things or move when he was upset. This new arrangement caused him great anxiety, and his fears were taking over his life. He had to learn to speak his boundary truth in a direct way instead of hiding.

This learned avoidance behavior usually develops at a young age in a household where the child couldn't directly state their feelings because the cost to do so was so high; the child was shut down, ridiculed, or met with passive-aggressive behavior. The passive-aggressive boundaries person doesn't know how to talk about their feelings; they just hope the other person gets the message through their snarky statements or behaviors. Essentially, they hide their true feelings because they don't know how others would deal with those feelings.

The passive-aggressive person may often use sarcasm, which is veiled anger. They may ghost a friend, feeling it's better than confronting the friend about a behavior. This leads to projecting and making up stories about feelings and behaviors that are rarely accurate. I learned to use sarcasm from my father and his father. When I was in therapy in my twenties, after a few sessions my therapist asked if we could talk about my anger. I was shocked and offended. *What do you mean, my anger?!* I had no idea how much rage I was sitting on, and if I did have any twinges of it, I thought I was disguising it well. But my sarcasm and passive-aggressiveness betrayed me and revealed to a trained listener the pain I was stuffing down.

At first, others may not pick up on passive-aggressive behaviors, but they do eventually see that they are being manipulated. Resentment then sets in, which further complicates the situation.

The following are examples of passive-aggressive boundaries:

- Making fun of someone to try to get them to stop a behavior.
- Shaming someone as they have shamed you.
- Making sarcastic remarks that you think are funny and clever in order to change someone else.
- Weaponizing incompetence; that is, retaliating by pretending to not know how to do something.
- Making plans and asking if it's okay after the fact.
- Giving but never accepting gifts (a form of control).
- Sabotaging yourself or someone else as a way to avoid facing something.
- Agreeing with everything, thereby avoiding conflict with others.
- Being the victim so you don't have to be responsible.
- Sneaking around and creating "me time" without telling a partner.
- Ignoring or neglecting a person or situation to make a point.
- Creating distractions from what the real issues are.
- Withdrawing from or ghosting a relationship with no explanation.

All of these passive-aggressive behaviors represent a pain that is coming out sideways because the person avoids setting clear boundaries. Passive-aggressive behaviors form a wall between people, sometimes resulting in more passive-aggressive, sarcastic behaviors because this is what the passive-aggressive boundaries person knows to do. These actions are designed to create an imbalance and put the passive-aggressive person in control.

Some people with passive-aggressive boundaries will overidentify with being a victim. This victim narrative coupled with passive-aggressive behaviors is a powerful defensive boundary, as it keeps people out and they feel a sense of control. I see this behavior as passive-aggressive boundaries because they are not usually interested in resolution or forgiveness, and their blaming language is a wounded boundary. Ownership of their feelings would require them to become vulnerable and emotionally available. They would have to relinquish their victimhood, own their shortcomings, connect with their pain directly, and admit their role in the situation. A false front protects their insecurities from being exposed. They pass everything through a wounded filter to detect anyone who may be out to hurt them. *Why do you always treat me this way? Why is everyone out to get me? Why is my life so screwed up?* They jealously guard these scorecards, which are powerful weapons that they can produce in a second when someone attempts to have a reasonable conversation toward a resolution. They brandish old hurts as if they just happened, keeping them sharp and ready to elicit shame and project hurt onto others, which mirrors the hurt they carry. The message is, *Don't see me; see my pain.*

If you recognize yourself in any of these passive-aggressive behaviors, know that what you feel is valid; it's the way the feeling is expressed that isn't a healthy boundary practice for relationships. This behavior pattern probably served you earlier in your life, and you probably saw other people in your family or friend group who behaved similarly. You may have learned that it was easier to avoid uncomfortable things by just doing what you want instead of learning how to compromise and talk through your feelings.

These passive-aggressive behaviors help you to feel in control and safe because some of your needs aren't being met. You may feel anger and frustration because others won't listen to you or do what you want. This is a bigger issue and ultimately means that you aren't being respected and your needs are not honored. You may be lost, resentful, stressed, tired, worried, confused, and not know how it got to this point. Know that this behavior grows out of a fear—fear of conflict, fear of not being seen (or seen), fear of not being able to control a situation or outcome, or fear that you aren't needed or wanted. Know that you can learn to speak your truth directly. You don't need to try to get your needs met in these indirect ways. Chances are, the people in your life know of your passive-aggressive ways and try to read your mind to figure out what you're trying to say. Learn to sit with your pain, your truth, and wrap more words around what you feel. Be clear about your needs with those in your life.

Remember that passive-aggressiveness is veiled anger. People with this type of boundary are angry about something; they feel hurt, used, or betrayed. If you recognize yourself here, see if you can open up about these hurts so that you can have a real discussion about them instead of using avoidant behavior. You may scoff at this and say there's nothing that can be done about it because if you could have dealt with this directly, you would have already done so. If you feel this strong resistance, you will benefit from outside help from a therapist.

Passive-aggressive boundaries keep us separate from others, as we hope they get the indirect message and read our minds so that everything will be resolved. This magical thinking only leads to prolonging the wounded pain. If you use this avoidant technique, be gentle with yourself. Practice being more direct. Express your pain more clearly, and try to see your part and their part in the situation.

Numbing-Out Boundaries

Numbing-out boundaries are about escapism and not dealing with something because it's too painful or it's easier to ignore because nothing has worked in the past. Examples of numbing-out boundaries are drugs and alcohol use, excessive sleeping, chronic online gaming, gambling, and overeating, to name a few. Another way of numbing out that is often normalized is overworking yourself to exhaustion as a way to not feel and to overcompensate. By escaping into these activities and substances, the person with numbing-out boundaries is saying, to themselves and the world, *Everything is too much right now. I need to distance myself because I feel overwhelmed*, or, *I'm depressed*, or, *I'm stressed*. They are saying they can't control their world and don't know how to set healthy boundaries to feel in control. Instead of using healthy boundary language to express any of this, they push down these feelings, hoping they will go away.

The person who numbs out actually has a lot of feelings in the moment. Numbing-out boundaries are set by distraction, avoidance, and escapism and are usually focused on anything but the real problem. An example of this distortion and disconnection with reality is when a person's house is on fire but they are obsessed that the lawn isn't mowed. They are focused on the wrong issue.

A numbing-out boundary is similar to other boundary types in that it is avoidant, but the behavior is not usually seen as a boundary. Numbing out often becomes a habit. There's a cause and effect: the indulgent behavior is a response to a feeling, and the behavior becomes the boundary statement. Instead of talking about and acknowledging their feelings, numbing-out boundaries people remove themselves by zoning out. This avoidant, self-soothing behavior is often learned at a young age and is most often seen in young people who constantly play video or online games.

Anything done in moderation once in a while is not a problem, but the problem develops when these numbing-out behaviors become the go-to response when the person feels overwhelmed. Anyone who has been in a relationship with an addicted person will tell you that once they start using, they aren't "there" anymore. The addicted person is making a statement that the rest of the household has to figure out. People who live with a workaholic will tell you they never see the person and don't know them anymore. The person who is doing the numbing out believes they aren't doing anything to hurt anyone else, so why is this a problem?

The following are examples of numbing-out boundaries:

- I don't want to talk about it, so I'm going to get high.
- I'm frustrated because I can't control my teenager, so I'm going to overspend money on things I don't need.
- I'm going to retreat to my depression nest and nap because I don't want to deal with life.
- I'm going to stay in denial about some realities in my life and reject anyone who tries to tell me otherwise.
- I'm going to get my emotional needs met through my kids and not my spouse.
- I'm going into my garage or man cave to grumble and withdraw from the family.
- It's easier to do my own thing than to ask others for help or to join me.
- I need to escape my family, so I'm going to play online games and not listen to them anymore.
- I'm worried about how we are going to pay for everything,

so I'm going to go to the casino and get drunk.
- I'm overwhelmed at work, so I'm going to stay up late and wear myself out playing video games. I can't tell anyone because they might not think I'm qualified for the job. I feel like an impostor.

Most people who use numbing-out boundaries see their activities as enjoyment and escape, not as a boundary. They don't see this as avoidant, unhealthy behavior. They don't recognize how they shut out others while they sleepwalk through life.

Numbing-out boundaries can look like a wall of boundaries and passive-aggressive boundaries. There are flavors of these boundaries that show up when we numb out because we are saying that we want to escape, we want the world to go away and shut it all out. The effect is the same; it's just a different boundary mechanism. The behavior becomes the nonverbal boundary.

> *Ask yourself, Am I putting up a wall of smoke, a wall of sleep, a wall of wine, a wall of screen time?*
> *What is bothering me that I am avoiding?*

If you recognize yourself doing numbing-out behaviors, spend some time looking underneath the activity to see if you can find the emotional reason for doing this. In other words, think about what you get out of it and how you feel before, during, and after. This is not about judging the behavior; instead, it's looking at the behavior as a symptom of a bigger issue. Are there things that you don't want to deal with, situations that are overwhelming or scary? These are normal feelings we all have, but you may be trying to deal with them on your own so you don't worry anyone else. Or maybe you're in a situation that feels hopeless and there's no way out. Maybe you feel that it won't do any good to talk about it anyway, so why bother. Maybe you have tried to talk about things and nothing came of it, so you just gave up—sort of quit and stayed.

Know that you are making a statement with your numbing-out boundaries, but the nonverbal message is not clear, and others don't know what you think and feel. Take some time to write out your feelings, just for yourself. Is there anything that you could share with someone else?

Numbing-out boundaries work for a while, but then you have to return to reality. The problem will still be there, the feelings will still be there, but I want you to know that talking about it with someone you trust will help you more than ignoring it will.

No Boundaries

People who have no boundaries are needless and wantless. They cater to others and give away their power. Having no boundaries means that others will fill in the vacuum by making decisions for them. No boundaries means there is a high potential to be abused, neglected, and victimized. No boundaries is ignoring gut instincts and not having a sense of what is okay and not okay, which creates an opening for enmeshment. Often people with no boundaries feel that having no boundaries is safer because they can pivot quickly and protect themselves. But this is far from the truth, as having no boundaries creates an opening for those who seek out victims to swoop in.

Having no boundaries is often the result of a highly dysfunctional childhood family or multiple traumatic experiences that reinforce the belief that trying to set any boundaries is fruitless. People with no boundaries do not have a sense of agency, sovereignty, or place in life. They are like a leaf in the wind and at the mercy of others. People with fuzzy boundaries have more boundaries than a person with no boundaries.

Do you feel you have no boundaries? To gain some insight,

look over the following questions without judgment, answer yes or no, and don't overthink your responses. There is no right or wrong; you are just getting a snapshot and exploring where you are with your boundaries right now. Write your answers in your notebook.

- Do I give others power to walk all over me?
- Do I play the victim in my relationships?
- Do I want to run away?
- Do I feel exhausted from doing things for others?
- Do I secretly wish others could read my mind and determine my needs?
- Do I secretly think, *If they loved me, they would know how I feel*?
- Do I test others' love for me?
- Do I wish to be invisible yet seen at the same time?
- Do I think others talk about me behind my back?
- Do I let others determine my reality and give me ideas about myself?
- Do I feel unworthy to set boundaries?
- Is it easier to distract myself with someone else's life than it is to look at my own?
- Do I continually doubt or question myself?

If you answered yes to more than half of these questions, you may have trouble setting any boundaries at all. Do you see any trends? Your "yes" answers show the thoughts and behaviors that reflect how having no boundaries shows up in your life. They are a reflection of the healing work that is needed and help bring an awareness of what you are carrying.

Keeping your new insights in mind, let's explore a little deeper to understand some of the inner child wounding that may have contributed to your having no boundaries. Answer the following questions in your notebook, giving deeper thought to your answers:

- Giving power away: Do I try to set boundaries but give up when I am told they are stupid or that I am making up things? What can I do differently?
- Internal boundaries: How good is my connection with my gut? Do I believe and trust in myself, or do I doubt myself? How well do I judge whether people are good for me or not?
- Self-awareness: Have I honestly examined what I think and feel about myself? What do I think and feel about myself now?
- Victim role: Do I play the victim in some relationships, like I'm not enough? Do I feel shame around this? If so, what can I do to move away from this role?
- Victim narrative: Do I blame others or the situation, thereby avoiding responsibility for outcomes? How would I feel if I took responsibility?
- Magical thinking: Do I just want everybody to get along and not have any problems? What would happen if I let others take responsibility for their own issues?
- Self-worth: Am I concerned others will not like me and abandon me if I set boundaries? How would I feel if I tried and they didn't abandon me?

If you connect to many of these descriptions and feel you don't have any boundaries, take a breath and know that you probably do have some boundaries, a line around some things that you won't let others cross. But the boundaries you have may not be robust enough to help you create a functional life and healthy relationships. Look over your responses and see yourself as a work in progress. You are coming a long way in understanding the BPS you had before and the one you want to create moving forward.

As you have learned, your sense of self and your boundary protection system are inherited from your childhood family, and you have carried these models, both healthy and unhealthy, into adulthood. Your boundaries correlate with how much inner child wounding you carry as an adult. Know that this can be healed. Healthy boundaries take a while to learn, so be patient with yourself. Our past informs us, but we are not shackled by it.

We come by our wounding honestly; everything we learned to do we felt was the right thing to do in that moment.

Extreme or No-Contact Boundaries

Extreme boundaries are the opposite of no boundaries and much harsher than bubble boundaries or even rigid walls of boundaries. An extreme boundary involves making a dramatic life change that we believe is the only way we can keep ourselves emotionally, physically, mentally, or sexually safe from another person. An example of an extreme boundary is when a person moves to a different state or country to get away from someone. It is an extreme last-ditch attempt get to a place of physical, emotional, and mental safety.

Someone who feels the need to set an extreme boundary has usually been through a lot to get to this point. They feel angry or hurt by something someone did to them, or they feel a great deal of fear about something real or imagined. They are willing to walk away from a relationship, a job, or a friendship as a response to this fear. They don't see any other alternative. However, some people want to establish an extreme boundary too quickly. They feel frustrated that the other person doesn't acknowledge their boundary, so they want to cut and run. People are often seduced by the idea of an extreme boundary because it initially seems like an easy, straightforward choice.

The following are examples of extreme boundaries:

- I am moving away and not telling you where I'm going.
- I'm blocking you from all contact.
- I am getting an order of protection against my adult child who abuses me.
- I will block you from all of my media and not acknowledge you.
- I will isolate, shut down, and say no to everything and anyone. I am too hurt by life.
- I'm not going to acknowledge you again even when we have to be at the same family function.

Extreme boundaries need to be seen as a last resort, not as a knee-jerk reaction or an easy choice. Extreme boundaries can cause a lot of pain, misunderstanding, and lost opportunity. They also take a lot of work to undo.

If you are tempted to establish an extreme boundary with someone in your life or have already done so, answer the following questions to see if this is or was the right choice for you:

- Have I examined my feelings about this person or situation in a grounded, reasonable way? What are these feelings?
- Have I explored and tried to set healthy boundaries with this person, yet they still disrespect me? What are my healthy boundaries?
- Do I feel that I've given my best effort to try to mend this relationship or situation while maintaining strong boundaries? What are some of the things I've tried?
- Do I feel abused or neglected by this person or situation?
- Do I feel the other person has been consistent in their disrespectful behavior, that it isn't a one-off occurrence?
- Do I read into things or make assumptions as to the other

person's position? If so, what could I try before setting an extreme boundary?
- Do I feel threatened in any way, where no amount of talking will keep me safe?
- Have I considered the consequences of setting such an extreme boundary? What are they?
- Are my boundaries violated no matter what I say or do?

If you answered these questions from a place of grounded clarity and still feel that an extreme boundary is your only option, then take care moving forward with it. It's important to have examined your feelings completely before you embark on this boundary choice. You need to feel resolved in your decision. It's easier to set clear boundaries when you are grounded, but if you feel rageful, angry, frustrated, or spiteful, take a moment and center yourself. These are all normal feelings when boundaries have been violated, so ask yourself again if you have explored all avenues with this person.

If you choose to set an extreme boundary, proceed with caution. This decision may come back to bite you. If you are not discerning and careful with your approach, your decision will only continue the wounded drama between you and the other person. I think of so many people who sit alone and lonely on the other side of the country, estranged from a close relative because an extreme boundary was created and no attempts were ever made to heal the rift. When asked why they created an extreme boundary, the answer is often because of something trivial.

I have worked with families who have had to create extreme boundaries with their adult children, and believe me, it was not an easy choice for these wonderful people. Their loved one had abused their good nature in multiple ways, and they had to set an extreme boundary as a last resort for their own emotional and physical safety. After much emotional and thoughtful consideration, they told the toxic person they were not welcome in their lives anymore. In some cases they got an order of protection that they keep renewing. This gut-wrenching but necessary choice hurt these people as much as the damage caused by their loved one did. These decisions came about only after many types of interventions and boundaries were applied to help save the relationship.

Take time with the choice of making an extreme boundary, as it takes much longer to repair than to hastily create.

You have learned a lot about defensive boundaries and how they can help us but also work against us. Maybe you've thought of other examples of defensive boundaries that you have used. Maybe it is easier for you to stay in a conflict-avoidant mode, betting that things are going to be okay if you don't say anything. If you relate to any of the defensive boundaries in this chapter, remember that you also have healthy, functional boundaries. The combination of defensive boundaries that were my go-to responses are still inside of me, and I can pull out these conflict-avoidant strategies when I need them. But I have learned that my suite of healthy boundary expressions help me stay more connected and emotionally free, which feels better than being defensively guarded and avoidant.

Seek out connections that work for you, where you feel like you can just be yourself. If you can't be yourself in a particular relationship, it may be because you think the other person judges you. If this is the case, think about setting a boundary to clarify your feelings. If you've tried this already, you may need to walk away. Take a moment to consider where you have reciprocal and respectful relationships, where you feel honored, heard, and seen. These are the types of relationships that are the gold standard to strive for so you can deepen your interactions and grow your connections. Look at these healthy relationships and consider what makes them work. Maybe it's feeling like-minded, or you just gel with the other person.

We need to be the change we want to see when it comes to boundary setting. Others will learn by our example and may be inspired to begin setting healthy boundaries in their relationships. Remember that you are doing more things right than wrong and that every day you make the best choices you know how to create the life that suits you right now. We are all doing the best we can with the tools we have. The message is to honor yourself, your feelings, and your needs. You are worth it.

CHAPTER NINE

Trauma Wounds and Boundaries with Manipulators

*There's nothing so dangerous for manipulators as
people who choose to think for themselves.*
—MEG GREENFIELD

We have covered many types of boundaries, internal and external, healthy and unhealthy, but there are special circumstances that call for specialized boundaries. The boundaries discussed in this chapter are for people who are in a relationship with a manipulator and those who are dealing with the aftershocks of trauma wounds while trying to set boundaries. The boundary protection systems in these situations often take more energy to maintain primarily because of the personalities involved, what's at stake, and coping with trauma memories. Since these circumstances are more complex and layered, we need to be more attuned to our needs and stay firmly grounded in our truth.

A Word of Caution

In situations with certain manipulators, healthy boundaries statements and actions are not advised. The communication techniques you have been learning are ways to acknowledge your feelings and stand up for yourself in order to help you deepen your connection to others. But sometimes the situation is highly activated or the parties involved are too lost in their own wounding, making it risky for you to express yourself.

The boundary styles that you have been learning so far are not recommended for those who are experiencing domestic violence (physical and sexual violence, economic control, psychological and emotional abuse), who are in a highly manipulative relationship or toxic environment, or who are experiencing extremely traumatic events. You can gain a lot of knowledge from this material, but please do not attempt to use the techniques outlined if you are in such a highly dysregulated environment. Doing so will often lead to more violence, control, or abuse and may put you or your children in danger. The boundary statements discussed in this chapter could be perceived by your abuser as a challenge or that you are trying to take over control; this will only embolden them to become more resentful and rageful.

If you have tried different ways to express your boundary needs on your own with someone who is abusive and this hasn't worked, please seek support and outside assistance. You will not be able to fix or navigate this situation on your own no matter how much you try to explain or reason. If you are in an environment like this, know that there are ways and methods for you to seek help safely and discreetly. You deserve to be safe and loved.

Here are some domestic violence resources for female and male victims of domestic violence in the United States:

National Domestic Violence Hotline: 800-799-7233
or www.thehotline.org

National Coalition Against Domestic Violence: www.ncadv.org

Boundaries with Manipulators and Narcissists

I now see behind the charming illusion: it was always about you and I was an afterthought. I no longer give you any more power. Controlling me no longer works.

Manipulators and people diagnosed with narcissistic personality disorder use controlling behaviors to get their needs met, but these descriptors are not equivalent even though they are often used interchangeably. Manipulators use tactics and techniques of control to throw us off balance, while narcissists are self-centered, lack empathy, and use sophisticated and layered tools of control and manipulation to get their needs met. A person can be a manipulator without being a narcissist, but being manipulative is a core tool both personality types use. A lot of people have narcissistic traits (more common) but would not meet the full criteria for narcissistic personality disorder. Unless I use the term "narcissist" to describe a specific set of traits, I use the blanket terms "manipulators" and "manipulation" to cover all. There is much to explore about this topic that is outside of the scope of this book. We will be exploring what it is like to be on the receiving end of manipulation. We tend to know when we are being manipulated, and no one likes it. As you will learn, clear and firm boundaries are the answer to this behavior.

The first thing to know about someone who has narcissistic traits is that, at a deep level, they feel that *they* are a victim of someone else or of circumstance. This perspective sets the stage to look behind their behavior to understand their motivation for controlling others. If they can control others by disrespecting boundaries, then *they* feel more in control, *they* feel safer. Their need for control comes from an insecurity, and they often feel wronged and attacked. This is why it is very hard to reason with a narcissist. Incredibly thin-skinned, they cannot take criticism, and they lack humility. They know all the buttons and how to get under the skin of others. They have little to no empathy, but they can easily read emotions and pretend to care about those around them. When they cannot manipulate, they will try to turn people against each other.

The second thing to know is that you do not need to explain, justify, or try to reason with a manipulator or someone with narcissistic traits to get them to understand your boundary or why you are setting it. They aren't interested in learning more about you or your boundary; they just want to get their needs met, and they see you in their way. The manipulator sees your attempt to set a boundary as an obstacle to be discarded; your boundaries are irrelevant and disposable. The more you try to reason and explain that what they are doing is hurting you, the more ammunition they gather to use against you. Their goal is to discredit you and your needs.

The third thing to know is that the manipulator or narcissistic-trait person needs a codependent as much as the wounded codependent needs them. This pairing completes the drama. For instance, when you don't state clear and consistent boundaries, the manipulator sees an opening and can use their wounded games against you. Without clear and consistent boundaries, you become a codependent enabler and thus part of the problem in the drama. Both the codependent and manipulator or narcissistic-trait person tend to have low self-esteem. Any sense of esteem they do have comes from other people; they do not generate it internally.

Manipulators have a secret agenda, but it's hard for outsiders to see it. They see the whole gameboard, are expert people readers, and are many steps ahead of us so they can get what they want, usually at our expense. The manipulator evaluates areas of weakness to exploit to get what they need from us. Our life spheres of emotions, time, sexual intimacy, or security, for example, become a source that feeds their needs while depleting ours. As a result of all of this manipulative behavior, we need a higher skill level of boundary setting to protect ourselves.

There are two types of manipulators and narcissistic-trait people: covert and overt. The covert manipulator is sly, sneaky, and well-rehearsed. They are the wolf in sheep's clothing and have learned to use their charm and wit to run over others while the target doesn't know they are being clobbered. This person is the master of gaslighting and backhanded compliments, all used to throw others off.

The overt manipulator doesn't care that others see their games. They are bold and brash and are used to getting their way by being a bully. This person thrives on chaos, the discomfort of others, and watching others squirm—that is their payoff.

Both overt and covert manipulators are deeply insecure. The last thing they want is for someone to see behind their false front and realize that they are a sham. If someone gets too close to figuring this out, the manipulator will get louder and bigger and use shaming and deflection to distract from being exposed. Both types of manipulators can spot a submissive person or a victim from a long way off, and they know how to get under their skin. Like emotional vampires, they need more than one codependent to feed off.

If you rehearse a conversation in your head with the other person as though you're preparing for a battle, chances are the other person is disrespectful and may be a manipulator. Your history with them has taught you that whatever point you make, they make a counterpoint that leaves you feeling unseen and unheard. Their need to have the last word is about control and domination. Your boundary is your truth, which is inconvenient for them. For them to honor your boundary, they would have to "give up" something or not feel in control. It is important to stay clear and direct with your message, and don't explain or try to reason why your boundary is your boundary.

The narcissist wants to feel powerful, not be in love.

My Story with Manipulators

As I discussed in the section My Inner Child Broken Boundaries in chapter 4, in my twenties I befriended people whom I looked up to and saw as strong, independent, and confident. They were everything I felt I wasn't. Some were probably narcissistic-trait people, and all were manipulative. My early journey with manipulators was a very difficult time in my life, when I was still learning about myself and my interactions with others. I wanted to include the following part of my story so you know that you can move on from manipulators and narcissists, as I have, and become whole again. Thankfully, I still have childhood friends and adult friends who are grounded, healed, and wonderful.

In my early twenties, from an emotionally wounded place, I projected onto the people in my life at that time a personal power that eluded me. I saw only the parts of them I wanted to see, who I needed them to be. When they were disrespectful or used me, I thought—or the codependent part of me wondered—what I did to cause them to treat me this way. I put onto them a misplaced loyalty and distorted projections, and I took the blame when things didn't go well. I turned over big parts of my self-worth to them and saw them as everything I felt I wasn't. I could not see any of their game playing because of my codependent, false-narrative wounding. Looking back, I see that there was no way I could have recognized their manipulations as red flags because I was operating from an incorrect idea of myself. Their manipulations are the smokescreen that keeps codependents from getting too close and guards against others being able to see their fears and insecurities. They don't want others to know how vulnerable they really are.

If these friends disrespected me, I would use reason or an explanation of my feelings or the situation to try to get them to understand my point of view. I would then try to have reasonable conversations, but they weren't interested in working things out with me; they just wanted to stay in their well-defended position. My futile attempt, along with my words, only gave them more ammunition to attack me with and to solidify their rigid, arrogant position. They would talk over me, discount what I said, and try to shame or gaslight me into a submissive state that they could control. They couldn't care less about having empathy for my feelings because it took away from their grandstanding and being center stage. I had not yet started therapy and did not know anything about boundaries. I did not have any way to garner a sense of equality in the relationship or develop tools of emotional self-protection.

The codependent thinks that the narcissist has a special key that they themselves need to feel complete. Codependents keep returning to this well and coming away empty and confused. We think they have something we will never know, and with their charming ways, we get sucked into their distorted dance. They know the power they can have over others, and they are always looking for the next person to extort and bring into their web. We turn our power over, and they sit back and grin with delight because they are getting the supply they need while their self-loathing and feelings of worthlessness are tucked away, well defended and camouflaged. They work hard to keep up this charming veneer, and if anyone sees the cracks in their hologram, they go after that person, throwing them under the bus to save themselves. They use other people to uplift themselves, curating an image that codependents cling to in a trauma-bonded way. The codependent carries a secret hope that some of this captivating magic will rub off on them.

Manipulators rarely want a reciprocal and respectful relationship as much as we do. They don't have the curiosity or interest to have an emotionally available connection. They keep returning to get the codependent sycophant's supply of supplication. They need us as much as we once thought we needed them. They don't want their supply to go away because their wounded ego needs to be fed, adored, idolized, and catered to.

As you learned, I saw how my mom would give in to and try to reason with my dad when he was being angry and manipulative. Her codependent enabling only served to embolden his behavior and continue the dance that he didn't want to end. When he was in his anxious rage, all he wanted was to verbally lash out in pain—a full, unbridled display of his wounding. Through therapy, I learned that my childhood emotional wounding and my mom's modeling of no boundaries created the template for enmeshment with the manipulators in my early adult life. The recognition that I continued the pattern was frightening—and liberating.

I eventually realized that I had to walk away from my narcissistic and manipulative friendships because my friends would discard or pretend they didn't hear any boundaries I set. No amount of my patient reasoning was going to change them because they did not think anything was wrong. This break was hard, but in the end it was the best way for me to look out for myself.

When we are ready to do the deeper work, we begin to see the patterns of the manipulator. We see them for who they are, and the distorted illusion begins to break down. As we heal and become stronger with our boundaries, the narcissist or manipulator pushes back. They feel the change in the dynamic, and their sixth sense knows they are losing ground. At this point they begin to double down and use shaming language, gaslighting techniques, and scorn to maintain their grasp on their position of power. They know that their shadow is being revealed and that we aren't falling for it anymore. This is when their victimhood is on full display. Exposed, they begin to see they can't manipulate us in the same way because we have seen behind their flimsy curtain. With their faulty game pieces now scattered on the floor, they retreat and move on to their next sitting target.

If someone is playing chess with you, get off the chessboard.

A relationship you can't easily walk away from, such as with a partner or family member, is a more complicated dynamic and requires more boundaries. As I healed and learned more about codependency and our family dramas, I began to use clear and consistent boundaries with my dad. The first step was that I had to know what my needs were and what I wanted to say or do when my dad would begin to manipulate and act out. This clarity gave me a sense of being anchored and grounded. I had a plan to deal with his uncertainty and the swirling chaos. I began to use all the tools I'm teaching you now.

Once you've worked through a lot of your pain to a place of healing, one of the approaches you can use to deal with manipulators is to become neutral and use strong, consistent boundaries. Do not give them the satisfaction of getting to you. Let them know that you see them for who they are, which is exactly what a manipulator hates. Remain grounded and detached enough to stay connected to yourself while maintaining your boundaries and objectivity.

Once you have new boundaries in place, the manipulation game isn't fun for them anymore. When you don't give them a supply of words or emotions to use against you, they will abandon you in a fury. They move on to new people (a fresh supply) to charm, cajole, and seduce, as your boundaries now bore them. *It just isn't fun when you can't make someone squirm.* If you are in a long-term relationship with a narcissist or manipulator, you can learn and apply all the boundaries you want, but it may not improve the relationship and they may not be enthralled with your new skills. They aren't interested in changing; they just want you to go back to the way you were, pre-boundaries.

To heal this codependent aspect, we need to recognize the wounded dance of the codependent and the narcissist. Boundaries give us the sight to see behind their pretense, where we realize they don't hold any more enchantment than we do, that they are flawed and hurting like us, just differently. By understanding the subconscious chemistry that brings the codependent together with the manipulator, we now carry the keys to our healed future. We no longer expect them to change. We understand the situation and our enabling role, but it doesn't feel like a victory. What we have now is the ability to create the boundaries we need to either have a clearer relationship with the narcissist or move on. When we heal our shadow self, we can recognize when others try to use our wounding against us for their gain.

If you related to parts of my story, see if you can find a glimmer of hope, and use the boundary tools you are learning to move on from the manipulators in your life.

I'm going into great detail explaining to you about the manipulator personality type to help you know that, one, you're not crazy for thinking these things, and, two, it's an uphill battle to establish working healthy boundaries with this type of personality.

All that being said, here are some guidelines to dealing with the manipulator or narcissistic-trait person:

- Be clear about what your boundaries are. Know that if you say maybe, they hear yes, and if you say no, they hear yes.
- Do not add to your boundary. If you say you feel hurt because they said a mean thing—*I'm hurt that you called me fat, and if you continue to do so I will have to reconsider if this relationship if good for me*—then this is the whole boundary statement.
- You can repeat your boundary statement, but stay focused and direct. You don't need to teach them why their actions or words hurt you.
- Remember that if you feel the urge to add to your words to get the manipulator to understand why you're upset, you open yourself up for them to use your words against you and you're going back to codependent behavior.
- Once you give them more words or reasoning (ammunition), they will spin this back and attack and ridicule you some more.
- Know that you will need to fight to maintain your sense of self, dignity, clarity, and place in a relationship with a manipulator.
- Your number one job with boundary setting with this type of person is to stay strong, clear, firm, and consistent. Protect yourself, as the manipulator is not interested in your protection.

Being in a relationship or working with a manipulator is exhausting, especially when you try to set boundaries with them. This is why so many people who are with a manipulator just give up and let them do or say what they want. They will say to the manipulator, *There's no winning with you. Whatever I say, you don't listen to me.* No matter how many boundaries you put in place, the manipulator will still want to blame you so they can stay in their victim space, perceiving your boundaries as a personal attack.

Manipulators use the tactic of wearing you down so you will roll over, give up, and swallow your words and sense of pride. It takes deep healing and boundary work to see the person you once thought of as magical and charming as a manipulative charlatan who quickly throws all of their smudged cards under the table.[6]

Another way manipulators control is through gift giving and love bombing, but their gifts always have strings attached. If you have someone like this in your life, you know how they will bring up what they've done for you or given you so you don't forget it. This conditional exchange casts a long shadow over the relationship and doesn't feel good because it's manipulative. Be careful what you accept from this person, as you may have to set the boundary (both internal and external) of *No, thank you.* Otherwise, they will not let you forget what they did for you or gave you and will use this to control you to get what they want in the future. A manipulator will blame you for your reaction to their toxic behavior, but they will never acknowledge how their actions are disrespectful to you.

> *If you've tried everything you know of to get the manipulator to respect and hear your boundaries and they continue to ignore you, it may be time to move on.*

Gaslighting is a tool used by manipulators to try to discredit our thoughts and feelings and make us feel as if we are going crazy. It is a form of emotional abuse they use to make us question our perception of reality. They will say something hurtful and then deny that they said what we heard them say. This technique turns

---

6 From Robert Jackman's foreword in *The Codependency Revolution: Fixing What Was Always Broken*, by Ross A. Rosenberg, Self-Love Recovery Institute, May 13, 2024.

our words back on us, and they work hard to convince us that what we saw, heard, or felt was all in our head. They try to make us feel that we and our feelings are the problem. They will say things like, *You're just making things up. You're the problem, not me. That never happened. Everyone else thinks you're crazy.* The gaslighter's main payoff is when they get the emotional reaction they've been waiting for: we blow up, cry in frustration, or give up and turn over our power, admitting defeat. Once we are spun around, they can confuse us even more to get what they want. They will carry this charade for as long as we try to convince them that we are not crazy and that we know what we saw, heard, or felt was real.

If you are in a relationship with a manipulator, you have probably tried many ways to get them to understand your feelings. They, in turn, have probably tried to talk you out of a feeling or gaslit you by trying to convince you that you are crazy or stupid for feeling the way you do. You also probably know that saying things back to them may enrage them more. Manipulators greatly dislike it when we are consistent and clear with our boundaries because we do not give them any more ammunition to attack us. When we are clear, we don't add to the chaos they thrive on, and they can't use their manipulative techniques against us to distract from the real issue.

Whether you realize it or not, you have developed some rules of behavior with the manipulator. You have learned to make yourself smaller to fit into their world, and you know what you can and can't discuss. This learned response limits your ability to be authentically yourself and creates shame. The next time you interact with a manipulator, observe yourself to see if you change for their comfort. See where you may have lost your way with your boundaries, and consider the types of boundaries you need to use with them. If your relationship needs better guardrails, talk through your feelings with a professional and assess your risk level in setting firmer boundaries with the manipulator in your life.

Know that after many years of refining their behavior, the manipulator will not likely give it up, as it's too great a risk for them—they don't want to know any differently. You may need to establish an extreme boundary by leaving the manipulator as a way to reclaim your dignity and sense of self. At the least, you need to have firm (not rigid) boundaries; otherwise, they will take a small opening and drive a truck through it. If you are trauma bonded with the manipulator—when your wounding fits into theirs like a puzzle piece—then breaking free is much harder. You may need to work with a skilled therapist to help you discern where you end and the manipulator begins, as the trauma-bonded person is lost in a confusing and twisted maze.

I'm not going to allow you to treat me that way anymore. If you continue, I will have to evaluate whether or not this relationship is good for me.

If you keep recycling in your mind past hurts from the manipulator, it means that a part of you really wants to work through this pain. Write out some symbolic letters to get this energy out of yourself. In this letter, say everything you'd like to say to the manipulator, even those things you know would never change their mind. Write down the imaginary fights that you have with them in your head. Putting this on paper and getting it out of you will help you feel lighter, and you will stop replaying what they did to you or what you want to say or do to them. It will relieve some of the pressure inside and help you to feel more whole. Most of the time you cannot have resolution in these situations; the best you can do is to become clear within yourself how you feel and what you would like to say if you could.

Our boundaries can become controlling when we push our needs onto someone else as a demand instead of simply stating them. We put our boundaries at their doorstep, and what they do on their side of the street is their choice.

When a manipulator tries to turn others against you, you can say to the manipulator or your friends, *Does this sound like something I would say?* People who know you will realize that, no, whatever the manipulator is trying to promote isn't anything you'd say. Stay in your clarity, as the person who is trying to control you is more insecure than they let on. Your boundary power has more energy than their gaslighting.

Remember that you do have options. If you're in a conversation, you can say things like, *I'm frustrated and want to talk with you today, but if you start blaming or shaming me, then the conversation will be done for the day.* Boundaries are the tools in your back pocket. These tools are there when you need them, but you don't need them all the time. You are learning to use this skill to protect yourself. Using your boundaries will give you a sense of comfort, control, and peace of mind. As you become clearer about your needs and boundaries, you will become acutely aware of when and how they are being violated and which boundary tool you need for the job.

People sometimes unconsciously adopt roles in what is known as a drama triangle. A concept developed by psychiatrist Dr. Stephen Karpman, the drama triangle describes dysfunctional social interactions between three people—the victim, the persecutor, and the rescuer—that keep the one who identifies as the victim (usually the manipulator) in place. Those who identify as victims often keep people in the other two roles to reinforce their victim narrative and so they don't have to change. Often, they are not interested in getting out of the drama triangle. This model is used to help people identify and change their roles and patterns of communication. What role do you play in your relationships? Sometimes the manipulator will put us in the role of the rescuer or persecutor to suit their needs. When you understand the drama triangle, you may start to see this play out in daily life.

If you recognize yourself as a manipulator, know that you learned these behaviors early on as a way to cope with situations that were out of your control, or you had insecure or scary feelings. Growing up, you may have had a parent or caregiver who celebrated you as royalty, which gave you a heightened sense of importance and entitlement, or you may have been treated very badly. You learned how to read people and gain a feeling of control when you could get your way and direct the situation. This empowered you, and you began to feel safe and powerful. You no longer felt like a victim; rather, you felt that you could, overtly or covertly, control others for your own comfort. However, this manipulation is disrespectful and hurtful to others.

You may not realize it, but other people know what you are doing. They feel your manipulations and games. You project your pain onto others and see in them things you don't like about yourself. Look over the course of your life. Maybe you've had failed relationships or lost jobs or friendships when people commented on your behavior. This wounded pattern will only create more hurt, and it's not the way out of the pain. There are many other ways to establish boundaries that don't involve controlling someone else for your comfort. Know that you can get help. A trained professional can guide you through this, but you will need to bring humility and a desire to heal.

All of these complicated, layered emotions take time to unpack and heal. Being in a relationship with a manipulator is challenging, as we have to have a sharp sense of when our boundaries are being violated and consistently set clear and firm boundaries all of the time. We have to protect ourselves, as they will not. Be gentle with yourself in the process. It took a while to get here, so it's going to take a while to heal and move on.

Trauma Wounding

Trauma impacts us at a deep level, often with long-lasting effects. Specifically, traumas disrupt our sense of self, safety, and agency, which then greatly influences our ability to set healthy boundaries. Trauma is the result of an accident, violence, combat, natural disaster, or the actions of an abuser or manipulator who disrespects our boundaries. Traumas can vary widely in nature, severity, and impact. Each person experiences trauma in their own way, and what can be traumatic for one person can be brushed off by another. Trauma can be from a one-time event, an ongoing series of events, or a long-term situation. There are different levels of traumas, but all forms can be addressed and new, stronger boundaries can be created.

Sometimes trauma survivors believe they cannot have any boundaries—which is related to feeling numbed out—or they create a rigid boundary protection system and become hyper-vigilant and aware. These defensive boundaries are the body's natural response following a trauma. Trauma survivors can also struggle with stating clear boundaries because their boundary protection system is overwhelmed. When their boundaries aren't respected, they internalize, thinking something is wrong with them or their boundary instead of blaming their abuser or the fact that they experienced a traumatic event. A unique defensive boundary system develops in response to the experience, the resulting trauma, and the reshaped worldview. Trauma survivors feel and experience things differently than those without trauma do.

People often minimize trauma as a way to get over it—*That happened to everyone when I was growing up*—but in order to heal trauma, we need to honor the experience and the emotion. The more we try to ignore trauma wounding, the louder it becomes—until we take notice. When we experience a trauma, our sense of boundary, agency, and control is stripped away, and we feel exposed, vulnerable, and without personal power. The world as we know it changes in an instant, and our perception and interpretation of situations become skewed. Past trauma shadows recycle inside of us, obscuring our perspective until they are healed. These are all natural symptoms of trauma.

Let's say a child is continually bullied in school and then bullied at home. This is ongoing trauma, and the child learns that there are potentially dangerous situations both inside and outside the house. They may lose their sense of boundaries and safety, and become hypervigilant, always looking out for aggressors. Their aggressors might tell them they can't say anything to anyone, so the child keeps silent because they don't want to get hurt. They learn to adapt and may try to avoid certain people, places, and situations. This cause and effect of the trauma shapes their relationship to their world and impacts how they think and feel. They may develop physiological and psychological reactions when they even think about being with other people. Some emotional aftershocks from bullying trauma include a low sense of self-worth, poor coping skills, no boundaries, being silent, withdrawing, avoiding, and perceiving threats when none are present. After repeated bullying, the child is worn down and unable to stop or prevent an aggressor from attacking—they give up. Their instinctive boundary protection system becomes practically nonexistent. They become blank and have numbed out their pain to survive the experience, resulting in having no boundaries.

If you feel you carry trauma, repeat this sentence to calm the part that carries the trauma: That time is over. There's nothing wrong with me. That's not happening now.

When we have experienced trauma, we may begin to make up stories about ourselves and our world that are sifted through a cloudy filter. We put ourselves down or believe everyone is out to get us. These misperceptions are called "cognitive distortions," and we begin to believe that these negative thoughts are who we are. We may try to protect ourselves by all-or-nothing thinking (no one can be trusted) or taking on too much responsibility or blame. Catastrophic thinking often grows out of trauma and impacts our ability to accurately assess what is happening in our world. In this same way, perfectionism grows out of childhood trauma, as the compulsion to be perfect covers up the shame effects of trauma. These cognitive distortions reinforce a broken BPS and contribute to the creation of a false narrative that we live by, which then greatly influences our ability to set healthy boundaries.

Until we heal our boundary protection system, the wounded part of us incorrectly interprets situations through a trauma lens. We take things personally and say to ourselves, *Something is wrong with me that they treated me that way. I'm somehow responsible for their behavior. I'm always screwing up.* Once we begin to heal our boundary protection system, we see life through a healed lens and say, *I deserve to be treated better. Whatever they are going through is their issue and is a reflection of where they are emotionally. I am worthy of healthy and respectful relationships.* Boundaries give us a platform to help us move out of a victim space into a sense of clarity, authenticity, and agency.

As a result of trauma and broken boundaries, we may have difficulty in adulthood discerning who is good for us and who may hurt us. Our "picker" is off, and we don't recognize red flags. We may be overly trusting of the wrong people, or we overgeneralize and see people and situations as threats because we are hypersensitive to any boundary violations. We put up huge walls, or we have no boundaries, letting everyone in—too much, too soon, too fast. Just as in childhood, we are vulnerable to others taking advantage of us because we carry the emotional signature of a victim, one that manipulators and bullies can sense. The trauma reaction is frozen in time, as though stuck in a snow globe, and the emotional reaction is timestamped to that event. We respond in the present as we did in the past because our trauma steps in front of us and directs the show.

As you learned in my story, when my mom and dad argued, my dad would raise his voice louder to silence the household. He used his aggressive anger to control the situation (probably his own anxiety) when he felt out of control. I learned to shut down, be quiet, and try to be invisible. I wanted the walls to swallow me up so I could escape his rage. Numbness and shutting down are the body's responses to trauma, which disconnects us from our source energy and often robs us of our voice. We retreat into a survival mode. Later, as a young adult, I had to find the confidence to express myself and reassure myself that I deserved to speak my truth. I had to learn that my voice had merit and value and that I could speak my truth without retribution. Trauma silences the authentic voice.

When I heard men or other boys my age getting loud and boisterous, my wounded interpretation of this behavior would overgeneralize, and my trauma wounding would think they were being aggressive. I would freeze, going blank and numb, which is what I learned as a child. Looking back, I now think they were just being boys and talking loudly or were excited, but my trauma wounding at the time interpreted their loudness as a threat, and I shut down and retreated. I had a conditioned response and simply reacted when I got triggered. Through therapy as an adult, I slowly learned how to be around loud men and not interpret their loudness as anger. It took a lot of work to heal and move past my conditioned trauma response. I learned I could be safe in speaking my truth, and my speaking up didn't mean I was being aggressive. Now I can sit across from a very angry person, hold space for this energy, and have compassion for their pain and fear. I have healed this part of me and am no longer triggered by their response, as I see it as their wounding coming forth. I've learned that anger is fear under great pressure.

Years ago, I worked with a young adult who had a lot of anxious symptoms, including obsessive-compulsive tendencies. He stepped into my office and bluntly asked me where the exits were and how many other people were on the floor of my building. I later learned that he had trauma experiences in his early life that had programmed this behavior. In his youth, he had been the lookout for a gang and had to have acute situational awareness that was above and beyond normal. As a result of this programming, he had to check out every place he went to because he was conditioned to do a threat assessment and determine how to protect himself. His present hyperaware, activated state was the result of this trauma. His trauma response was on constant alert and assessing potential danger, even in the safety of my office. His boundary system was hypervigilant and overactive, running everything through this wounded filter, interpreting everyday events as threats. His trauma had conditioned him to have rigid boundaries.

When a traumatic event happens, we often go into a survival mode of fight, flee, fawn, or freeze. When we experience trauma, we "check out"—what is known as dissociation—so we can survive the event. Dissociation is the body's instinctive trauma boundary response to protect our emotional core. Long after the traumatic event, we can dissociate when triggered, and then replay the trauma movie, usually from start to finish. There is much more information about trauma and dissociation that is outside of the scope of this book, but for now, if you think you dissociate because of a trauma, know that this is (was) your natural response to trauma and that you are doing your best with this overwhelming emotional data. If you feel you have lingering effects of a trauma such as dissociation or numbing out, or have bigger reactions to events than normal, you may want to be evaluated for post-traumatic stress disorder. This is treatable, and you do not have to carry these symptoms around. Please seek help to work through this recycling pain. Know that you can heal the trauma, gently move out of this state, and shut down the trauma movie so you don't replay it anymore.

Trauma Assessment

If you have experienced trauma, you may have a hard time setting boundaries with anyone. Understanding the origins of this poor or nonexistent BPS will greatly help you to move forward and start healing this wounding. The following questions will help you see where you are now.

Sit in a safe, quiet space and become still inside. Take your time to answer the following questions in your notebook to assess if you carry trauma wounding. Know that some of the questions may be challenging to think about because they may spark memories that you try to avoid. The questions are not diagnostic but are meant to give you a snapshot of where you may need some boundary help in going deeper in your healing work.

- Do you have memories that keep recycling and that are hard to move past?
- Are there people in your life that you avoid because of what they have said or done to you?
- Do you wish that the trauma movie in your head would

just stop?
- Do others say you seem spacey at times and drift off?
- Do you look away, go blank, and have a hard time refocusing?
- Do you get triggered by things that don't seem to bother other people?

Answering yes to any one of these questions could point to something that upsets you, trauma wounding from your past, or a current situation that may be impacting your ability to set healthy boundaries. Hold space for this. Know that there are ways to get help and learn to embody a feeling of calm and safety. Breathe, and know that you are learning many tools that will help make your life easier. If there are things you cannot move past on your own, meet with a trauma professional to go deeper into the symptoms you have identified.

My boundaries protect me from being hurt as I once was.

Is there a part of your trauma past that shows up today and impacts your ability to set boundaries? Know that this can be healed, that what you learned can be unlearned. Healing work does not erase the past, but it does put it into a place where you can safely examine and hold what happened. Your memories will still be there; you will just be able to hold them without cringing, feeling regret, or being scared.

Trauma and Boundary Setting

Boundary violations are like a punch in the gut. You know in your gut when something doesn't feel right, so even if you can't put your finger on it, it is probably because a boundary was violated. The important thing to remember is that if you feel dishonored or are unsure if a boundary violation has occurred, it probably has.

As you are learning, when we experience repeated trauma and boundary violations we feel defeated and worn down by the experience. When our "no" responses are not heard and our boundaries ignored, we get the mistaken idea that our boundaries are wrong or that we should give up the idea of having any at all. Often we stop trying and resign ourselves to this is how it is. We internalize this cognitive distortion and believe it is somehow our fault that the other person doesn't listen to us. But this distortion is from looking through the trauma lens of our codependent wounding. It is our victimhood coming forth.

When in doubt, set a boundary and keep yourself safe; honor your feelings. Later, assess what happened. Ask yourself, *Was the situation dangerous or harmful? Was the other person good or bad? How did my gut feel?* Take your time with this. Trauma hides inside of us, and many people don't realize that they have dormant trauma memories that influence their perception, causing them to misread red flag trauma cues. As a result, boundary violations are ignored or overlooked, as in, *Oh, everybody yells at me that way.* Or, as we begin to wake up to our trauma wounding, we become hypervigilant and startled at the slightest sight, sound, smell, or touch that reminds us of our trauma.

Consider working with a professional, and look into eye movement desensitization and reprocessing, which is a technique to help you to turn down the volume from past traumas. It can help you heal this pain and move on with your life. As you become clearer about what is a boundary violation and what is not, you will feel a sense of power over events and know what kind of boundary you need for each situation. You can learn to discern what is an actual threat and what is a shadow of wounding from your past.

> *Right now I'm not treated as if I'm worthy,*
> *but I know deep down inside that I am.*
> *I am learning how to speak my truth*
> *and look out for myself.*

As you are learning, there are many ways boundary violations can show up in your life. It's important to check in with your gut, determine the violation, and decide your next step. If you keep replaying what someone said or did to you and it feels like a violation, remember that—if it is safe for you to do so—you can always go back to the person after the situation has passed and speak your truth, as it will set you free. For example, *I felt hurt by what you said to me the other day.* This action will let past or present aggressors know that you are standing firm and will not let yourself be hurt anymore in that way. More importantly, you will hear yourself state your boundary and stand up for and protect yourself. Even if the other person continues their behavior, you know that you used your boundary tools to look out for yourself in ways your younger self could not. Your boundary truth will set you free from the looping trauma response.

As I mentioned at the beginning of the chapter, if you are in a domestic violence or verbally aggressive situation right now, I do not recommend that you set boundaries just yet, as this may enrage and activate your abuser to do more violent things toward you. Seek out a professional and have them guide you to a safer place. Call 988 or 911 to find safety and guidance. You've always been and will always be worth protecting.

Lindsay's Story

Lindsay's boyfriend recently broke up with her. She felt he hadn't been nice to her and never did what she wanted. She swore off dating for a while. She asked her parents, Mary and Frank, if they could come over and help her hang pictures in her new apartment. Her mom said they could come over at five-thirty for a bit, but they were getting ready to go out of town and couldn't come any other time or stay very long. Lindsay bluntly said, "That won't work for me. I go to the gym then, and I have to go shopping." Mary said that she and Frank were squeezing time into their schedule to come over, so why couldn't Lindsay change her schedule?

Mary was upset that Lindsay would not accommodate their offer. The message Lindsay was sending was that her time was worth more than theirs. Lindsay's rigid boundaries were uncaring and unbending, especially considering her parents were trying to help her. Lindsay had a habit of not treating her parents very well when she was hurting emotionally. Over the years her parents saw this and began setting stronger boundaries with their daughter. Mary learned to stop giving in to Lindsay's needs because she saw that it enabled this bad behavior and compromised Mary's boundaries.

Rigid boundaries are useful when others are abusive or repeatedly violate our boundaries, but that wasn't the case with Lindsay's parents. Lindsay set up her rigid walls when she was bullied in grade school and in response to the hurt she felt from her boyfriend's recent rejection. Lindsay's hurt activated her rigid boundaries with her parents, treating them as if they had violated her boundaries.

Lindsay's story is an example of using a defensive boundary type that doesn't fit the situation; it's a knee-jerk reaction based on past trauma. Her parents have learned to stay strong with their healthy boundaries when Lindsay's trauma wounding shows up. Lindsay feels safe with her rigid boundaries, but they enable her trauma wounds, telling her she can't trust anyone and needs to stay guarded.

Unhealed traumas can affect our ability to say yes when we want to because doing so may make us vulnerable. A frozen trauma response is to say no to everything, which becomes a wall reinforced by this fear. Saying no in this context becomes a rigid boundary to keep out the unknown danger or exposure. As a result, the overuse of no becomes the limiting cage that keeps us safe, but it also reinforces the trauma wounding and the cognitive distortion that we can't protect ourselves. Saying no to everything may be an old, broken boundary system. Consider this next time you say no when you want to say yes. Discern whether it is a knee-jerk response to something new, which the trauma brain interprets as exposure or danger. Ask, *Is this me or my trauma talking?*

It's important to assess whether the boundary style you bring into a relationship fits the one you're with, someone else, or if it is old trauma wounding. If you feel you recycle trauma wounds in your life, please talk with a therapist who understands trauma. You can heal this wound.

Many people walk around with unhealed trauma. They learn to live with it, but it festers in the shadow, impacting how they feel about themselves and how they look at life. Traumas don't just go away on their own; they sit in dusty corners, waiting until we are ready, if ever, to face, hold, and heal them. Our subconscious knows when we are ready to consciously hold our trauma truth. It will bubble up and come out when ready. You don't need to hunt for your trauma. When the time is right, it will present itself for you to hold so that you can heal and move on unencumbered.

What I have found is that this spontaneous unfurling of trauma memory is not a bad thing; it is a portal to emotional freedom. Feeling or remembering the trauma may be hard and sting, but the emotional freedom that waits for you on the other side will allow you to move on with wings spread.

This chapter has looked at many types of boundaries we use in complex situations. You've learned that one of the more challenging aspects of boundary setting is learning to set boundaries with manipulators and those with narcissistic traits. The manipulator is only interested in getting their needs met and will talk over or ignore any boundaries you bring forth. Stay strong in your boundary truth when manipulators show up in your life. You don't need to lose yourself in their wounded dance.

You also learned that when we carry unhealed traumas, setting boundaries can be a tremendous emotional risk. Unhealed trauma often shuts down our ability to set boundaries. Take some time with this reflection, and give yourself permission to work with a trauma therapist to gently unfold this pain you've carried for so long. Trauma separates us from our authentic self, shaking us to our core, the world we once knew shattered in a million pieces. There is hope on the other side of this darkness. Boundary setting helps us to regroup, find our words, and allow the authentic self to become grounded in a post-trauma reality.

Know that your trauma can be given a voice, an opening for the opportunity to be healed. Be gentle with yourself, and find a skilled practitioner to help you heal. You are worth it.

I numbed out and became frozen because of my trauma. As I open up to myself, a deep thaw unclenches the grip on this wounding. I'm learning I have a voice, and my boundaries shatter the illusion that I have no power.

CHAPTER TEN

Unique Boundaries

When you finally learn that a person's behavior has more to do with
their own internal struggle than you, you learn grace.
—ALLISON AARS

Sometimes life is messy and the boundaries that work for us in one life sphere don't translate to other spheres. These situations call for the use of new boundary knowledge to assess what we need for each unique experience.

In this chapter we will explore the effects of intergenerational trauma and the challenges many people experience in setting boundaries with their families and cultures. These are boundary stretches, especially when there is a great price to pay for speaking one's truth in families that are traditional and hierarchical. We will also look at the need for healthy boundaries when we are the caretaker for elderly parents. I will give you my insights to what I have personally experienced with elder care, the unique challenges of being in a caregiver role, and how family dynamics change when the adult child switches roles and takes care of aging parents.

Intergenerational Trauma and Cultural Taboos

Intergenerational traumas are familial emotional wounds that are passed down from one generation to the next. These are the spoken and unspoken wounded traditions of how family members relate to each other. They are an accepted way of life and span the arc of time. Examples of passed-down emotional wounding are abuse, neglect, enmeshment, control, and one part of the family not talking to another. As you learned in chapter 4, this dysfunctional lineage becomes an accepted family norm instead of being seen as harmful or unproductive. When these behaviors are questioned, the response is, *Well, this is just how we do it in our family*. They are woven into the family tapestry, which holds secrets, shame, and pain alongside celebrations, births, deaths, and anniversaries. All of these elements and the unspoken rules blend into a unique family soup that everyone inside understands. Trying to set new boundaries within this family system is very challenging, as this goes against the entrenched mindset. I will give you internal boundary examples in this context, which will help provide perspective so you don't remain lost in the family dance. Since the emotional wounds are deeply rooted, this type of boundary setting works best as an internal process rather than external boundary declarations.

Many older generations steadfastly don't want the family dance to change. They hold on to the familiar even when they know it's not right or that the rest of the world has moved on. Younger generations see the intergenerational trauma more clearly and often don't want to continue interwoven wounded patterns. Some boundary solutions are not easy to define, especially when there are family members who want to hold on to these norms and try to control you or an outcome instead of respecting your needs. Those who are outside of the family and culture think that it would be easy to speak your truth and go against the system, but these familial rules are often reinforced with shame and guilt. The long-established message is that family tradition outweighs personal interests and needs, and your boundaries don't have a place here.

Note that the boundaries I discuss in this context are for consideration and are not necessarily ideal for every situation, which is why this chapter is titled Unique Boundaries. Only you know your family and culture, and only you can determine how you can express yourself within this context. Also note that the boundaries we will discuss tend to fall into the category of defensive boundaries and other techniques to help keep you grounded in the middle of a family storm.

Boundaries in this context are often perceived by elders as being selfish and not considerate of the greater good of the family. Within some families and cultures, standing up for yourself, speaking your truth, or asserting yourself to an elder or senior family member is perceived as disrespectful. The understood and unspoken rule is to not question your elders. Elders come first, then everyone else. This inability to have what many would regard as a reasonable conversation can lead to a great disruption within the family. This creates tremendous consternation for the person who wants to speak their truth because they know the price they will pay for this self-expression. Retribution often comes in the form of being scolded or shamed back into their family role, reinforcing the familial or cultural rules and hierarchy. In some families, this means rejection, ostracization, and banishment.

Older generations are proud of the traditions they uphold, but they are often scared to let go of what they know, so they hold a firm grip on their version of how things should be. The message is that to be in this family, you need to remember your place and not talk back or be disrespectful. The subtext is that you cannot advocate for yourself or set boundaries—the elders in the family set the rules. They don't want their traditions to die. Unfortunately for younger generations, these traditions can include elements of intergenerational trauma.

In these family dynamics, most people just go through the motions and do what their elders ask of them. They follow the family dance, push their own boundary needs deep down, and hide what they think or do. If you are in a situation where others try to make you smaller and control your life, you can decide how much or how little you will engage with them. You probably have some control and can put limits around your involvement.

In severe cases, when someone is highly controlling, you may need to push down emotions and become stoic and neutral as a boundary survival skill to navigate interactions. (See the previous section on manipulators.) In these situations, it is important to be formal and polite with elders and do what is asked, then get out of firing range. These are boundary-adjacent tools that you don't use with anyone else, but you need to use them in this context to keep steady. These defensive boundaries are a passive resistance so you can stay safe in the field of dysfunction. It's not an ideal boundary by any stretch, but it is one way for you to stay as emotionally intact as you can so you don't lose yourself and turn over all of your power. Look at the situation objectively so you can come up with a way to navigate this tense environment and create emotional safety within as you gradually disengage and distance yourself from the dysfunction.

As with any boundary you state, this is, first, for yourself to hear. Even if you are able to express your boundary to the other person and they can hold it for you, they probably won't change their mind. In some families, there is an intergenerational wound that is carried and passed down, reinforcing the necessity to maintain family traditions over individual wants. They believe family business is family business and want things to stay private. They don't see the need for outside help. The message from older generations is that they have sacrificed for the good of the family, and so should you. They do to you what was done to them. Of course, there are good parts to this, but when their needs conflict with your independence, the boundary protection systems clash.

The bottom line is to come to terms with how things are and then find a way to navigate the complex situation. We can't easily divorce our families, so we have to find an equilibrium within ourselves, a place for this reality to live. These situations are hard to reconcile, as you may deeply love your family and cultural traditions, but there's a part of you that doesn't want to get swallowed up and lost in the wounded dance. You can be persistent and steadfast—remember that boundary work is about honoring *your* feelings. Those who love you deeply may not understand why you need a certain boundary, but that is not the point. The point is that you hear yourself being protective and loving toward your parents and elders, and yourself, by expressing a boundary with clarity and certainty—even if you are the only one to hear it.

When it is not feasible to bring up your boundary needs, I recommend that you first become clear within yourself about how you feel regarding a boundary violation. Then you can at least acknowledge the knotted-up emotion inside of you through writing or talking about your feelings with a trusted friend. Naming your feelings gives them agency and will relieve some of the built-up pressure around the issue. You could write a symbolic letter to the person, but I advise you to *not* give or share the letter. You can say or write something like, *I'm so upset and frustrated that my mom won't listen to me and wants me to move back home because she's lonely, but I have established my own life.* After you've written out your feeling statement, sit with it and reflect, as there are probably more things you want to say. This work is a solitary journey. It is for you and no one else, for when you can't go to the other person to express yourself or work with them toward an understanding. If there were a simple answer, you would have already found it. You've probably tried all manner of reasoning or even had other people intervene on your behalf, but the other person won't budge, so the unresolved hard feelings marinate in their own stew. Since you can't express your boundary and feelings outwardly, this internal work will be harder, and it may take longer to work through the feelings. Dealing with family dynamics is complicated with layered emotions, and there is rarely a simple answer to the problem. The struggle becomes how to honor the family while honoring yourself.

You can apply your new boundary knowledge to other situations such as work or a place where you can't speak your boundary truth. Boundaries are not straightforward in these situations, and staying neutral is not always sustainable. Have clarity within yourself about what you will and will not do, who you are and who you are not. Take things one day at a time.

Caregiver Boundaries

Caregivers are some of the most empathetic people on the planet. Caregivers who have good internal and external boundaries let caring, giving energy flow through them, and they seem to have an endless supply of compassion. Many highly sensitive people make great caregivers, as their empathy is seemingly endless. Those who have been in a caregiving field for a long time have learned to set strong, healthy limits and boundaries, which is a mark of self-empathy mastery. They have learned how to give and be available to those in need without giving themselves away. They give from their well, but they don't let their own well run dry because they know to also give themselves nourishment.

Those who give everything they have without replenishing themselves tend to burn out quickly. They give to others as a way to help themselves feel good. This type of caregiver becomes a self-serving caretaker, a person who does so much for others but whose own life is a mess. They have poor boundaries and do not take care of themselves. This lack of internal boundaries often has roots in inner child wounding that is carried over from their family of origin. If a child learned to cater to and take on their parent's burdens at a young age, they probably learned the enmeshed role of the caregiver. The key to regaining balance is to have empathy and give to others while also giving to yourself. Being a healthy caregiver requires self-respect and self-love.

Many people try to increase their self-esteem by doing for others. They will overdo and exhaust themselves to show their love and to prove that they are a good person, they have value. They love the person and want to help out, but giving all of themselves without good self-care is an overcompensation that unconsciously replays or tries to repair family-of-origin issues. This hero behavior is a wounded expression and is not sustainable, as it creates too much stress and leads to burnout. If you think you are playing out old wounding in your caregiving capacity, see a therapist to uncover where the wounding began and how to heal this pattern.

Many adult children now take care of their parents, which creates an upside-down family hierarchy. Some aging parents do a good job of turning over control and letting the adult children help out and, in fact, are grateful. But others refuse to give up control. They question their adult children and may even think they are out to get them or steal their money. They grip on to the last vestiges of feeling in control. Various dementia symptoms may also present in older adults, which further complicates the work the adult child must do, such as finding out where the bank books are or if there is a will or powers of attorney for healthcare and finances. The message for adult children caregivers is to be patient and set clear boundaries with yourself and your parent.

It's hard to help people who don't want to be helped. They may not be ready to receive your generosity, no matter what your best intentions are.

For elders or those who are otherwise impaired, their refusal is often one of the only controls they have left. Be patient, as they are watching their independence evaporate in front of their eyes. Ask open-ended questions when you interact with them. If you ask yes-or-no questions, you will almost always get a no. A good internal boundary with dementia patients is to remember that when they are paranoid, angry, and lashing out, this is almost always the illness talking. The sweet person you knew is deep inside, under a thick cotton of confusion.

Make sure to set clear boundaries about what you can and cannot do, and be clear with your limits, which will help you manage your energy and frustration level. Don't try to be a hero. Elders often become highly dependent and want only one person to help them because they know and feel safe with them. They don't realize the toll it takes on the caregiver. Set clear boundaries up front, before a pattern of dependence is established, as this will be harder to change the longer it goes on.

To be a successful caregiver, speak in a caring, empathetic tone and set limits, such as *I can help you out for a couple of hours today, but then I have other things to do,* or, *You will need to get someone else to help lift you out of bed because I don't have the strength to do that.* At some point you may need to say to yourself, *I did the best I could.* Some people have so many needs that you can't address them all. Ideally, you should be one of many who help out. If you are getting burned out, look to elder care resources and faith communities for assistance.

Caregivers often try to bring the person they are taking care of into their reality instead of meeting them in their reality, where they are. When this happens, priorities clash and the caregiver gets frustrated that the older person will not go along with new ideas. One caregiver boundary is to assess what their reality is and then consider the reality you want to bring them into. The older person simply wants the familiar and what they know and understand. Thoughtful attempts by a caregiver to set up activities, adult day care, physical therapy, education, musical events, or outings may be met with a lot of resistance if this is not something the older person did when they were younger. You need to find the balance between what would help them and what they can stretch into. Neither of you wants a tug-of-war. The more you can create a bridge to their world, the better you can reach them and respect their boundaries. A caregiver's internal boundary is about respecting the elder's agency, independence, and abilities even when we can see all of the things they could be doing.

Know that you are still a good person when you set boundaries with someone you love. Do what you can, know your limits, and feel good about helping them. Empathy is a value to nurture and embrace, not something to overuse and disrespect. Learn to give yourself a large serving of self-empathy to help reinforce your boundary system.

Grounding Yourself

Whenever we deal with a challenging situation for a long period of time, there's a risk that we will lose ourselves in it. Their problems become our problems, and the boundaries get fuzzy. One way to help keep this distinction clear is to use grounding techniques that get you back into your own body, emotions, and thoughts. Worrying about them is not going to make them better, and chances are it will fill you with anxiety over things you cannot control. One technique to stabilize is to write out a list of five to ten things you know to be true about yourself. For example: *I'm a good son/daughter; I'm a good partner; I'm a good driver; I love my children; I'm a hard worker.* Put this list in a place that is easy to access, like on your phone or on a piece of paper in your car. Read these truths when you are feeling lost in someone else's drama.

This grounding list is meant to be used when you feel imbalanced, thrown off, and disoriented about where you end and someone else begins. It is for the times when others' needs are louder in your head than your own. In a calm voice, out loud or to yourself, repeat three times these statements you know to be true. Check in with yourself and calm your breath, slow down your heartrate, and put both feet on the floor. I know some people who need to do this before they have an interaction with those in their lives who are domineering, manipulative, or angry. This helps them to stay true to themselves and remember their truth.

Mark's Story

Mark came to see me years ago. He talked about the friendships he had with people at work and how much he enjoyed his job. He spoke of his workmates in glowing terms and felt a comradery with them. As time went on, he began to understand the importance of having a healthy boundary protection system. He started to notice that a couple of his buddies at work would put him down in what he thought was just friendly banter. His wounding didn't allow him to hear the shaming—he heard it as guy talk, but it also felt like when he was bullied as a kid. He was confused about his feelings around this because he liked these guys and didn't want to feel this way. He tried to shake it off, but it was an odd mix of uncomfortably familiar feelings.

As Mark's healing progressed, a thick curtain was pulled back, and he began to hear and feel the criticism in the form of sarcasm, shaming, and passive-aggressive behaviors. As time went on, he realized that his coworkers had always spoken to him in that way and that he had not had a good BPS to recognize the red flags. One day, he found the courage to approach his friend Chris. He told Chris that he didn't appreciate being put down for how he played basketball in front of others. Chris was caught off guard, as Mark hadn't spoken up before. Flippantly, Chris pushed it off, saying that they were just joking. The kidding continued, and Mark resolved to speak up again the next time it happened.

It didn't take long. As they warmed up on the basketball court, Chris, grinning, said something sarcastic about Mark's playing. Mark said, "Man, that's not funny. It really bugs me when you say that." Chris apologized and said he didn't mean anything by it. This was a big step for Mark. Chris, realizing that Mark was acting differently, came back later and apologized again. Mark shared his trauma as a boy being bullied by his brothers, and Chris said he was actually bullied as well. This connection was a healing experience for both of them, as they learned something about each other and themselves.

When we speak up as adults and set boundaries we are able to defend ourselves with words and actions we did not have as children. It's hard to put a boundary out there, especially if you were bullied at a young age and feel those same feelings now as you did then. Trust yourself when this old wound reveals itself. Speak up and hear yourself protecting yourself in ways you wish you could have when you were younger. This is how we heal with boundaries.

We have more in common with each other than we realize. Even though people look like adults, sometimes there's a wounded kid inside fighting to find protection and safety.

*Your value does not decrease because of
someone's inability to see your worth.*

You've learned how to relate to family members when they cling to familiar ways of interacting that no longer fit your boundary style. You've also learned that intergenerational trauma is not easily healed and requires great patience as you set internal boundaries to navigate complex family dynamics.

You also learned key boundary points to remember when you interact as a caregiver. It's hard not to lose ourselves when our love and tears cloud our view and all we want is for them to be better and out of pain. Our natural instinct is to do all we can to make it all better, but these situations are usually complex, and a simple answer is not enough. Know that you can do your part, but you cannot do all of the parts. When you are a caregiver, ask for help from others, as the person you take care of may not be able to ask for more help.

Whenever we interact within our family system there is a potential for a lot of emotion to get stirred up. Sometimes our boundary knowledge goes out the window and we revert to old behaviors to cope. This work is not about perfection but about trying your best, restarting conversations if you need to, and having compassion for yourself and others. Use your creativity as you bring in the different boundary types that you need for these unique situations. You are developing robust boundary tools that you can call on when needed.

CHAPTER ELEVEN

Stepping into Emotional Freedom

A boundary is not that at which something stops,
but that from which something begins.
—MARTIN HEIDEGGER

You've come a long way, from learning about the basics of boundary setting to understanding its power. As you continue to do this work, you will notice that people who are aligned with your new attitude will be drawn to you. They will want to hang out with you because they are emotionally healthy, too. Like attracts like. Your newfound boundary language empowers your authenticity, bringing forth the you that's been waiting, wanting to show up.

Those who don't connect with how you are living your life with boundaries and authenticity will begin to drift away. Those who are stuck may be confused and resentful of you, feeling that you are not nice anymore or that you have changed. They miss swimming with you in a dysfunctional and unhealthy boundary pool that once defined your connection. They want you to go back to the enmeshed toxic soup because they know how to play that game. They are unsure about these boundaries you are setting, which to them may sound mean, controlling, and exclusionary. In moments of uncertainty, others will project their pain onto you, wanting you to go back to the before time. But bigger horizons are calling to you. This change is because you are expanding and stepping into a grander version of yourself, your inner healer having patiently waited for you all this time.

Others may not be used to hearing you express yourself in such a clear manner, and they may be irritated that you aren't falling in line with what they want you to do. This is normal. Some of your friends, family, and coworkers may not want the relationship dynamics to change because, as you've learned, this means they will have to change how they interact with you. This is frightening to someone who has poor boundaries and doesn't respect other people's boundaries. They may continue to believe they can change your mind about how you feel or what you want to do. As you look back over your history, you may be able to see that you trained your friends to hear your no as a maybe that they could transform into a yes—but no longer.

Hopefully, you have friends and family that will be excited for you and proud that you are honoring your truth and standing up for yourself. People have all sorts of reactions to boundaries. Honor yourself, and stand firm in all the ways you have now learned instead of giving in for someone else's comfort. It's liberating when friends and others validate our boundaries, as we feel seen, heard, and held. Your voice, your truth, deserves to be known. Be patient with yourself and others as you walk this path to emotional freedom.

> *Walking the path out of the shadows of illusion takes courage, tenacity, and hope.*

Stay strong and clear on your journey, listen to your gut, speak your truth, and others will follow your lead. Those who love you want the best for you, even if that means they have to give up an idea they have of you or change in some way to accommodate your new boundaries. You have learned how to check in with your feelings, speak intentionally, and get your point across in a way that others can clearly know your boundaries.

Uncharted Lands

Setting boundaries can lead you down a totally new path in your relationships and open you up to feeling, maybe for the first time, a sense of emotional freedom. If you are brave and trust the new boundaries that you set, you will be able to stand strong in this new arena. You will feel solid as you express your new boundaries, and you will know deep in your core that you speak your truth. You will be amazed when you state your boundaries, others respect them, and you feel more whole. You will continue to learn more about yourself through this process.

Others who are disrespectful of you may try to get their way by ignoring, rejecting, and ridiculing your boundaries. You will need to use the boundary skills you have learned to reinforce and defend them as you would protect a precious treasure. After all, boundaries are one of the major elements that defines your relationship to others. A simple example is a friend who repeatedly cancels lunch plans on you. At some point, you will probably want to set a boundary and stop making lunch plans with them. It just doesn't feel right to keep injuring yourself with disappointment and hurt because of their carelessness. You honor yourself and your truth by no longer putting yourself out there to be rejected. You look out for yourself in ways that you did not do before. You have learned to pay attention to the power you hold for yourself and the power you give away to others. You will clearly hear, see, and feel when there is a boundary violation, and you will reflexively know how you want to respond to protect yourself.

As you heal, your friends will begin to feel the change in your energy and how you show up. They may misinterpret your boundaries, but most of this is their projection. You will be able to tell who has done their boundary work by their reaction to your boundaries. As you've learned, people who don't have good boundaries may see your new boundaries as a personal attack or that you are being mean or controlling. When you are consistent, good friends will want to work with your new boundaries. They will want the best for you.

With healthy boundaries, I feel like a fuller version of me; more of me is now present. There's an easy freedom for me to show up authentically as who I am.

We take on a responsibility with boundaries. We learn that we have to look out for ourselves, and in doing so, there may be casualties along the way. But the lion's share of proceeds from healthy boundary setting far outweighs what we have to let go of.

Doing the Work

As you develop your boundary protection system you will have successes and times when setting boundaries do not go as you had hoped. Sometimes you will create healthy, solid, strong connections, and sometimes you will go back to your old behaviors. This push and pull is a natural way that most people learn a new skill; you're not going to be an expert right away. You may also start to notice gaps in areas where you need to develop a specific set of boundary skills to help a relationship become more respectful and reciprocal. You may also recognize after the fact when you should have stated a boundary but missed it. Know you can go back at a later time to clear this up so your boundary system feels intact.

Review the circle exercise you completed in chapter 3 and notice where you have safe connections. Once you interject more boundaries into the mix, notice where a connection feels reciprocal, grounded, and nurturing. Then look at those areas where the connection feels uneven, where you walk away feeling not so good about yourself or the situation. Just observe yourself using the tools you've learned; notice what works for you and where you need reinforcement. This isn't about judging yourself; it's using your discernment to determine your role as either a conscious creator or an impulsive reactor.

This new boundary language takes energy. You may sometimes think that it would be easier to go back to the old way. You may have used your childhood BPS for decades, but it probably didn't give you the quality of life you were looking for. We need to give to our adult selves what we didn't receive in childhood. We need to be our own functional parent, reassuring, encouraging, praising, and loving ourselves. With your new boundary knowledge you can establish the BPS that works for you today, setting aside the old defensive patterns that kept you feeling separate from others.

The temptation in this work is to look at how other people react to your boundary setting and readjust these boundaries for their comfort. While you do want to observe these interactions, remember that others are not the barometer for how you are doing. Just because they don't like it when you say no doesn't mean your no is bad. You learn this by checking in with yourself: Do you feel proud when you stand up for yourself? Do you feel a sense of accomplishment when you state your needs? Bring this work back to yourself and check in with yourself first to see the changes you are making with your healing, then look at what is going on in your relationships.

Others may continue the same behaviors, not respecting your boundaries or ignoring you. As you continue healing, you will see more clearly their respect or lack thereof. It will become crystal clear who can walk this journey with you. Stay focused on your work, and be consistent within yourself and with others. Remember that others usually don't want us to change because it means that they have to change. Bringing your boundaries into a relationship is an invitation to take it to the next level of healing.

The more we set boundaries, the deeper we integrate them and begin to feel more whole, present, and available.

If you don't feel like there's any movement within yourself or in a relationship, reassess your boundaries. Check in and determine whether you have clarity or if you are giving mixed messages, either to yourself or the other person, or both. In some relationships, it may be difficult for you to own your truth, or you may skirt an issue and be indirect with your communication, fearing you may lose the relationship if you are honest. Perhaps you don't want to cause an argument, and you cringe at the idea of bringing up an old topic again. This avoidance is natural, it's a fear, but you are stronger than you realize. If the fear continues to hold you back, reevaluate your options and consider whether or not this relationship is good for you. Determine whether you've used your new boundary skills to form solid connections and deepen the relationship. Ask yourself what the fear is that holds you back from letting someone in a little more. See if you can determine if this is inner child wounding showing up, fearfully holding you back, stifling your voice.

As you've learned, boundaries are more than *I'm responsible only to myself and you are responsible only for yourself*. There is a mutually shared respect and reciprocity that helps us to feel connected and joined with others. Remember that boundaries are not about abandoning others but about honoring our needs and theirs within the context of the relationship.

If you believe you are setting healthy boundaries but a specific relationship dynamic does not improve, know that you are making more progress than you think. You are learning so much about yourself and seeing and feeling relationships more completely. With all of the boundary work you are doing, you are able to look through a healed lens and recognize the stagnation. Being able to see this means that you have done a lot of healing work because you may not have recognized this at all in the past. When relationships don't change no matter how much you work on yourself and speak your truth, look at what you can change and control, then evaluate whether or not the relationship is fulfilling or if you are just going through the motions out of habit. What does your reciprocity gauge tell you? Does this feel like an even exchange? Are you both putting in the effort, or are you doing all the heavy lifting?

Maintaining Boundaries

Sometimes setting boundaries is the easy part. The hard part is reinforcing and maintaining them, especially if people around you disrespect and challenge them. If you stay strong and maintain your boundaries, then others will have to adjust how they interact with you, or you may need to move on from them.

Remember, some people will disrespect the boundaries you fought so hard to create by trying to wear you down so you will let them go. As a reminder, here are some ways that disrespect happens:

- They use sarcasm and shaming language or make fun of your words.
- They ignore your needs and do what they want.
- They say yes, I hear you, but they keep disrespecting you.
- They touch you when you have said not to or haven't given permission.

- They directly or indirectly make threats or ultimatums.
- They try to talk you out of a feeling or tell you how you feel.

Stay strong and consistent with yourself and this work. Transitioning to setting healthy boundaries consistently is challenging because you are learning a new skill and practicing it every day. Take heart and stay strong, as this liminal space is where you are moving from an old way of behaving into a new, expanded paradigm. This transformation takes patience, consistency, and a belief in yourself.

When we're young, we want to please others and make them happy. When we get older, we want to please ourselves.

Following are several ways to maintain your boundaries. Keep this list handy to refer to as you get stronger in setting healthy boundaries:

- Write out the boundaries you need in special circumstances or with certain people as a reminder to yourself.
- Say your boundary statements out loud. Get used to the words, and feel their energy and power. What do you need to say to yourself or others to make your life better?
- State your boundaries clearly to others so there is no ambiguity.
- If someone asks why you have a certain boundary, simply restate it. "I feel hurt when you say this to me," for example. Don't apologize for or explain the boundary.
- Keep practicing your boundaries with those who respect them. Build up your boundary muscle.
- Remember, you do not need to defend, explain, or justify a boundary. If you do this, people who do not respect

your boundary will get the idea that your boundary is negotiable.

As you work on setting boundaries, notice how the wounded parts of you may try to go back to familiar ways of avoiding setting boundaries. See this pull as coming from the part of you that is afraid of the unknown, or the traumatized part that has gotten burned before. Gently encourage yourself to stay true to yourself, true to the path that you can intuitively feel will take you toward healing and feeling whole.

Review your evaluation of your life spheres in chapter 2. Knowing what you know now, would you evaluate them the same, or have you applied your new boundary skills so that your assessments have changed? Do you now allocate your energy differently to create balance in most of your life spheres? Have your priorities shifted because of what you have learned about boundaries and balance?

Growing into Your Boundaries

Boundaries are akin to butterfly wings: quiet, durable, adaptable, and strong, empowering the butterfly with the freedom of flight and opportunity.

We change, heal, grow, and shift over time. We are still ourselves, but each day we become a more expanded version of ourselves as we interact with life and learn and understand more. Relationships are dynamic, and gaps and challenges occur even in established, solid, functional connections. If you notice a disconnect, ask yourself what you can control or change within yourself without compromising your boundaries in order to make the connection feel functional again.

When your outside world doesn't reflect how you feel inside, this doesn't mean that you are doing something wrong. It means you cannot control other people or all situations. Through consistent boundary setting, over time you will attract and cultivate relationships that are fulfilling, reciprocal, and rewarding. This work is about taking ownership of your life choices instead of looking for others to change for your comfort. You have developed your own unique boundary signature over time. It probably works for relationships that are reciprocal and respectful, but your BPS may need some reinforcement in those relationships that are dishonoring. Be honest with yourself and evaluate whether you see people for who they really are rather than who you need them to be.

During those times on your healing journey when you feel stuck or stranded on an island of suffering and can't see a way out, know that there are ways to form bridges of connection to get you off the island. Look to others in your life who help ground you and provide emotional safety to help you get to a regulated space. They form a bridge to help you to see the way through and out of the pain. You don't need to be alone, and with healthy boundaries, you are learning how to have connections. A good sign that you are moving in the right direction is when you feel open to developing intimacy, connection, and life-enriching experiences that are separate from the actual outcomes. In other words, outcomes will vary, but with a strong core of boundaries, you will be able to navigate many different situations in real time.

Moving from one way of interacting with yourself and the world to another takes energy. Healing doesn't happen overnight, but through consistent effort, you will begin to see relationships become easier, and some relationships may fall away. Your new boundary language will become integrated into your daily life, and you will more easily recognize when you need a certain type of boundary. With consistent practice, your boundaries will become second nature. They are an as-needed tool in your back pocket, easy to access.

> *I'm free now. I'm back to the me that*
> *had been waiting there all this time.*

As you heal big parts of yourself with consistent, healthy boundaries, you create an environment for your lost inner child to trust that you can consistently defend yourself; that part no longer has to step forward with wounded defensiveness. This wounded part is tentative to trust and has defended you for a long time, so you have to show that part of yourself that you are setting new and healthy boundaries. Once healthy boundaries are established, this frozen wounding can thaw and rejoin with the authentic self, no longer needing to impulsively react with defensiveness when a trigger shows up. What this means practically is that when you set functional boundaries, your inner child sees and realizes that the adult you is protecting all of you. The inner child knows at a deep level it no longer needs to show up with wounded tools of yelling, shutting down, and so on to defend you. If your eight-year-old self used to show up and get defensive, this part will now be able to feel safe and witness the adult self setting boundaries. The inner child heals because you are now protecting yourself with healthy boundaries instead of using defensive and avoidant wounded responses.

When you have clarity with your boundaries, you will discern who and what you are, who you are not, what you need, and what no longer serves you. You align with yourself and see yourself clearly, maybe for the first time. You now know a lot about boundaries, and you can start using this knowledge to imagine and manifest the life you want to create. Your functional adult self is protecting all of you so you can show up authentically.

Welcoming Your Authentic Self

To heal, we need boundaries.
Healing requires us to be vulnerable and open.
Vulnerability requires boundary tools so we feel safe.
When we feel safe, we can enter into a state of healing.
Healing happens in a state of love and authenticity.
It is a gift we give ourselves.

Your strong boundaries, your attunement, and your connection with self will attract and resonate with others who have done their healing work. Connections and disconnections will happen naturally. You will see who is able to grow with you—even if it's a stretch for them. And you will begin to recognize who is stuck in their wounding and why, for all sorts of nonjudgmental reasons, they can't progress with you. You will speak your authentic truth within the context of the situation, and the boundaries you will feel will be the best ones to express your needs.

When you set consistent boundaries, you reinforce your support system. You move out of a dysfunctional dance and into a place of newfound clarity. There is a sense of predictability when you use healthy boundaries, and you can rely on yourself to be dependable. You have learned how to check in with your gut-level energy system, discern how you feel, and know how to create a boundary statement that works for you. You are learning to trust yourself and your new boundary tools. Consistent boundaries will help you be the same person in all of your life spheres, as you will no longer change yourself for someone else's comfort.

Defend your boundaries as if you are defending a castle filled with treasure. Only you know the specific protection you need to stay strong and free within your world.

There is an emotional freedom that is generated from the consistent use of boundaries. At the beginning of the book I referenced people you may know who seem to have it all together. Now you have a better idea of how they have shaped their world with the effective use of boundaries. Now you know how they were able to bring their authentic selves forward. Emotional freedom comes from knowing you have the right tool for the right job, feeling confident, aware, and prepared. Life still has ups and downs, but now you have a functional tool kit to give you the strength to face situations that you avoided before. You are able to meet someone, assess what you pick up from them with your gut-level reaction, and respond with a healthy boundary.

Boundary work involves compassion for yourself and others. All is in the right order, even when things seem out of place and rocky. Transitions are messy, and most of us experience growing pains at any age. When we stretch and challenge ourselves, we flex our boundary muscle and open ourselves up to living the life we dream about.

You are making this happen.

The more healthy boundaries we set,
the more clarity we have.
The more clarity we have,
the more parts of us feel
connected, safe, and authentic.
The more we step into our new boundary power,
the more we feel fully integrated with the true self.
We have set ourselves free.

Through this work, you can now see more of the boundary types you and others use. You can see where others use their boundary type to pull you in or push you away. You can see how their and your boundary protections systems have worked to shape interactions with others. Learning about boundaries teaches us about ourselves and our world. This is an introspective work that pulls back the heavy curtain of denial and illusion, highlighting what works and doesn't, what's healed and what isn't. We more clearly see what has been hiding in plain sight.

We all want to be liked and loved. I believe this need to feel connected sits deep within the heart. Know that even when you say no to someone and think that will disconnect you from them, it actually connects you deeper because now this person knows more about you. Now this person knows you love and respect yourself enough to stand up for yourself. Showing this vulnerability takes courage, respect, and love, all of which you embody.

As much as you are making this happen, so are those in your life who honor your truth. They hold space for the part of you that needs to be seen and heard. When you set a boundary, those who respect you hold your boundary and honor it, listening and responding to your needs. Thank them for being a valuable person in your life, for respecting your needs, and for reciprocating your actions. It's nice for them to get this feedback, as we don't often hear praise as adults. We come home to ourselves as we heal—it's a full circle moment, rejoining with the authentic self.

You know so much more about yourself than you did when you began this journey. You have given yourself permission to go deep within and hold some uncomfortable truths. You have learned how to recognize your needs and express them in a clear and consistent manner. You are honest with yourself and the relationships you have inherited and created. You stepped up to the challenge and faced your fears. Build on what you have learned through this work and make your boundaries work for you. Create a life of ease and authenticity as you use your new boundary skills.

You are stepping into the emotional freedom that was always available to you. Now you can claim and express your needs clearly. You have learned how to communicate your feelings in ways that others can hear. You no longer recycle your pain; you express what is going on inside of you, and each time you do this, you strengthen your core.

To paraphrase Maya Angelou, when we know more, we can do better. That's what you are doing: you are learning how to live your life in a better way so as to create more positive interactions and outcomes. You are giving yourself the great gift of healing and emotional freedom so that you can feel strong in your core, knowing that you are embodying your authentic self each day. You are bringing forth the life you want to live. You have found the courage to set healthy boundaries.

Be brave as you confidently claim your courage, protecting yourself with your boundaries, your truth. You are deserving and more than worth it.

Blessings on your healing path.

You did the best you could
with what you knew at the time.
Don't let new wisdom
lead you to condemn yourself
over old struggles.
Forgive yourself and move forward.
—MORGAN RICHARD OLIVER

Feelings Inventory

The following tables contain lists of words you can reference to describe emotional and physical feelings. The words are divided into two categories: feelings we have when our needs are satisfied, and feelings we have when our needs are not met. When you have a gut reaction to a situation, check in with this feeling, then refer to the chart below to find the word or words that best describe the feeling.

Feelings When Your Needs Are Satisfied

AFFECTIONATE	CONFIDENT	GRATEFUL	PEACEFUL
compassionate	**empowered**	appreciative	calm
friendly	**open**	moved	clear headed
loving	**proud**	thankful	comfortable
open-hearted	**safe**	touched	centered
sympathetic	**secure**		content
tender		**INSPIRED**	equanimous
warm	**EXCITED**	amazed	fulfilled
	amazed	awed	mellow
ENGAGED	animated	wonder	quiet
absorbed	ardent		relaxed
alert	aroused	**JOYFUL**	relieved
curious	astonished	amused	satisfied
engrossed	dazzled	delighted	serene
enchanted	eager	glad	still
entranced	energetic	happy	tranquil
fascinated	enthusiastic	jubilant	trusting
interested	giddy	pleased	
intrigued	invigorated	tickled	**REFRESHED**
involved	lively		enlivened
spellbound	passionate	**EXHILARATED**	rejuvenated
stimulated	surprised	blissful	renewed
	vibrant	ecstatic	rested
HOPEFUL		elated	restored
expectant		enthralled	revived
encouraged		exuberant	
optimistic		radiant	
		rapturous	
		thrilled	

Feelings When Your Needs Are Not Satisfied

AFRAID	CONFUSED	EMBARRASSED	TENSE
apprehensive	ambivalent	ashamed	anxious
dread	baffled	chagrined	cranky
foreboding	bewildered	flustered	distressed
frightened	dazed	guilty	distraught
mistrustful	hesitant	mortified	edgy
panicked	lost	self-conscious	fidgety
petrified	mystified		frazzled
scared	perplexed	**FATIGUE**	irritable
suspicious	puzzled	beat	jittery
terrified	torn	burnt out	nervous
wary		depleted	overwhelmed
worried	**DISCONNECTED**	exhausted	restless
	alienated	lethargic	stressed out
ANNOYED	aloof	listless	
aggravated	apathetic	sleepy	**VULNERABLE**
dismayed	bored	tired	fragile
disgruntled	cold	weary	guarded
displeased	detached	worn out	helpless
exasperated	distant		insecure
frustrated	distracted	**PAIN**	leery
impatient	indifferent	agony	reserved
irritated	numb	anguished	sensitive
irked	removed	bereaved	shaky
	uninterested	devastated	
ANGRY	withdrawn	grief	**YEARNING**
enraged		heartbroken	envious
furious	**DISQUIET**	hurt	jealous
incensed	agitated	lonely	longing
indignant	alarmed	miserable	nostalgic
irate	discombobulated	regretful	pining
livid	disconcerted	remorseful	wistful
outraged	disturbed		
resentful	perturbed	**SAD**	
	rattled	depressed	
AVERSION	restless	dejected	
animosity	shocked	despair	
appalled	startled	despondent	
contempt	surprised	disappointed	
disgusted	troubled	discouraged	
dislike	turbulent	disheartened	
hate	turmoil	forlorn	
horrified	uncomfortable	gloomy	
hostile	uneasy	heavy hearted	
repulsed	unnerved	hopeless	

About the Author

Robert Jackman is a best-selling author, inner child expert, trauma specialist, and board-certified psychotherapist with the National Board of Certified Counselors who has been helping people on their healing path in his private practice for over twenty-five years. A graduate of Loyola University of Chicago and National Louis University, his five books are therapist recommended and have been read by over 100,000 people worldwide. All of his books are translated into multiple languages. He has taught master's-level classes at NLU and led outpatient groups in clinics and hospitals. Robert has been a guest speaker on Sirius XM radio, numerous podcasts, panels, and telesummits on codependency, boundary setting, couples communication, inner child work, grief and loss, mindfulness, and the role of spirituality in healing, and has participated in numerous retreats for Victories for Men. His work has been featured in counseling journals and referenced in psychological research.

Robert is a Reiki Master and uses energy psychology in his practice and in his personal development. He believes in the power of healing through self-awareness, self-compassion, and a strong therapeutic alliance between client and therapist. He considers himself a codependent in recovery and is always working on his healing path, setting boundaries, nurturing his relationships, and connecting with his authentic self.

For more information about Robert, upcoming events, and his books, *Healing Your Lost Inner Child* and the *Companion Workbook, Healing Your Wounded Relationship, The Tender Path of Grief & Loss,* and *The Courage to Set Healthy Boundaries,* please visit www.theartofpracticalwisdom.com and follow him on his YouTube channel, The Art of Practical Wisdom.